Building European Union

Building European Union

A documentary history and analysis

edited by Trevor Salmon and Sir William Nicoll

MANCHESTER UNIVERSITY PRESS
MANCHESTER AND NEW YORK

distributed exclusively in the USA by St. Martin's Press

Published by Manchester University Press
Oxford Road, Manchester M13 9NR, UK
and Room 400, 175 Fifth Avenue, New York, NY 10010, USA

Distributed exclusively in the USA by
St. Martin's Press, Inc., 175 Fifth Avenue, New York, NY 10010, USA

British Library Cataloguing-in-Publication Data
A catalogue record for this book is available from the British Library

Library of Congress Cataloging-in-Publication Data
Building European Union: a documentary history and analysis /
edited by Trevor Salmon and Sir William Nicoll
   p. c.
Includes bibliographical references
  ISBN 0-7190-4445-6 (hardcover) – ISBN 0-7190-4446-4 (pbk.)
  1. European federation—History. 2. European federation—History—
Sources. 3. Europe—Economic integration—History. 4. European
Union—History. I. Salmon, Trevor C. II. Nicoll, William.
JN15.B79 1997
337.1'4—dc20   96–26854
                                        CIP

ISBN 0-7190-4445-6 *hardback*
ISBN 0-7190-4446-4 *paperback*

First published 1997

01 00 99 98 97   10 9 8 7 6 5 4 3 2 1

Typeset by Carnegie Publishing, Preston
Printed in Great Britain by Bell & Bain Ltd, Glasgow

Contents

List of abbreviations

CAP	Common Agricultural Policy
CCP	Common Commercial Policy
CET	Common External Tariff
CFSP	Common Foreign and Security Policy
CJHA	Cooperation in the fields of Justice and Home Affairs
CMEA	Council for Mutual Economic Assistance
Coreper	Committee of Permanent Representatives
CSCE	Conference on Security and Cooperation in Europe
EC	European Community
ECB	European Central Bank
ECJ	European Court of Justice
ECSC	European Coal and Steel Community
ECU	European Currency Unit
EDC	European Defence Community
EEA	European Economic Area
EFTA	European Free Trade Association
EIB	European Investment Bank
EMI	European Monetary Institute
EMU	Economic and Monetary Union
EMS	European Monetary System
EP	European Parliament
EPC	(1) European Political Cooperation (2) European Political Community
ERM	Exchange Rate Mechanism (of the EMS)
ERP	European Recovery Programme
EU	European Union
Euratom	European Atomic Energy Community
GATT	General Agreement on Tariffs and Trade
IGC	Inter-governmental Conference

IMF	International Monetary Fund
MEP	Member of the European Parliament
MLF	Multilateral Force
NATO	North Atlantic Treaty Organization
OECD	Organization for Economic Cooperation and Development
OEEC	Organization for European Economic Cooperation
OJ	Official Journal
OOP	Office for Official Publications (of the European Community)
QMV	Qualified Majority Vote/Voting
SEA	Single European Act
SEM	Single European Market
SMEs	Small and medium size enterprises
TEU	Treaty on European Union
WEU	Western European Union
WTO	World Trade Organization

Introduction

The development of the European Community and of European Union has created a mountain of documents, some ephemeral, some enduring. Along with the thousands of meetings which made or unmade decisions, the documents chart the visions, aspirations, triumphs, disappointments and despair of the protagonists. Some are arid exercises in legal drafting. Some are utterances of noble purpose. Some are rodomontade and bombast. Of them there will be no end – the continuous technical improvement in communications both swells the demand for messages and provides a copious supply of them.

There are twin dangers. The sheer bulk of paper tends to discourage the reading of it. Things are laid aside until a favourable moment comes for them to be read and marked. The management of the accumulating stock gets out of hand. Despite the sophisticated data retrieval apparatus now available – and perhaps because of the torrents of academic and journalistic appraisal of the events – the actual texts tend to be displaced by impressions, partial recollections and tendentious interpretations of them.

This book attempts an antidote. It sets out to collect together what the authors believe to be key documents and to talk about them as briefly as is consistent with presenting them in their contexts. The documents are what those concerned said they were doing. Some of the writings ultimately led nowhere. Some inspired the writer's or writers' adherents to overcome obstacles. Some advanced the cause of European integration, others opposed it.

This collection does not include extracts from the founding or amending Treaties of the European Community or European Union (with two small exceptions), since these are widely available and commented upon.

Any selection from what practitioners sometimes call the *florilegia* of European literature must be draconian and open to objection. Everybody has his or her own ideas about what was and is vital and everybody is more or less right. This is our minimal compilation, based on our collective experiences.

In this endeavour we have been aided by the sterling Gina Wilson of St Andrews University, who has transformed innumerable texts in different formats with grace and patience. The Editors apologize if any material herein is subject to copyright and will be pleased to include appropriate acknowledgements in any further edition.

Document 1

William Penn, the English Quaker, having been expelled from Oxford in 1660 for his nonconformist beliefs, travelled widely on the continent and saw at first-hand the aftermath of the Thirty Years War (1618–48). This experience strengthened his belief in the healing power of brotherly love, which it was to be his lifelong mission to promote.

In 1693 he published his 'Essay towards the Present and Future Peace in Europe by the Establishment of an European Dyet, Parliament, or Estates', subtitled (in Latin) 'blessed are the peacemakers', and 'Let arms yield to the robe' (of the parliamentarian).

It was a proposal for the establishment of a European Parliament in which decisions on disputes among the participants would be taken by a three-quarter majority vote, weighted according to their respective economic power.

The Essay had no effect on the continuing European wars. Recourse to arms remained the preferred way of resolving disputes.

The Penn essay is included in the present collection not for the effects it had on European history but as one example of the many plans, proposals and reflections on the integration of Europe as an alternative to its disintegration.

William Penn, 'An Essay towards the Present and Future Peace of Europe, by the Establishment of an European Dyet, Parliament, or Estates', 1693

IV. Of a general peace, or the peace of Europe, and the means of it

Now if the sovereign princes of Europe, who represent that society, or independent state of men that was previous to the obligations of society, would, for the same reason that engaged men first into society, viz. love of peace and order, agree to meet by their stated deputies in a general diet, estates, or parliament, and there establish rules of justice for sovereign princes to observe one to another; and thus to meet yearly, or once in two or three years at farthest, or as they shall cause, and to be styled, the sovereign or imperial diet, parliament or state of Europe; before which sovereign assembly, should be brought all differences depending between one sovereign and another, that cannot be made up by private embassies, before the sessions begin; and that if any of the sovereignties that constitute these imperial states shall refuse to submit their claim or pretensions to them, or to abide and perform the judgement thereof, and seek their remedy by arms, or delay their compliance beyond the time prefixed in their resolutions, all the other sovereignties, united as one strength, shall compel the submission and performance of the sentence, with damages to the suffering party, and charges to the sovereignties that obliged their submission: to be sure Europe would quietly obtain that so much desired and needed peace, to her harassed inhabitants; no sovereignty in Europe, having the power, and therefore cannot show the will to dispute the conclusion; and consequently, peace would be procured, and continued in Europe . . .

[. . .]

VII. Of the composition of these imperial states

The composition and proportion of this sovereign part, or imperial state does, at the first look, seem to carry with it no small difficulty what votes to allow for the inequality of the princes and states. But with submission to better judgements, I cannot think it invincible: for if it be possible to have an estimate of the yearly value of the several sovereign countries, whose delegates are to make up this august assembly, the determination of the number of persons or votes in the states for every sovereignty, will not be impracticable . . .

I pretend to no manner of exactness, but go wholly by guess, being but for example's sake. I suppose the empire of Germany to send twelve; France, ten; Spain, ten; Italy, which comes to France, eight; England, six; Portugal, three; Sweedland, four; Denmark, three; Poland, four; Venice, three; the Seven Provinces, four; The Thirteen Cantons, and little neighbouring sovereignties, two; dukedoms of Holstein and Courland, one: and if the Turks and Muscovites are taken in, as seems but fit and just, they will make ten a piece more. The whole makes ninety. A great presence when they represent the fourth; and now the best and wealthiest part of the known world; where religion and learning, civility and arts have their seat and empire. But it is not absolutely necessary there should be always so many persons, to represent the larger sovereignties; for the votes may be given by one man of any sovereignty, as well as by ten or twelve: though the fuller the assembly of states is, the more solemn, effectual, and free the debates will be, and the resolutions must needs come with greater authority. The place of their first session should be central, as much as is possible, afterwards as they agree.

VIII. Of the regulation of the imperial states in session

To avoid quarrel for precedency, the room may be round, and have diverse doors to come in and go out at, to prevent exceptions. If the whole number be cast into tens, each choosing one, they may preside by turns, to whom all speeches should be addressed, and who should collect the sense of the debates, and state the question of a vote, which, in my opinion, should be by the ballot, after the prudent and commendable method of the Venetians . . .

It seems to me, that nothing in this imperial parliament should pass, but by three-quarters of the whole, at least seven above the balance . . . All complaints should be delivered in writing, in the nature of memorials; and journals kept by a proper person, in a trunk or chest, which should have as many differing locks, as there are tens in the states. And if there were a clerk for each ten, and a pew or table for those clerks in the assembly; and at the end of every session, one out of each ten, were appointed to examine and compare the journal of those clerks, and then lock them up as I have before expressed, it would be clear and satisfactory . . . I will say little of the language in which the session of the sovereign estates should be held, but to be sure it must be in Latin or French; the first would be very well for civilians, but the last most easy for men of quality . . .

The conclusion

I will conclude this my proposal of an European, sovereign, or imperial diet, parliament, or estates, with that which I have touched upon before, and which falls under the notice of every one concerned, by coming home to their particular and respective experience within their own sovereignties. That by the same rules of justice and prudence, by which parents and masters govern their families, and magistrates their cities, and estates their republics, and princes and kings their principalities and kingdoms, Europe may obtain and preserve peace among her sovereignties. For wars are the duels of princes; and as government in kingdoms and states, prevents men being judges and executioners for themselves, overrules private passions as to injuries or revenge, and subjects the great as well as the small to the rule of justice, that power might not vanquish or oppress right, nor one neighbour act an independency and sovereignty upon another, while they have resigned that original claim to the benefit and comfort of society; so this being soberly weighed in the whole, and parts of it, it will not be hard to conceive or frame, not yet to execute the design I have here proposed . . .

Document 2

Richard Coudenhove-Kalergi (1894–1972) was of Flemish and Cretan stock. His mother was Japanese. Born a citizen of the Austro-Hungarian Empire, he became Czech and later French. He fled from Vienna after the Anschluss in 1938 and settled down in Switzerland.

His most notable publication was 'Pan-Europa' in 1923. It was an appeal for European unity, via Franco-German reconciliation, in the face of possible invasion by Russia and of American and British economic and industrial domination.

A leading convert to his cause was Aristide Briand, at different times French Foreign Minister and Prime Minister. Briand became Honorary President of the Pan-Europa movement which Coudenhove-Kalergi founded in Vienna in 1923. Briand launched at the League of Nations in Geneva on 4 September 1929 (See Document 3) an initiative for European union.

In February 1930, Mr Winston Churchill applauded the Briand initiative and said:

Among innumerable sparks that flash and fade away there now and again gleams one that lights up not only the immediate scene, but the whole world. So when the idea of the United States of Europe drifted off upon the wind and came in contact with the immense accumulation of muddle, waste, particularism and prejudice which had long lain piled up in the European garden, it became quite evident that a new series of events had opened. The resuscitation of the Pan-European idea is largely identified with Coudenhove-Kalergi.

*It was at the same time that Mr Churchill uttered the phrase often quoted to clarify or otherwise his sense of Europe: 'But we have our own dreams and our task. **We are with Europe, but not of it.**'*

When Count Coudenhove-Kalergi returned to Europe after the war, he found himself eclipsed by pro-European activists like Altiero Spinelli (See Documents 5). He helped Mr Churchill to compose the speech which the latter delivered in Zurich on 18 September 1946 (See Document 10). He founded in 1947 the European Parliamentary Union. By then many other actors and organizations were striving for an ever-closer union. In 1965 Coudenhove-Kalergi broke with colleagues in the Pan-European Union and with the European Movement by publicly supporting the European policies of President de Gaulle: 'Realistically, the next stage is to set up, in agreement with the Vth Republic, a European confederation led by a council of governments and helped by international organizations.'

Richard Coudenhove-Kalergi, 'Pan-Europe', 1923

Europe as a political concept does not exist. The part of the world with that name covers peoples and States in chaos, a powder keg of international conflicts, the breeding ground of future conflicts. This is the European Question: the mutual hatred of Europeans for each other poisons the international atmosphere and is a perpetual worry to even the most peace-loving countries of the world . . . The European Question will be resolved only by the union of the peoples of Europe. This will come about either voluntarily, by the construction of a pan-European federation or coercively by Russian conquest . . .

As a political notion, Europe comprises all the democratic States of the continent, plus Iceland, linked to Denmark in a personal union. The small part of Turkey in Europe belongs politically to Asia . . . I know that there will be difficulty in getting that designation accepted and that it will be objected that a Europe without Russia and without England cannot be called 'Pan-Europe' or 'Complete Europe'. This objection, which is based on theory, has no significance . . .

The advocates of Greater Europe cannot imagine the United States of Europe without England. They want the British Empire to be a member State of the European Federation. Under this policy, what Europe gained in strength it would lose in cohesion. If Europe included Australia, Canada and South Africa, it would not be Europe, but an intercontinental Empire . . . This Greater Europe would split into two dissimilar parts: 1. English language countries spread across the world, currently part of the British Empire and 2. the coherent complex of non-English European States . . .

The whole of the European Question comes to a head in the Russian problem. The principal aim of European policy should be to prevent a Russian invasion. To avoid it, there is only one answer: united Europe . . .

The . . . danger for Europe is of certain States, and especially Germany turning to Russia. Politically speaking, Germany is closer to Russia today than it is to the Western States. It refuses to join the League of Nations, but it has concluded the Rapallo Treaty of Friendship with Russia. A large part of Germany hopes that in alliance with Russia it could tear up the Treaty of Versailles and once again partition Poland . . .

But if Europe wants to win in the competition with the great economic regions of England and America, it must show itself to Russia as an economic unit. As long as it is fragmented internally by tariff barriers, it cannot compete with the other empires . . .

To scupper the needed creation of a European Customs Union [the enemies of pan-Europe] will call for international free trade; to scupper the pact of European guarantee, they will ask for a pact of intercontinental guarantee; to scupper the United States of Europe they will call for the United States of the world . . .

Only the reconstruction of Europe, undertaken broad-mindedly, on federalist and democratic bases can put right economically the fragmentation of Austria-Hungary and the mutilation of Germany. Statesmen who are better at tearing down rather than building up are dilettanti and demagogues. They must vanish from the political scene and make room for constructive leaders . . .

The greatest obstacle to the realization of the United States of Europe is the thousand year rivalry between the two most populous nations of Pan-Europe: Germany and France . . .

The historic moment would have come for the two nations, freed from their dynasties, to bury the ambitions and aspirations of their sovereigns with their thirst for glory, to find reconciliation in working together for the reconstruction, union and progress of Europe . . .

But the essence is to recognize the common Franco-German destiny. As long as the politics of Europe were also the politics of the world, the things that divided the two countries had the upper-hand over what brought them together. Today when the future of Europe is at stake, in the face of the other continents, French and German interests converge more and more. The ruin of one of these countries would necessarily bring about the ruin of the other. Therefore there must arise between them a solidarity of reason even if there is not yet place for a solidarity of love . . .

If France . . . recognizes that it cannot destroy Germany without putting itself in danger of death, it must . . . resolutely take the path of reconciliation. This path has only one destination: pan-Europe. Therefore, close collaboration with a democratic and peaceful Germany, reconciliation on the basis of justified war indemnities, a customs union to join together German coal and French ore with the aim of creating a pan-European iron and steel industry, a treaty for the settlement of disputes and security, protection against Russia, a common defence against forces of reaction, disarmament, common reconstruction of the European economy and finances, the establishment of a pan-European federation . . .

There is only one radical way to resolve the problem of European frontiers equitably and lastingly: not redrawing the frontiers but suppressing them.

The European who is peaceloving and renounces any redrawing of frontiers must put all his energy into obtaining their suppression for national and economic reasons . . .

The crowning act of pan-European efforts would be the constitution of the United States of Europe on the model of the United States of America. Europe would present itself as a single entity *vis à vis* other continents and world powers, and inside the Federation every State would have the maximum of liberty. Pan-Europe would have two chambers. The Chamber of the Peoples would be made up of 300 members, in the ratio of one per million inhabitants. The Chamber of the States would have twenty-six representatives of the twenty-six European governments . . .

This standard of love and of the spirit must, one day, fly from Portugal to Poland on the empire unified in peace and liberty.

Documents 3

Aristide Briand became Minister of Foreign Affairs in the French Government in 1925. He had little faith in the League of Nations as an instrument to ensure peace. His own policy was what he called 'apaisement', by which he meant positive measures to prevent the outbreak of wars. Incidentally, that was the understanding of the term by Mr Chamberlain, the later British Prime Minister. However, the English translation took on a different meaning later − giving in to the dictators.

Briand believed that peace in Europe depended upon Franco-German reconciliation. He found a ready listener in his German opposite number, Gustav Stresemann. Stresemann's own objectives were to secure the revival of Germany as a power in Central Europe, along with the revision of the Eastern boundary as it had been redrawn by the Treaty of Versailles.

A new understanding with France was a sine qua non *for Stresemann's aims.*

Briand and Stresemann knew that a purely Franco-German initiative would cause widespread alarm. There needed to be a European framework. Briand moreover had to bide his time. His Prime Minister, Poincaré, was hostile both to measures which might seem to be favourable to Germany and to any which drew inspiration from the advocates of European union. Poincare retired in 1929 and Briand became Prime Minister, retaining in his own hands the foreign affairs portfolio.

On 9 September 1929, at the autumn session of the League of Nations in Geneva, Briand delivered a carefully nuanced speech on Europe, 'with some misgivings and timidity'.

European members of the League of Nations asked Briand to prepare a memorandum to amplify his ideas. The 'Briand Report' was published on 1 May 1930. It was not an inspiring document and the world had meanwhile changed round it. The Wall Street crash began in October 1929. Stresemann died in the same month. The Briand Report cautiously changed the thrust of the original approach, by proposing the setting up of European political structures as the necessary foundation for an economic system which should become: 'a common market for the raising of human welfare to the highest possible level across the territories of the European community.'

The Briand Report found few friends. Briand suggested that the League should set up a committee to study 'European union'. The committee met, but gave up its task when Briand died in 1932. The project was dead.

M. Briand, Foreign Minister of France, 'Memorandum on the Organization of a Regime of European Federal Union Addressed to Twenty-Six Governments of Europe', 1930

No one doubts today that the lack of cohesion . . . constitutes, practically, the most serious obstacle to the development and efficiency of all political or juridical institutions on which it is the tendency to base the first attempts for a universal peace organization . . . [similarly the] scattering of forces limits . . . the possibilities of enlargement of the economic markets, the attempts to intensify and improve industrial production . . . the search for a formula of European cooperation in connection with the League of Nations, far from weakening the authority of this latter must and can tend only to strengthen it . . . The policy of European union to which the search for a first bond of solidarity between European Governments ought to tend, implies in fact, a conception absolutely contrary to that which may have determined formerly, in Europe, the formation of customs unions . . . that is to say, to constitute in fact an instrument of struggle against States situated outside those unions.

[. . .]

It is important, finally, to place the proposed inquiry under the general conception that in no case and in no degree can the institution of the federal bond sought for between European Governments affect in any manner the sovereign rights of the States, members of such a *de facto* association.

It is on the basis of absolute sovereignty and of entire political independence that the understanding between European Nations ought to be effected. Furthermore, it would be impossible to imagine the least thought of political domination in an organization deliberately placed under the control of the League of Nations, the two fundamental principles of which are precisely, the sovereignty of States and the equality of rights. And with the rights of sovereignty, is it not the very genius of every nation which can find in its individual cooperation in the collective work the means of affirming itself still more the respect of the traditions and characteristics special to each people? . . .

II

1. *Necessity of a representative and responsible organ in the form of regularly establishing the 'European Conference'*, composed of representatives of all European Governments which are members of the League of Nations and which would be the essential directing organ of the European Union, in liaison with the League of Nations . . .

Observation

In order to avoid any predominance in favour of one European State over the others, presidents of the European Conference should be elected annually and function in rotation.

2. *Necessity of an executive organ, in the form of a permanent Political Committee*, composed of only a certain number of members of the European Conference and assuring, in practice, to the European Union its organization for study at the same time as its instrument of action.

The composition and powers of the European Committee, the manner of designation of its members, the organization of its presidency and of its regular or extraordinary sessions, should be determined at the next meeting of European States.

III

1. *General subordination of the economic problem to the political.* All possibility of progress towards economic union being strictly determined by the question of security, and this question being intimately bound up with that of the realizable progress towards political union, it is on the political plane that constructive effort looking to giving Europe its organic structure should first of all be made. It is also on this plane that the economic policy of Europe should afterwards be drawn up, in its broad outlines, as well as the special customs policy of each European State.

The contrary order would not only be useless, it would appear to the weaker nations to be likely to expose them, without guarantees or compensation, to the risks of political domination which might result from an industrial domination of the more strongly organized States.

It is therefore logical and normal that the justification of the economic sacrifices to be made to the whole should be found only in the development of a political situation warranting confidence between peoples and true pacification of minds. And even after the actual accomplishment of such a condition, assured by the establishment of a regime of constant and close peaceful association in peace between the peoples of Europe, there would still be needed, on the political plane, the intervention of a higher feeling of international necessities to impose on the Members of the European community, in favour of the collectivity, the sincere conception and effective prosecution of a truly liberal tariff policy.

2. *Conception of European political cooperation* as one which ought to tend towards this essential end: a federation built not upon the idea of unity but of union; that is to say, sufficiently flexible to respect the independence and national sovereignty of each of the States, while assuring them all the benefit of collective solidarity for the settlement of political questions involving the fate of the European community or that of its Members . . .

3. *Conception of the economic organization of Europe* as one which ought to tend to this essential end: a *rapprochement* of the European economic systems effected under the political responsibility of the Governments working in unison.

With this purpose in mind, the Governments might definitively associate themselves in an act of a general nature and of principle which would constitute a simple pact of economic solidarity, the purpose which they intend to set as the ideal end to their tariff policy (establishment of a common market to raise to the maximum the level of human well-being over all the territories of the European community). With the help of such a general orientation, immediate efforts could be undertaken practically for the rational organization of European production and exchanges, by means of the progressive liberation and the methodical simplification of the circulation of goods, capital, and persons, with the single reservation of the needs of national defence in each State . . .

IV

1. *Determination of the field of European cooperation,* particularly in the following spheres:

(a) *General economy.* The effective realization, in Europe, of the programme drawn up by the last economic conference of the League of Nations; the control of the policy of industrial unions and cartels among various countries; examination and preparation of all future possibilities regarding the progressive lowering of tariffs etc.

(b) *Economic equipment.* Realization of coordination between great public works executed by European States (routes for heavy automobile traffic, canals, etc.).

(c) *Communications and transit.* By land, water, and air: regulation and improvement of inter-European traffic; coordination of the labours of the European waterways commissions; agreements between railways; European regime of posts, telegraphs and telephones; radio-broadcasting rules etc.

(d) *Finances.* Encouragement of credit interded for the development of the economically less developed regions of Europe; European market; monetary questions, etc.

(e) *Labour* . . . questions having a continental or regional character, such as the regulation of the social consequences of inter-European emigration (application by one country to another of laws respecting labour accidents, social insurance, workers' pensions, etc.).

(f) *Hygiene* . . .

(g) *Intellectual cooperation.* Cooperation by universities and academies; library and artistic relations; centralization of scientific research; improvement of the press system in relations between agencies and in transportation of newspapers, etc.

(h) *Interparliamentary relations . . .*

(i) *Administration . . .*

[France believed that] for purely practical reasons . . . [plans and comments] should adhere to as elementary a conception as possible of the subject of consultation: not because that it is its wish to limit the possibilities of future development of a federal organization of Europe, but because, in the present state of the European world and for the sake of increasing the chances of unanimous consent to the first concrete proposal of conciliating all the interests and all the special situations involved, it is of great importance to keep to the initial data of several very simple views. Likewise, the best method is to proceed from the simpler to the more complex, and to trust to time in the task of assuring, with life, by a constant evolution and by a kind of continuous creation, the full expansion of the natural resources which the European Union might contain.

Internal British Foreign Office Minute on the Briand Plan, 1930

It is submitted that the attitude of His Majesty's Government towards M. Briand's proposals should be one of caution, though cordial caution. Neither the real meaning of the proposals nor the real nature of M. Briand's intentions can be elucidated without much further information than has yet arrived from Paris and other European centres. The proposals in the first place concern Continental Europe more directly and fully than they do this country. It therefore appears right and proper and politically advisable that His Majesty's Government should not commit themselves to any definite view of the proposals till the countries primarily concerned have spoken their minds . . .

If the proposals are impracticable, as in part they appear to be, there is surely no reason why His Majesty's Government should take upon themselves the onus of turning down something which Germany and Italy, who are far more directly concerned, will do themselves . . . If, however, the proposals are capable of being used to make a new start on practical lines in the improved economic (and perhaps subsequently also political) cooperation, opposition on the part of His Majesty's Government might at this stage do real harm. On this hypothesis what would seem necessary would be careful study of the course of events coupled with a discriminating sympathy for all such reorganizations of Europe as is not in unjustified contravention

of British rights and interests, of the peculiar and indissoluble con-
nexion of the British Isles with the world-wide territories of the British
Empire and of prestige and efficiency of the League of Nations which
is the sheet anchor of British policy . . . it is suggested that . . . [Gov-
ernment] should confine themselves to an expression of warm
sympathy with the high ideals of European cooperation . . .

Reply from the British Government, 1930

[. . .]

3. . . . The French Government hope that by their proposals they may
promote closer cooperation among the nations and Governments of
Europe, and thus strengthen the safeguards against another European war.

4. With this purpose His Majesty's Government . . . are in the fullest
sympathy. It is an axiom of His Majesty's Government that the first
of British interests is peace, and measures calculated to ensure peace
will therefore secure their ready and warm support . . .

5. His Majesty's Government . . . are also in agreement with the
French Government in thinking that it is primarily in respect of economic relations that closer cooperation between the nations of Europe
is urgently to be desired.

6. . . . While . . . the independence and national sovereignty of each
country have to be respected, as well as the special ties affecting
particular groups of nations, much can be done by political authorities
to promote a wider outlook on economic questions, and, in so far as
political action is directed to that object . . . the United Kingdom agree
to the proposal made in the Memorandum for the association of
economic and political authorities.

7. . . . [The UK is] not confident that mature examination will show
that the establishment of new and independent international institutions is either necessary or desirable.
[. . .]

9. . . . an exclusive and independent European union of the kind
proposed might emphasize or create tendencies to inter-continental
rivalries . . .

10. . . . [The UK] believes that the purpose that the French Government have in view can be effectively secured by so adapting the
proposals . . . as to bring them fully within the framework of the

League . . . [and are] convinced that it would be possible, perhaps by establishing European Committees of the Assembly, of the Council and of the technical organizations . . . to create whatever machinery is required for promoting closer European cooperation without incurring the risks and difficulties which a system of new and independent institutions might involve . . .

Document 4

Britain and France declared war on Germany in September 1939 following the German invasion of Poland. In the winter and spring of 1939–40, the two sides played a 'phony war', each staying behind its own defensive lines. On 10 May 1940, a German offensive opened in France, Belgium and Luxembourg.

The German advance continued south of the River Somme, and reached Rouen and the Seine on 9 June. With Italy invading the south of France on 10 June, the French Generalissimo, Weygand, advised his Government, which had fled to Tours, to seek an armistice. M. Reynaud, Prime Minister, began the process of seeking British agreement to France negotiating separately for peace.

M. Jean Monnet, businessman, organizer of allied war supply in the First World War, later Deputy Secretary of the League of Nations, was in London. He conceived the need for a dramatic gesture to keep France in the war: 'France and Britain must join their destinies in the war, and beyond'. He was the principal draftsman of the 'Declaration of Union' of 16 June 1940. Mr Churchill, who had become the British Prime Minister, was not enthusiastic, but accepted the need for an imaginative gesture.

In the crush of events, confusion was inevitable. The impression in Tours was that the offer of Anglo-French union had been withdrawn when Britain replied to M. Reynaud's request to be released from the obligation to pursue the fight against Germany. Two messages were sent to the British ambassador. One conveyed the declaration. The other required France, as a condition for seeking peace, to despatch the French Fleet to British harbours. The messages were then cancelled when Mr Churchill decided to meet the French Government in Tours forthwith. Before he could leave, the French Government began to disintegrate. Although M. Reynaud urged acceptance of the Declaration of Union, his colleagues, led by his deputy, Marshal Pétain, indignantly rejected it. They believed that the war was already lost and that Britain faced certain defeat. According to Marshal Pétain: 'to make a union with Britain is fusion with a corpse'.

Winston Churchill and General de Gaulle, 'Declaration on Franco-British Union', London, June 1940

At this most fateful moment in the history of the modern world, the Governments of the United Kingdom and the French Republic make this declaration of indissoluble union and unyielding resolution in their common defence of justice and freedom against subjection to a system which reduces mankind to a life of robots and slaves.

The two Governments declare that France and Great Britain shall no longer be two nations, but one Franco-British Union.

The constitution of the Union will provide for joint organs of defence, foreign, financial, and economic policies.

Every citizen of France will enjoy immediately citizenship of Great Britain; every British subject will become a citizen of France.

Both countries will share responsibility for the repair of the devastation of war, wherever it occurs in their territories, and the resources of both shall be equally, and as one, applied to that purpose.

During the war there shall be a single War Cabinet, and all the forces of Britain and France, whether on land, sea, or in the air, will be placed under its direction. It will govern from wherever best it can. The two Parliaments will be formally associated. The nations of the British Empire are already forming new armies. France will keep her available forces in the field, on the sea, and in the air. The Union appeals to the United States to fortify the economic resources of the Allies, and to bring forth her powerful material aid to the common cause.

The Union will concentrate its whole energy against the power of the enemy, no matter where the battle may be.

And thus we shall conquer.

Documents 5

The Fascist Government of Italy imprisoned its dissidents on the island of Ventotene. Their discussions led to the drafting of the Ventotene Manifesto, one of whose principal authors was Altiero Spinelli (1907–86).

The Manifesto is a call for the establishment of European socialism and an attack on all totalitarianism, whether Fascist, Nazi or 'ultra-collectivist'

Communist – and on the Catholic Church, characterized as the 'natural ally of all reactionary regimes'.

It advocates European unity, dismissing as vain any declarations of neutrality, non-aggression pacts and the League of Nations. But its Europeanism is largely incidental to the demand for social reform and individual freedom.

Spinelli developed the European proposal in his further writing on 'The United States of Europe and the various political trends' (1941–42). It was the basis of the rest of his political life, as a writer, Commissioner in Brussels and Member of the directly elected European Parliament (as an 'independent Communist'). His monument as a European Parliamentarian is the Draft Treaty establishing the European Union (See Document 43).

Ernesto Rossi and Altiero Spinelli, 'The Ventotene Manifesto', August 1941

Every nation has an equal right to organize itself as an independent State . . . The concept of national independence has been a powerful stimulus to progress . . . But this concept carried within itself the seeds of capitalist imperialism which our generation has seen develop until it produced totalitarian States and unleashed the world wars . . .

The absolute sovereignty of the nation States has caused each one of them to try to dominate the others. Moreover, each tries to extend its sphere of influence over an even larger area . . . The inevitable result of this desire to dominate is the hegemony of the strongest State over all the others, which are subjected to it . . .

The problem which must first be solved is the final abolition of the division of Europe into sovereign national States. Without this, any progress made will be appearance only . . . People are now much more in favour of a federal reorganization of Europe than they were in the past. The harsh experiences of the last ten years have opened the eyes even of those who had no wish to see; they have also brought about numerous circumstances favourable to our ideal.

Every thinking man now appreciates that it is impossible to maintain a balance of power among the independent European States so long as militarist Germany exists side by side with them. Nor will it be possible to reduce Germany to small pieces or hold it down after it has been defeated. In proof of this, it has become clear that no European country can remain apart while the others wage war; . . . [T]he futility, even the harmfulness, of institutions like the League of Nations, has been demonstrated; they pretend to guarantee international law, but without the military force needed to enforce their decisions, and they respect the absolute sovereignty of their member States . . . The manifold problems which bedevil the international affairs of the continent have become insoluble: definition of the boundaries in areas of mixed populations, protection of rights of ethnic minorities, outlets to the sea for inland countries, Balkan question, Irish question, etc. All of them could most easily be resolved by a European Federation. Historically, similar problems arising between the petty principalities which went to make up the larger national unities lost their bitterness on being transformed into relations between one province and another.

On the other hand, the disappearance of the sense of security which had resulted from the impregnability of Great Britain, . . . the collapse of the French army . . . and, above all, awareness of the serious danger of universal subjugation, all are circumstances favouring the establishment of a federal regime which would bring today's anarchy to an end . . .

Altiero Spinelli, 'The United States of Europe and the Various Political Trends', 1942

[. . .]
But the international order can also be created in a way more suited to our basic demands, namely a federal system. This would allow each State to develop its national life in the way best suited to the level and character of its civilization, but it would deprive its member States of those elements of sovereignty which enabled them to assert their selfish aims; it would create and administer a corpus of international law to which all States would be equally subject.

The federal authority should be entrusted with powers that would ensure the permanent abolition of exclusivist national policies. It must have the sole power to raise and employ armed forces (which would also be responsible for public order within States), to conduct foreign policy, and to fix the administrative boundaries of the member States so as to satisfy basic national requirements and see that ethnic minorities are not mistreated. It would take steps to abolish protectionist barriers and prevent their re-erection: it would issue a single federal currency; it would ensure full freedom of movement for all citizens within the federation, and would administer all colonies, i.e. all territories still incapable of self-government.

To perform these tasks effectively there must be a federal magistrature, an administrative apparatus independent of the individual States. The federation must levy directly from the citizens the taxes necessary for the functioning of these bodies; it must possess a legislature and organs of control based on the direct participation of citizens, not merely representatives of the federated States.

Such, in outline, is the organization which can be called the United States of Europe, and which is the indispensable condition for the elimination of imperialism and militarism.

Given Europe's predominance in the world, even today, as a centre of civilization, and the fact that its quarrels have always made it the epicentre of world conflict, the final pacification of our continent under federal institutions would be the greatest step towards world peace that could be taken at the present juncture.

Document 6

The 'White Rose' resistance movement was active in Munich in the summer and autumn of 1942. The notable members were the brother and sister Hans (born 1918) and Sophie (born 1921) Scholl. They were arrested in February 1943 and guillotined.

Hans and Sophie Scholl, 'The White Rose Movement', 1942

What must we learn from the outcome of this war, which was never a national one?

The imperialistic idea of power, wherever it is found, must be made harmless for all time. Selfish Prussian militarism must never again come to power. Only broad and generous cooperation among European nations can provide the foundation for a new structure. Every centralized power, such as the Prussian State tried to exercise in Germany and Europe, must be nipped in the bud. The Germany of the future must be federal. Only a healthy, federal political organization can today put new life into exhausted Europe. Workers must be freed by reasonable socialism from their state of abject slavery. The illusion of economic self-sufficiency must disappear from Europe. Every nation and every individual has a right to the goods of this world!

Freedom of speech and conscience, protection of the individual citizen against the criminal use of force by the State – these are the foundations of the new Europe.

Support the resistance movement – distribute leaflets!

Document 7

Although deeply involved in the 'Franco-French' negotiations among rival leaders to set up the Committee of National Liberation, Jean Monnet in Algeria found time to reflect on what would follow in France and more widely in Europe after peace.

On 5 August 1943 he set some of his thoughts down on paper: a European entity (without Britain), with French participation essential; the widening of the market; the sterilization of key defence industries.

M. Monnet left Algiers on 5 November 1943, to return to Washington and take part in the preparations for administering France after its liberation.

M. Jean Monnet, 'Algiers Memorandum', August 1943

There will be no peace in Europe if States are reconstituted on a basis of national sovereignty with all that implies in terms of prestige politics and economic protectionism. If the nations of Europe adopt defensive positions again, huge armies will be necessary again. Under the future peace treaty, some nations will be allowed to re-arm; others will not. That was tried in 1919; we all know the result. Intra-European alliances will be formed; we know what they are worth. Social reform will be impeded or blocked by the sheer weight of military budgets. Europe will be reborn in fear.

The nations of Europe are too circumscribed to give their people the prosperity made possible, and hence necessary, by modern conditions. They will need larger markets. And they will have to refrain from using a major proportion of their resources to maintain 'key' industries needed for national defence and made mandatory by the concept of sovereign, protectionist States, as we knew them before 1939.

Prosperity and vital social progress will remain elusive until the nations of Europe form a federation of a 'European entity' which will forge them into a single economic unit . . . Our concern is a solution to the European problem. The British, the Americans, the Russians have worlds of their own into which they can temporarily retreat. But France is bound to Europe. France cannot opt out, for her very existence hinges on a solution to the European problem. Developments on the European scene in the wake of imminent liberation, will inevitably prompt the three major powers to protect themselves against Europe and hence France. For no agreement into which France might be drawn with Britain, America or Russia could cut her off from Europe, with whom she has so many intellectual, material and military ties.

Document 8

With Germany triumphant, its allies, puppet regimes and the neutrals were apprehensive about their place in the postwar world. It appeared to the German Foreign Office that they needed reassurances to offset Anglo-American propaganda and to secure their stronger political support for the war effort. It was also necessary to weaken American resolve – what better way than by showing that the USA was fighting against something it had itself achieved – a Union of the States?

Work on the plan for the postwar reconstruction and political organiz-ation of Europe began in the flush of victory and spread over the period of reverses, notably the defeat at Stalingrad on 31 January 1943.

On 21 March 1943, the Foreign Minister, Joachim von Ribbentrop (1893–1946), approved a memorandum on the establishment of a Euro-pean confederation, also described in the papers as a 'European community'. It was ostensibly designed to secure lasting peace in Europe (from which Britain would be isolated) and to bring an end to European particularism.

Although Ribbentrop apparently believed that he had the ear of the Führer he was mistaken. Hitler roundly dismissed the plan. His Germany was hegemonic and did not need to promise the rest of Europe anything.

'Draft "Annex on European Confederation"' approved by German Foreign Minister, Joachim von Ribbentrop, March 1943

Foundation of the European Confederation

The Governments of the German Reich, Italy, France, Belgium, the Netherlands, Denmark, Norway, Finland, Estonia, Latvia, Lithuania, Slovakia, Hungary, Rumania, Bulgaria, Serbia, Greece, Croatia and Spain have resolved to form a European Confederation.
[. . .]

The instrument establishing the European Confederation, . . . includes the following provisions.

1. In order to give tangible expression to the common destiny of European peoples and to ensure that wars never again break out among them, the States here represented have for all time established a European Confederation.

2. The members of the Confederation are sovereign States and guarantee one another's freedom and political independence. The organization of their internal affairs is a matter for the sovereign decision of each of them.

3. The member nations of the Confederation will jointly defend the interests of Europe in every direction and protect the European continent against external enemies.

4. The States of the Confederation will conclude an alliance for the defence of Europe, the plans for which will be drawn up in due course.

5. The European economy will be organized by the member States on the basis of a uniform plan arrived at by mutual agreement. Customs barriers among them will be progressively abolished.

6. While preserving their national character, the States united in the Confederation will conduct intensive cultural exchanges with one another.

7. The European States which are not founder members of the Confederation are solemnly invited to join it.

8. All details of the organization of the European Confederation shall be laid down in a Confederal Act, which will form the subject of consultation after the war by all the Governments concerned.

Document 9

Representatives of the national resistance movements in Denmark, France, Italy, Norway, Holland, Czechoslovakia, Yugoslavia and Germany itself gathered in Geneva in May 1944 to adopt a common policy on how Europe should be organized after the fighting. Despite their specific local experiences, many resistance groups were also conscious of their common experiences. Draft Declaration I reflected both their solidarity and their belief in 'sound federal links'. A draft declaration on European Federation,

Declaration II, had been prepared by Altiero Spinelli and his fellow political prisoner, Ernesto Rossi, who had also worked on the Ventotene document (See Document 5).

Some Members of the Resistance Groups in Europe, 'Draft Declaration II on European Federation', Geneva, May 1944

Manifesto

The peoples of Europe are united in their resistance to Nazi oppression. This common struggle has created among them a solidarity and unity of interests and aims which demonstrate their significance and value by the fact that the representatives of the European resistance movements have come together to draft this declaration expressing their hopes and aspirations regarding the future of peace and civilization.

[. . .]

The lack of unity and cohesion between the different parts of the world make it impossible to tackle immediately the task of creating a federal world organization. At the end of this war we shall have to limit ourselves to the building up of a less ambitious world organization – which should however permit of development in a federal direction – in the framework of which the great powers will have the task of guaranteeing collective security. It will not be, however, an effective instrument of peace unless the great powers are organized in such a way that the spirit of peace and understanding can prevail.

It is for this reason that, within the framework of this world organization, a more radical and direct solution must be found for the European problem. European peace is the keystone in the arch of world peace. During the lifetime of one generation Europe has twice been the centre of a world conflict whose chief cause was the existence of thirty sovereign States in Europe. It is a most urgent task to end this international anarchy by creating a European Federal Union.

Only a Federal Union will enable the German people to join the European community without becoming a danger to other peoples.

Only a Federal Union will make it possible to solve the problem of drawing frontiers in districts with mixed population. The minorities will thus cease to be the object of nationalistic jealousies, and frontiers will be nothing but demarcation lines between administrative districts.

Only a Federal Union will be in a position to protect democratic institutions and so to prevent politically less developed countries becoming a danger to the international order.

Only a Federal Union will make possible the economic reconstruction of the Continent and the liquidation of monopolies and national self-sufficiency.

Only a Federal Union will allow a logical and natural solution of the problems of the access to the sea of those countries which are situated in the interior of the Continent, of a rational use of those rivers which flow through several States, of the control of straits, and, generally, of most of the problems which during recent years have disturbed international relations.

It is not possible at present to determine the geographical frontiers of a Federal Union which would guarantee peace in Europe. We must, however, state that from the outset such a Union must be strong enough to avoid the risk of either being used as a mere sphere of influence by a foreign State or of becoming the instrument of the political ambitions of one of its member States. Furthermore it must from the beginning be open to all countries which entirely or partly belong to Europe and which wish to join it and are qualified to do so.

The Federal Union must be based upon a declaration of civil, political and economic rights which would guarantee democratic institutions and the free development of the human personality, and upon a declaration of the rights of minorities to have as much autonomy as is compatible with the integrity of the national States to which they belong.

The Federal Union must not interfere with the right of each of its member States to solve its special problems in conformity with its ethnical and cultural pattern. But, in view of the failure of the League of Nations, the States must irrevocably surrender to the Federation their sovereign rights in the sphere of defence, relations with powers outside the Union, international exchange and communications.

The Federal Union must possess the following essential features:

1. A government responsible not to the governments of the various member States but to the peoples, who must be under its direct jurisdiction in the spheres to which its powers extend.

2. An army at the disposal of this government, no national armies being permitted.

3. A Supreme Court acting as authority in interpreting the Constitution and deciding cases of conflict between the member States or between the member States and the Union . . .

Document 10

In 1942, writing to his Foreign Secretary Anthony Eden, Mr Churchill, as Prime Minister, expressed the hope that the European family 'may act unitedly as one under a Council of Europe. I look forward to a United States of Europe with reduced barriers to trade and movement, and where the economy of Europe could be studied as a whole'. His fundamental position, however, remained that noted in the commentary on Document 2 – 'We are with Europe, but not of it'.

This crucial distinction was not apparent to many in Europe in the period 1945–49. In 1946 Churchill spent much time touring Western Europe and receiving widespread public homage. Speaking in Zurich on the occasion of receiving an Honorary degree he used the phrase 'We must build a kind of United States of Europe'.

Mr Winston Churchill, 'Speech in Zurich', September 1946

If Europe were once united in the sharing of its common inheritance, there would be no limit to the happiness, to the prosperity and glory which its three or four hundred million people would enjoy. Yet it is from Europe that have sprung that series of frightful quarrels, originated by the Teutonic nations, which we have seen even in this twentieth century and in our own lifetime, wreck the peace and mar the prospects of all mankind.

And what is the plight to which Europe has been reduced? Some of the smaller States have indeed made a good recovery, but over wide areas a vast quivering mass of tormented, hungry, care-worn and bewildered human beings gape at the ruins of their cities and homes . . .

Yet all the while there is a remedy which, if it were generally and spontaneously adopted, would as if by a miracle transform the whole scene, and would in a few years make all Europe, or the greater part of it, as free and as happy as Switzerland is today. What is this sovereign remedy? It is to re-create the European Family, or as much of it as we can, and provide it with a structure under which it can dwell in peace, in safety and in freedom. We must build a kind of United States of Europe . . .

Much work has been done upon this task by the exertions of the Pan-European Union which owes so much to Count Coudenhove-

Kalergi . . . [to] . . . Briand . . . [and to] that immense body of doctrine and procedure, which was brought into being . . . [by] . . . the League. The League did not fail because of its principles or conceptions. It failed because these principles were deserted by those States who had brought it into being. It failed because the Governments of those days feared to face the facts and act while time remained. This disaster must not be repeated . . .

. . . President Truman had expressed his interest and sympathy with this great design. There is no reason why a regional organization of Europe should in any way conflict with the world organization of the United Nations. On the contrary, I believe that the larger synthesis will only survive if it is founded upon coherent natural groupings. There is already a natural grouping in the Western Hemisphere. We British have our own Commonwealth of Nations. These do not weaken, on the contrary they strengthen, the world organization. They are in fact its main support. And why should there not be a European group which could give a sense of enlarged patriotism and common citizenship to the distracted peoples of this turbulent and mighty continent . . .

I am now going to say something that will astonish you. The first step in the re-creation of the European Family must be a partnership between France and Germany. In this way only can France recover the moral leadership of Europe. There can be no revival of Europe without a spiritually great France and a spiritually great Germany. The structure of the United States of Europe, if well and truly built, will be such as to make the material strength of a single State less important. Small nations will count as much as large ones and gain their honour by their contribution to the common cause. The ancient states and principalities of Germany, freely joined together for mutual convenience in a federal system, might each take their individual place among the United States of Europe. I shall not try to make a detailed programme . . .

But I must give you a warning. Time may be short . . . If we are to form the United States of Europe or whatever name or form it may take, we must begin now . . .

Our constant aim must be to build and fortify the strength of UNO. Under and within that world concept we must re-create the European family in a regional structure called, it may be, the United States of Europe. The first step is to form a Council of Europe. If at first all the States of Europe are not willing or able to join the Union, we must nevertheless proceed to assemble and combine those who will and those who can . . . In this urgent work, France and Germany must take the lead together. Great Britain, the British Commonwealth of Nations, mighty America, and I trust Soviet Russia – for then indeed all would be well – must be the friends and sponsors of the new Europe and must champion its right to live and shine.

Document 11

The great wartime coalition between the United States, Britain and the Soviet Union was already fraying before the end of the war in 1945. By 1947 the wartime alliance fractured completely, for the most part because of Soviet expansion.

Britain, which had been supporting Greece and Turkey against communist rebellions, announced in the winter of 1946–47 that it could no longer do so. After 15 weeks of frantic activity the American administration responded with the Truman Doctrine on 12 March 1947, in which President Truman told the American Congress that: 'It must be the policy of the United States of America to support free peoples who are resisting attempted subjugation by armed minorities, or by outside pressure'. Initially developed in response to the Greek and Turkish crises, it reflected the prevailing view that the situation in Western Europe was no less threatening.

On 5 June 1947 Secretary of State, George C. Marshall launched the idea of a Programme for European Recovery, of which the key for the future of Europe was the belief that 'The program should be a joint one, agreed to by a number, if not all, European nations'. This proved to be a catalyst to bring Western Europe together. Equally important it contributed significantly to the economic recovery of Europe, as the Plan restored the social and economic infrastructure of Europe. The aid was offered to the whole of Europe, but Stalin enforced rejection by Soviet satellites. Under the ERP, the United States gave some $13,150m to sixteen West European States.

Secretary of State, George C. Marshall, 'Speech at Harvard University', June 1947

In considering the requirements for the rehabilitation of Europe, the physical loss of life, the visible destruction of cities, factories, mines, and railroads was correctly estimated, but it has become obvious during recent months that this visible destruction was probably less serious than the dislocation of the entire fabric of European economy . . . Machinery has fallen into disrepair or is entirely obsolete . . . The breakdown of the business structure of Europe during the war was complete . . . But even given a more prompt solution of these difficult problems, the rehabilitation of the economic structure of Europe quite evidently will require a much longer time and greater effort than has been foreseen . . .

The truth of the matter is that Europe's requirements for the next three or four years of foreign food and other essential products – principally from America – are so much greater than her present ability to pay that she must have substantially additional help or face economic, social, and political deterioration of a very grave character.

The remedy lies in breaking the vicious circle and restoring the confidence of the European people in the economic future of their own countries and of Europe as a whole. The manufacturer and the farmer throughout wide areas must be able and willing to exchange their product for currencies, the continuing value of which is not open to question . . .

Our policy is directed not against any country or doctrine but against hunger, poverty, desperation, and chaos. Its purpose should be the revival of a working economy in the world so as to permit the emergence of political and social conditions in which free institutions can exist. Such assistance, I am convinced, must not be on a piecemeal basis as various crises develop. Any assistance that this Government may render in the future should provide a cure rather than a mere palliative. Any government that is willing to assist in the task of recovery will find full cooperation, I am sure, on the part of the United States Government. Any government which manoeuvres to block the recovery of other countries cannot expect help from us. Furthermore, governments, political parties, or groups which seek to perpetuate human misery in order to profit therefrom politically or otherwise will encounter the opposition of the United States.

It is already evident that, before the United States Government can proceed much further in its efforts to alleviate the situation and help start the European world on its way to recovery, there must be some agreement among the countries of Europe as to the requirements of the situation and the part those countries themselves will take in order to give proper effect to whatever action might be undertaken by this Government. It would be neither fitting nor efficacious for this Government to undertake to draw up unilaterally a programme designed to place Europe on its feet economically. This is the business of the Europeans. The initiative, I think, must come from Europe. The role of this country should consist of friendly aid in the drafting of a European programme and of later support of such a programme so far as it may be practical for us to do so. The programme should be a joint one, agreed to by a number, if not all, European nations. An essential part of any successful action on the part of the United States is an understanding on the part of the people of America of the character of the problem and the remedies to be applied . . . With foresight, and a willingness on the part of our people to face up to the vast responsibility which history has clearly placed upon our country, the difficulties . . . can and will be overcome . . .

Documents 12

The international tensions that contributed to the Truman Doctrine and Marshall Plan continued unabated. Indeed, they intensified with the Soviet formation in September 1947 of Cominform. A further drama was the Communist coup d'etat of February 1948 in Prague. The split in Europe between East and West and the continuing apparent hostility of the Soviets, led many Western leaders to contemplate the need for a Western defensive alliance. They recognized too that they would have to show that they were trying to do something for themselves, before they could hope to attract American commitment to their security.

On 17 March 1948 representatives of Belgium, France, Luxembourg, the Netherlands and the United Kingdom signed the Brussels Treaty pledging themselves to a common defence and to strengthen their economic and cultural ties. The main carrier of the economic objective was the Organization for European Economic Cooperation, established in April 1948, and charged with carrying through the European Recovery Programme.

In September 1948 within the Brussels Treaty framework the Western Union Defence Organization was created, but it was overtaken by the North Atlantic Treaty signed on 4 April 1949.

The outbreak of the Korean War in June 1950 provoked demands for a European army and the re-arming of Germany (See Documents 17). When the proposed European Defence Community failed, the problem remained of German participation in Western defence. The five Brussels Treaty powers, the United States and Canada, as well as Italian and German representatives amended the 1948 Brussels Treaty, via the so-called Paris Agreements. These allowed for German membership of NATO, for Italian and German membership of the Western European Union, the re-named Western Union Defence Organization, and changed the 1948 commitment to take steps in the event of renewed German aggression to the objective 'to promote the unity and to encourage the progressive integration of Europe'. Also of note in the original Brussels Treaty is Article 10 (Article 12 of the amended 1954 Treaty), which is of contemporary relevance, and much mis-quoted.

'The Treaty of Economic, Social and Cultural Collaboration and Collective Self-Defence', Brussels, March 1948

Resolved . . . to afford assistance to each other, in accordance with the Charter of the United Nations, in maintaining international peace and security and in resisting any policy of aggression; to take such steps as may be held to be necessary in the event of a renewal by Germany of a policy of aggression; to associate progressively in the pursuance of these aims other States inspired by the same ideals and animated by the like determination;
[. . .]

Article 1

Convinced of the close community of their interests and of the necessity of uniting in order to promote the economic recovery of Europe, the High Contracting Parties will so organize and coordinate their economic activities as to produce the best possible results, by the elimination of conflict in their economic policies, the coordination of production and the development of commercial exchanges.

The cooperation provided for in the preceding paragraph, which will be effected through the Consultative Council referred to in Article 7 as well as through other bodies, shall not involve any duplication of, or prejudice to, the work of other economic organizations in which the High Contracting Parties are or may be represented but shall on the contrary assist the work of those organizations.

Article 2

The High Contracting Parties will make every effort in common, both by direct consultation and in specialized agencies, to promote the attainment of a higher standard of living by their peoples and to

develop on corresponding lines the social and other related services
of their countries.

The High Contracting Parties will consult with the object of achieving the earliest possible application of recommendations of immediate
practical interest, relating to social matters, adopted with their approval in the specialized agencies. They will endeavour to conclude
as soon as possible conventions with each other in the sphere of social
security.

[. . .]

Article 4 [Article 5 of the revised 1954 Treaty]

If any of the High Contracting Parties should be the object of an armed
attack in Europe, the other High Contracting Parties will, in accordance with the provisions of Article 51 of the Charter of the United
Nations, afford the Party so attacked all the military and other aid
and assistance in their power . . .

[. . .]

Article 7

At the request of any of the High Contracting Parties, the Council
shall be immediately convened in order to permit the High Contracting Parties to consult with regard to any situation which may
constitute a threat to peace, in whatever area this threat should arise;
with regard to the attitude to be adopted and the steps to be taken in
case of a renewal by Germany of an aggressive policy; or with regard
to any situation constituting a danger to economic stability.

[. . .]

Article 10 [Article 12 of the revised 1954 Treaty]

The present Treaty . . . shall enter into force on the date of the deposit
of the last instrument of ratification and shall thereafter remain in
force for fifty years.

After the expiry of the period of fifty years, each of the High Contracting Parties shall have the right to cease to be a party thereto
provided that he shall have previously given one year's notice of
denunciation . . .

'Protocol Modifying and Completing the Brussels Treaty', Paris, October 1954

Inspired by a common will to strengthen peace and security;

Desirous to this end of promoting the unity and of encouraging the progressive integration of Europe;

Convinced that the accession of the Federal Republic of Germany and the Italian Republic to the Treaty will represent a new and substantial advance towards these aims; . . .

Article 1

The Federal Republic of Germany and the Italian Republic hereby accede to the Treaty as modified and completed by the present Protocol . . .

Article 2

The sub-paragraph of the Preamble to the Treaty: 'to take such steps as may be held necessary in the event of renewal by Germany of a policy of aggression' shall be modified to read: 'to promote the unity and to encourage the progressive integration of Europe' . . .

Article 3

The following new Article shall be inserted in the Treaty as Article 4: 'In the execution of the Treaty the High Contracting Parties and any organs established by Them under the Treaty shall work in close cooperation with the North Atlantic Treaty Organization'.

'Recognizing the undesirability of duplicating the Military Staffs of NATO, the Council and its agency will rely on the appropriate Military Authorities of NATO for information and advice on military matters'. [. . .]

Documents 13

The Hague Congress of 7–10 May 1948 represented a high point of federal aspirations in the immediate postwar period, but as seen in Document 14, its immediate outcome was a setback for federalists in the form of the Council of Europe.

Those meeting in The Hague attended as private individuals, but represented a variety of the transnational groups which had emerged both during and after the war, and which by and large, were convinced that the postwar political system required to be radically different from its prewar predecessor.

In 1947 an attempt was made to coordinate these groups. An early outcome of that effort, under the influence of Duncan Sandys, Churchill's son-in-law, was the Congress of Europe. Some favoured a mass movement approach, but Sandys and others opted for an international assembly of prominent public figures. Over 800 attended, including twelve former Prime Ministers, and François Mitterrand, the future President of France.

The Political Resolution was approved with only a handful of votes against in committee and unanimously by the plenary. It was widely reported in the press and captured widespread public interest.

The Economic Resolution, heavily influenced by the Marshall Plan and the creation of the OEEC, nonetheless previewed much of what was to come later.

A more immediate result was to be the creation of the Council of Europe in 1949 (See Document 14).

'The Hague Congress Political Resolution', May 1948

[Acknowledging] an unprecedented menace to the well-being and the security of the peoples of Europe . . .

The Congress:

1. Recognizes that it is the urgent duty of the nations of Europe to create an economic and political union in order to assure security and social progress.

2. Notes with approval the recent steps which have been taken by some European Governments in the direction of economic and political cooperation, but believes that in the present emergency the organizations created are by themselves insufficient to provide any lasting remedy.

3. Declares that the time has come when the European nations must transfer and merge some portion of their sovereign rights so as to secure common political and economic action for the integration and proper development of their common resources.

4. Demands the convening, as a matter of real urgency, of a European Assembly chosen by the Parliaments of the participating nations, from among their members and others, designed:

a)   to stimulate and give expression to European public opinion;

b)   to advise upon immediate practical measures designed progressively to bring about the necessary economic and political union of Europe;

c) to examine the juridical and constitutional implications arising out of the creation of such a union or federation and their economic and social consequences;

d) to prepare the necessary plans.

5. Considers that the resultant union or federation should be open to all European nations democratically governed and which undertake to respect a Charter of Human Rights, and resolves that a Commission should be set up to undertake immediately the double task of drafting such a Charter and of laying down standards to which a State must conform if it is to deserve the name of a democracy. Declares that in no circumstances shall a State be entitled to be called a democracy unless it does, in fact as well as in law, guarantee to its citizens liberty of thought, assembly and expression, as well as the right to form a political opposition.

Requests that this Commission should report within three months on its labours.

6. Is convinced that in the interest of human values and human liberty, the Assembly should make proposals for the establishment of a Court of Justice with adequate sanctions for the implementation of this Charter, and to this end any citizen of the associated countries shall have redress before the court, at any time and with the least possible delay, of any violation of his rights as formulated in the Charter.

7. Declares its conviction that the sole solution of the economic and political problems of Germany is its integration in a federated Europe.

8. Considers that any union or federation of Europe should be designed to protect the security of its constituent peoples, should be free from outside control, and should not be directed against any other nation.

9. Assigns to a united Europe the immediate task of establishing progressively a democratic social system, the aim of which shall be to free mankind from all types of slavery and from all economic insecurity, as political democracy is intended to protect it against the exercise of arbitrary power.

10. Declares that the union or federation must have as one of its objectives the improvement of economic, political, social and cultural standards of or in independent or associated territories, without prejudice to the ties which now bind its constituent parts to other countries beyond the seas.

11. Declares that the creation of a united Europe is an essential element in the creation of a united world.

'The Hague Congress Economic and Social Resolution', May 1948

The Congress:

1. Recognizes that no attempt to rebuild the economy of Europe upon the basis of rigidly divided national sovereignty can prove successful.

2. Affirms the urgent need for an economic union in Europe.

3. Declares that this union must maintain and progressively adjust the economic ties which at present link the countries of Europe with the Dominions and associated States or dependent territories overseas.

4. Welcomes the initial measures taken by certain Governments towards closer economic cooperation, or towards regional groupings; . . .

5. Urges all the Governments concerned forthwith to proclaim their determination to promote economic union and to put into effect the immediate economic measures required.

   These should include measures designed:

Trade

1. To remove step by step and, as soon as possible, finally abolish the obstacles to trade within the union which result from quotas and import or export prohibitions.

2. To reduce and, wherever possible, completely eliminate customs duties between the member States.

Currency

1. To restore budgetary equilibrium which is a first essential for the stability of currencies in each country and to reduce by all available means – including monetary policy – the disparities of prices and wages which are incompatible with the freedom of the exchanges.

2. To take early steps to establish multilateral clearings or, through the adjustment of exchange values, to set up areas within which the exchange of goods shall not be handicapped by currency controls.

3. Thus to pave the way for the free convertibility of currencies and

the gradual restoration of freedom of trade among the countries of Europe.

Production

1. To promote a common programme for the development of agricultural resources and the provision of the necessary equipment, in order to provide Europe with the highest possible nutritional standard.

2. To encourage technical or regional industrial specialization and the renewal and modernization of the technical means of production.

3. To draw up and carry into effect a programme of development and production for the basic industries of the whole area; this should include:

(a) the production and fair distribution of the coal resources of united Europe as well as the expansion of its electric power;

(b) the coordination and rationalization of communications;

(c) the utilization in general of resources and equipment of European countries in conformity with the needs of their peoples.

Labour

1. To raise to the greatest possible extent the standard of living of the populations of Europe . . .

2. To promote the mobility of labour to the maximum possible extent, while assuring to migrant workers and their families the standards of wages, social security, living conditions, and conditions of employment prevailing in the country to which they come.

3. To coordinate their economic policies so as to secure full employment.
[. . .]

Ultimate objectives

6. The Congress considers that in addition to these first measures, steps should also be taken to achieve, progressively, within the union:
[. . .]

(e) the free circulation of capital;

(f) the unification of currencies;

(g) the coordination of budgetary and credit policy;

(h) a full customs union, involving the abolition of all barriers to the movement of goods between the countries of the union and the application to non-member countries of tariffs low enough not to interfere with the normal flow or hinder the development of world trade;

(i)   the coordination of social legislation.

[. . .]

Document 14

In August 1948 the Belgian and French Governments supported proposals for the creation of a European parliamentary assembly, with real powers and taking decisions by majority vote. In October the Council of the Brussels Treaty set up a 'Committee of 18' to study this, the Hague proposals and British counter-proposals for an inter-governmental ministerial body. In January 1949 the Foreign Ministers of the five Brussels Treaty powers agreed in principle to the establishment of a Council of Europe, based on the British inter-governmental model, rather than the supranational alternatives. The Statute was signed in London in May 1949 by ten States, the Brussels five plus Denmark, Ireland, Italy, Norway and Sweden; others rapidly followed.

In 1948–49 many continental Europeans were still very anxious for British involvement in their endeavours for the future, and though disappointed by the limited competence of the new body, were ready to compromise to secure British participation. The Irish and Scandinavians, who had had different wartime experiences from the others, generally favoured the inter-governmental rather than supranational approach.

Most federalists had hoped the new body would have limited functions but real powers and would be the constituent assembly of the new United States of Europe. Both dreams were dashed. The Council of Europe was given very wide functions but no real power, given the unanimity rule.

One important initial success, and a lasting monument to the Council was the signing of the Convention for the Protection of Human Rights and Fundamental Freedoms in November 1950.

'Statute of the Council of Europe', London, May 1949

The Governments of . . .

Convinced that the pursuit of peace based on justice and international cooperation is vital for the preservation of human society and civilization;

Reaffirming their devotion to the spiritual and moral values which are the common heritage of their peoples and the true source of individual freedom, political liberty and the rule of law, principles which form the basis of all genuine democracy; . . .

Article 1

1. The aim of the Council of Europe is to achieve a greater unity between its members for the purpose of safeguarding and realizing the ideals and principles which are their common heritage and facilitating their economic and social progress.

2. This aim shall be pursued through the organs of the Council by discussion of questions of common concern and by agreements and common action in economic, social, cultural, scientific, legal and administrative matters and in the maintenance and further realization of human rights and fundamental freedoms . . .
[. . .]

4. Matters relating to National Defence do not fall within the scope of the Council of Europe.
[. . .]

Article 3

Every member of the Council of Europe must accept the principles of the rule of law and of the enjoyment by all persons within its jurisdiction of human rights and fundamental freedoms, and collaborate sincerely and effectively in the realization of the aim of the Council . . .
[. . .]

Article 20

Resolutions of the Committee of Ministers . . . require the unanimous vote of the representatives . . .
[. . .]

Article 22

The Consultative Assembly is the deliberative organ of the Council of Europe. It shall debate matters within its competence under this Statute and present its conclusions, in the form of recommendations, to the Committee of Ministers.

Documents 15

The unity of the 'United Nations' who had fought the war as allies had collapsed by 1944–45. Even the Western allies were divided over the postwar settlement. France governed the Saar, and treated it almost as a colony. The Ruhr was administered by the International Ruhr Authority, consisting of representatives of the USA, the UK and France.

France needed German coal for its own recovery plan. But France also wanted to maintain restrictions on the recovery of Ruhr heavy industry, fearful of competition from German steel. The Germans resented the controls imposed upon them and were upset by what appeared to be French attempts to detach the Saar permanently from Germany.

M. Jean Monnet was appointed Commissioner for the first French National Plan in January 1946. The Plan took account of French control of Saar industry and of the restrictions which France wanted to maintain on the industrial power of the Ruhr.

By 1949 Monnet was beginning to think about planning on a European basis. He made some overtures to London, but became convinced that the British Government was not prepared to enter into a closer economic union.

In March 1950, the German Chancellor, Dr Konrad Adenauer, suggested the fusion of France and Germany, modelling himself, so it seemed to Monnet, on the proposed Anglo-French Union of 1940. The proposal was ill-received in France.

Monnet sought some other effective means of embedding France and Germany in a common interest. In April 1950, returning from a walking tour, he reflected on an allied conference due to be held in London on 10 May, at which France would foreseeably come under Anglo-American pressure to accept an easement of the constraints on Germany. On 1 May 1950, M. Robert Schuman, French Foreign Minister accepted Monnet's idea for a Franco-German Coal and Steel Pool. On 3 May 1950, M. Monnet presented to him and to the French Prime Minister, M. Bidault, a fuller statement of the argument for the project. On 7 May, M. Monnet and his team met to draft the Declaration which M. Schuman was to make on 9 May 1950.

Monnet and the French were keen to involve the UK but after the negotiations leading to the Council of Europe (See Document 14) were wary and realistic. In the aftermath of the Schuman Declaration there was a series of convoluted talks and exchange of notes between the French and British. The key stumbling block was a proposed draft French communiqué, to be accepted by all those participating in the negotiations, which committed them to the principles of 'pooling' production and the institution of a 'new higher authority whose decisions will bind'.

Jean Monnet, 'Memorandum to Robert Schuman and Georges Bidault', May 1950

Whichever way you turn in the situation in the world today, you meet only deadlock, whether it is the growing acceptance of the inevitability of a war, the German problem, the continuation of French recovery, the organization of Europe, even the place of France in Europe and in the world.

To get out of such a situation there is only one way: concrete and resolute action, bearing on a limited but decisive point, changing it fundamentally and systematically changing the very terms of the whole set of problems.

It is in this spirit that the attached proposal has been devised. The following reflections summarize the findings which led to it.

I

Minds have fixed on a simple and dangerous objective: the Cold War.

Every proposal, every action is seen by public opinion as a contribution to the Cold War.

The Cold War has as its objective to make the adversary yield; it is the first phase of a real war.

This outlook creates among ruling circles a rigidity of mind which characterizes the pursuit of a single objective. The search for solutions to problems disappears. Rigidity of mind and of objective all round inevitably lead to a collision which is in the logic of the outlook. The collision means war.

In fact, we are already at war.

We have to change the course of events. To do that, we have to change the spirit of men. Words are not enough. Only immediate action, bearing on one essential point can change the present stasis. The action must be deep, real, immediate and dramatic. It must be able to change things and bring to life the hopes which people are on the point of losing belief in. It will thus give the peoples of 'free' countries hope in objectives which are further off than those for which they are working and will arouse in them active determination to pursue them.

II

The German situation is rapidly becoming a dangerous cancer for peace in the near future, and for France at once, if the Germans do not point themselves towards hope and collaboration with free peoples.

The situation cannot be settled by German unification, because it would require US/USSR agreement, unimaginable at this time . . .

We must not seek to settle the German problem which cannot be settled with what we have in hand. We have to change what we have by transforming it.

We have to undertake a dynamic action which will transform the German situation and lift up German spirits. We must not look for a static settlement using only what we at present have.

III

The continuation of French recovery will be stopped short if the question of German industrial production and its competitive capacity is not settled rapidly.

The basis of the superiority which French industrialists have always acknowledged in Germany is its production of steel at a price with which France can barely compete. From this they draw the conclusion that the whole of French production is handicapped.

Germany is already asking to increase its steel production from 11 to 14 million tons. We will refuse, but the Americans will insist. In the end we will, with some reservations, give way. At the same time, French production will run flat or even fall.

It is enough to state these facts to be spared the need to describe the consequences in elaborate detail: Germany expanding, German export dumping; French industries' demands for protection; stopping or fudging the liberalization of trade; re-creating the prewar cartels; possible direction of German expansion towards the East, a prelude to political agreements; France falling back into the ruts of curtailed protected production.

The decision which will bring about that situation will be embarked upon, if not taken, at the London conference, under American pressure.

[. . .]

With the proposed solution comes the disappearance of the question of the dominance of German industry, which would instil fear in Europe, would be the cause of constant trouble; and in the end would prevent the union of Europe and would afresh bring about the loss of Germany itself. On the contrary, the solution creates for German, French and European industry the conditions for common expansion in competition, without dominance.

From the French point of view, such a solution places national industry at the same starting point as German industry, eliminates the export dumping which the German steel industry would otherwise practise, and gives the French steel industry its share of European expansion, without fear of dumping and without the lure of the cartel. Industrialists' fears, which would involve Malthusianism, the end of 'liberalization' and in the end the return to the ruts of the past will be eliminated. The greatest obstacle to the continuation of French industrial progress will have been seen off.

IV

Until now, we have been engaged in an effort to secure the economic, military and political organization of the West: OEEC, Brussels Treaty, Strasbourg.

Two years of experience, OEEC discussions of payments agreements, the liberalization of trade etc., the armaments programme submitted to the last meeting in Brussels, the discussions in Strasbourg, the efforts – still without concrete result – to reach a Franco-Italian Customs Union show that we are making no real progress towards the goal which we set ourselves: the organization of Europe, its economic development and its collective security.

No matter how much England wants to collaborate with Europe it will never agree to anything which could loosen its ties with the Dominions, or to enter into commitments with Europe going beyond those which America itself would undertake.

Germany, the essential element in Europe, cannot become involved in the organization of Europe as things stand, for the reasons given above.

It is certain that the continuation of action undertaken along the lines in which we are at present engaged leads nowhere and moreover risks not seizing the time when the organization of Europe would be possible . . .

We must abandon the forms of the past and embark on the road of transformation both by the creation of economic conditions on a common base and by the establishment of new authorities accepted by national sovereignties.

Europe has never existed. The sum of sovereignties meeting in Councils does not make up an entity. We must genuinely create

Europe, so that it reveals itself to itself and to American opinion and so that it has confidence in its own future . . .

V

At the present time, Europe cannot be born without France. France alone can speak and act . . .

Robert Schuman, 'Declaration', May 1950

World peace cannot be safeguarded without the making of creative efforts proportionate to the dangers which threaten it. The contribution which an organized and living Europe can bring to civilization is indispensable to the maintenance of peaceful relations. In taking upon herself for more than twenty years the role of champion of a united Europe, France has always had as her essential aim the service of peace. A united Europe was not achieved and we had war.

Europe will not be made all at once, or according to a single plan. It will be built through concrete achievements which first create a *de facto* solidarity. The coming together of the nations of Europe requires the elimination of the age-old opposition of France and Germany. Any action taken must in the first place concern these two countries.

With this aim in view, the French Government proposes to take action immediately on one limited but decisive point. It proposes that Franco-German production of coal and steel as a whole be placed under a common High Authority, within the framework of an organization open to the participation of the other countries of Europe.

The pooling of coal and steel production should immediately provide for the setting up of common foundations for economic development as a first step in the federation of Europe, and will change the destinies of those regions which have long been devoted to the manufacture of munitions of war, of which they have been the most constant victims.

The solidarity in production thus established will make it plain that any war between France and Germany becomes not merely unthinkable, but materially impossible. The setting up of this powerful productive unit, open to all countries willing to take part and bound ultimately to provide all the member countries with the basic elements of industrial production on the same terms, will lay a true foundation for their economic unification. This production will be offered to the world as a whole without distinction or exception, with the aim of contributing to raising living standards and to promoting peaceful achievements.

In this way there will be realized simply and speedily that fusion of interests which is indispensable to the establishment of a common economic system; it may be the leaven from which may grow a wider and deeper community between countries long opposed to one another by sanguinary divisions.

By pooling basic production and by instituting a new High Authority, whose decisions will bind France, Germany and other member countries, this proposal will lead to the realization of the first concrete foundation of a European Federation indispensable to the preservation of peace.

To promote the realization of the objectives defined, the French Government is ready to open negotiations on the following bases:

The task with which this common High Authority will be charged will be that of securing in the shortest possible time the modernization of production and the improvement of its quality; the supply of coal and steel on identical terms to the French and German markets, as well as to the markets of other member countries; the development in common of exports to other countries; the equalization and improvement of the living conditions of workers in these industries.

To achieve these objectives, starting from the very conditions in which the production of member countries is at present situated, it is proposed that certain transitional measures should be instituted, such as the application of a production and investment plan, the establishment of compensating machinery for equating prices, and the creation of a restructuring fund to facilitate the rationalization of production. The movement of coal and steel between member countries will immediately be freed from all customs duty, and will not be affected by differential transport rates. Conditions will gradually be created which will spontaneously provide for the more rational distribution of production at the highest level of productivity.

In contrast to international cartels, which tend to impose restrictive practices on distribution and the exploitation of national markets, and to maintain high profits, the organization will ensure the fusion of markets and the expansion of production.

The essential principles and undertakings defined above will be the subject of a treaty signed between the States and submitted for the ratification of their national parliaments. The negotiations required to settle details of application will be undertaken with the help of an arbitrator appointed by common agreement. He will be entrusted with the task of seeing that the agreements reached conform with the principles laid down, and, in the event of a deadlock, he will decide what solution is to be adopted. The common High Authority entrusted with the management of the scheme will be composed of independent persons chosen by common agreement between the Governments. The Authority's decisions will be enforceable in France, Germany and other member countries. Appropriate measures will be provided for means of appeal against the decisions of the Authority.

A representative of the United Nations will be accredited to the Authority, and will be instructed to make a public report to the United Nations twice yearly, giving an account of the working of the new organization, particularly as concerns the safeguarding of its specific objectives.

The institution of the High Authority will in no way prejudice the methods of ownership of enterprises. In the exercise of its functions, the common High Authority will take into account the powers conferred upon the International Ruhr Authority and the obligations of all kinds imposed upon Germany, so long as these remain in force.

'Anglo-French Discussions Regarding French Proposals for the Western European Coal, Iron and Steel Industries', May 1950

The British Prime Minister, Mr Attlee, 11 May 1950

It is the declared policy of the Western Powers to promote the entry of Germany as a free member into the comity of European nations. The French proposals are designed to facilitate that process and must consequently be regarded as a notable contribution towards the solution of a major European problem. The proposals also have far-reaching implications for the future economic structure of participating countries; and this aspect will require very careful study by His Majesty's Government and the other Governments concerned. His Majesty's Government will approach the problem in a sympathetic spirit and desire to make it clear at the outset that they welcome this French initiative to end the age-long feud with Germany and so bring unity and peace to Europe . . .

Minute of meetings between M. Jean Monnet, and Sir Edwin Plowden, the Chief Planning Officer to His Majesty's Government

It became clear in the course of these talks that the French Government

felt it desirable that the acceptance by other Governments of the principles set out in the French communiqué of 9 May should precede any working out of the practical application of their proposals.
[. . .]

[The French from the outset made clear they were] anxious that the British Government should associate itself with the French initiative . . . They pointed out that if it were desired to reach concrete results it was necessary that the Governments should be in agreement from the beginning on the principles and the essential undertakings defined in the French Government's document, but that the numerous problems which would arise from putting the project into effect would require discussions and studies which would have to be pursued in common with the object of achieving the signature of the proposed treaty . . .

Reply by the British Government, 31 May 1950

[. . .]

After the most careful study of the French Memorandum, it remains the view of His Majesty's Government that to subscribe to the terms of the draft communiqué enclosed in the French Government's Memorandum of 25 May would involve entering into an advance commitment to pool coal and steel resources and to set up an authority, with certain supreme powers, before there had been full opportunity of considering how these important and far-reaching proposals would work in practice. His Majesty's Government are most anxious that these proposals should be discussed and pursued but they feel unable to associate themselves with a communiqué which appears to take decisions prior to, rather than as a result of, intergovernmental discussions . . .

Document 16

The Treaty establishing the European Coal and Steel Community, signed in Paris on 18 April 1951 and due to expire in 2002, opens with a ringing preamble and then goes on to create the Coal and Steel Community.

The Treaty creates a High Authority, non-elected and vested with wide powers, the exercise of some of which depends upon the unanimous assent of the Council, representing the Governments of the member States.

M. Monnet had seen no need for a Council of Ministers, and little for a Parliamentary Assembly. He yielded on both, largely at the insistence of the Netherlands and Belgium, but the Assembly remained consultative only, apart from its power to dismiss the High Authority as a body by a vote of two-thirds of its membership.

The 'Merger Treaty' creating a single Council and a single Commission of the European Communities and to that extent amending the ECSC Treaty was signed in Brussels on 8 April 1965. One of the changes was the deletion of the word 'supranational' from the description of the duties of a member of the single Commission (new article 10). This word had fallen out of favour with the six member States.

'The Treaty Establishing the European Coal and Steel Community', Paris, April 1951

Considering that world peace can be safeguarded only by creative efforts commensurate with the dangers that threaten it, . . .

Convinced that the contribution which an organized and vital Europe can make to civilization is indispensable to the maintenance of peaceful relations,

Recognizing that Europe can be built only through practical achievements which will first of all create real solidarity, and through the establishment of common bases for economic development, . . .

Anxious to help, by expanding their basic production, to raise the standard of living and further the works of peace, . . .

Resolved to substitute for age-old rivalries the merging of their essential interests; to create by establishing an economic community, the basis for a broader and deeper community among peoples long divided by bloody conflicts; and to lay the foundations for institutions which will give direction to a destiny henceforward shared, . . .

Have decided to create a European Coal and Steel Community . . .
[. . .]

Article 9 [In 1951 original]

The members of the High Authority . . . shall refrain from any action incompatible with the supranational character of their duties.

Article 10 [as amended in 1965 Merger Treaty]

The members of the Commission . . . shall refrain from any action incompatible with their duties . . .

Documents 17

On 25 June 1950 North Korean forces invaded South Korea. This attack was widely perceived in the West as a possible precursor or diversion to a Soviet attack on West Berlin or Western Europe. In this situation, the United States began to think about the reservoir of manpower in West Germany. In 1950, however, few Europeans were willing to envisage a re-armed Germany.

Robert Schuman himself had made clear during the ratification debate on the North Atlantic Treaty in the French National Assembly that: 'Germany is unarmed and will remain unarmed . . . It is unthinkable that she should be allowed to join the Atlantic Pact as a nation empowered to defend or help defend other nations'. Even the new German Government was not willing to contemplate a reconstituted Wehrmacht, although in December 1949 their new Chancellor, Adenauer, said he might be able to envisage 'a German contingent in the army of a European federation, under European command'.

Against this background, Mr Churchill, leader of the British opposition party, made a celebrated speech in the Consultative Assembly of the Council of Europe. The resolution which he proposed was passed by eighty-nine votes to five. Churchill is thus often seen as the 'father' of the idea of a European army.

Monnet and others were equally concerned about the turn of events, and especially that they might undermine the progress on the negotiations about the Schuman Plan (See Document 15) by raising fears in and about Germany. Monnet and the same team that worked on the Schuman Plan thus began to evolve a proposal in the military area. The French Prime Minister, René Pléven, announced the Pleven Plan to the French National Assembly on 24 October 1950. He said that France now recognized that since Germany would benefit from the Atlantic Pact system, it should contribute to the system of defence for Western Europe. He thus proposed 'the creation, for our common defence, of a European army tied to political institutions of a united Europe'.

The Pléven Plan and European Defence Community Treaty broadly followed the ECSC model, as can be seen in this Document, but they ran into a series of objections. Many doubted whether an allied command structure would be efficient; many in France were doubtful about the ultimate subordination to NATO, and thus America; and even more im-

portantly, there was a strong reluctance to relinquish governmental control over the State's armed forces. More particularly, changes soon occurred in the French Government, France became even more disastrously embroiled in Indo-China, and growing unease developed about the concessions required of the French in the Treaty, giving up what the new Germany had not yet acquired, control of a national army. At root too there remained a deep unhappiness about re-arming Germany.

Nonetheless, the European Defence Community Treaty and accompanying protocols were signed in Paris on 27 May 1952 by all six members of the ECSC. Four of them ratified the Treaty. In Germany the Social Democrats opposed it, but were defeated. By the summer of 1954 the Italians were close to ratifying, but the French were not. Their partners refused a French request for major revisions to the Treaty, and at the end of August 1954 the French National Assembly on a procedural motion rejected the Treaty.

Since the issues that caused the proposal had not gone away, something still had to be done. The result was the revamping of the 1948 Brussels Treaty by the Paris Agreements of 1954, which led to the Western European Union and the membership of the Federal Republic of Germany in NATO in 1955 (See Documents 12).

Mr Winston Churchill, 'Speech to the Consultative Assembly of the Council of Europe', August 1950

I am very glad that the Germans, amid their own problems, have come here to share our perils and augment our strength . . . There is no revival of Europe, no safety or freedom for any of us, except in standing together, united and unflinching . . .

Now, however, suddenly the lightning-flash in Korea, and the spreading conflagration which has followed it, has roused the whole of the free world to a keen and vehement realization of its dangers, and many measures are now proposed which, if they had been taken two years ago, would at least have yielded fruit by now . . .

I do not doubt that, as the realization of our mortal danger deepens, it will awaken that sense of self-preservation which is the foundation of human existence, and this process is now going forward . . . We in this Assembly have no responsibility or executive power, but we are bound to give our warning and our counsel. There must be created, and in the shortest possible time, a real defensive front in Europe. Great Britain and the United States must send large forces to the Continent. I have already made my appeal to Germany. France must again revive her famous army. We welcome our Italian comrades. All . . . must bear their share and do their best . . . Those who serve supreme causes must not consider what they can get but what they can give . . .

Not only should we reaffirm, . . . our allegiance to the United Nations, but we should make a gesture of practical and constructive guidance by declaring ourselves in favour of the immediate creation of a European army under a unified command, and in which we should all bear a worthy and honourable part. Therefore, . . . I beg to move that:

The Assembly in order to express its devotion to the maintenance of peace and its resolve to sustain the action of the Security Council of the United Nations in defence of peaceful peoples against aggression, calls for the immediate creation of a unified European army subject to proper European democratic control and acting in full cooperation with the United States and Canada.

'The European Defence Community Treaty', Paris, May 1952

Determined in cooperation with the free nations and in the spirit of the Charter of the United Nations, to contribute to the maintenance of peace, more particularly by ensuring the defence of Western Europe against any aggression in close collaboration with organizations having the same purpose;

Considering the fullest possible integration to the extent compatible with military necessities, of the human and material elements of their Defence Forces assembled within a supranational European organization to be the best means for the attainment of this aim with the necessary speed and efficiency;

Convinced that such integration will lead to the most rational and economical use of their countries' resources, in particular through the establishment of a common budget and common armaments programmes;

Determined thereby to secure the expansion of their military strength without detriment to social progress;

Anxious to preserve the spiritual and moral values which are the common heritage of their peoples, and convinced that within the common force formed without discrimination between the member States, national patriotism, far from being weakened, will be consolidated and harmonized in a broader framework;

Recognizing that this is a new and essential step towards the creation of a united Europe;

Have resolved to set up a European Defence Community . . .

Article 1

The High Contracting Parties, by the present Treaty, set up among themselves a European Defence Community, supranational in character, comprising common institutions, common armed forces, and a common budget.

Article 2

1. The objectives of the Community are exclusively defensive.

2. Consequently, under the conditions set forth in this Treaty, it shall ensure the security of member States against any aggression by taking part in Western defence within the framework of the North Atlantic Treaty; by integrating the defence forces of the member States; and by the rational and economical employment of their resources.

3. Any armed attack against any of the member States in Europe or against the European Defence Forces shall be considered an armed attack on all member States. The member States and the European Defence Forces shall afford to the State or forces so attacked all the military and other aid in their power . . .
[. . .]

Article 9

The armed forces of the Community, hereinafter known as the 'European Defence Forces', shall be composed of units made available to the Community by its member States, with a view to their fusion under the conditions laid down in this Treaty.

No member State shall recruit or maintain national armed forces other than those for which provision is made in Article 10 below.

Article 10

1. Member States may recruit and maintain national armed forces intended for employment in non-European territories for whose defence they have assumed responsibility, together with home-based units necessary for the maintenance and relief of such forces.

2. Member States may also recruit and maintain national armed forces for the fulfilment of international missions accepted by them,
[. . .]

5. The total size of the national armed forces referred to in the present Article, including maintenance units, shall not be so large as to jeopardize the contribution of any member State to the European Defence Forces, as determined by agreement between the Governments of the member States.

Article 18

1. The competent Supreme Commander responsible to the North Atlantic Treaty Organization shall, subject to the proviso in paragraph 3 below, be authorized to ensure that the European Defence Forces are organized, equipped, trained and prepared for their duties in a satisfactory manner. As soon as they are ready for service, these forces, subject to the proviso referred to above, shall be placed at the disposal of the competent Supreme Commander responsible to the North Atlantic Treaty Organization who shall exercise over them such authority and responsibilities as devolve on him by virtue of his mandate and, in particular, shall submit to the Community his requirements as regards the articulation and deployment of the forces; . . .

2. In time of war, the competent Supreme Commander responsible to the North Atlantic Treaty Organization shall exercise over the forces referred to above the full powers and responsibilities as Supreme Commander conferred upon him by his mandate.

3. In the case of units of the European Defence Forces assigned to internal defence and the protection of the sea approaches of the territories of member States, determination of the authorities to whom they shall be subordinate for Command purposes and employment shall depend either on NATO conventions concluded within the framework of the North Atlantic Treaty or on agreements between NATO and the Community.

Article 38

The Assembly [of the European Defence Community, and the same as the ECSC Assembly] shall also examine problems arising from the co-existence of different agencies for European cooperation already established or which might be established, with a view to ensuring coordination within the framework of the federal or confederal structure . . .

Article 120

1. The present Treaty shall be applicable to the European territories of member States.

[. . .]

3. By a unanimous decision of the Council, after parliamentary approval where necessary in accordance with the constitutional rules of each member State . . .

European defence formations may be stationed on territories other than those envisaged in paragraph 1 . . .

Document 18

Pléven spoke in October 1950 of the need for a 'single European political and military authority' (See Document 17). Discussions on a European army and defence community were likely to require discussions on foreign policy and a political community.

In September 1952 the Foreign Ministers of the Six asked the ECSC Assembly in conjunction with a number of co-opted members to study the creation of a European Political Community and draft a Treaty.

The seventy-eight member 'constitutional committee', under the Presidency of M. Paul Henri-Spaak, produced by March 1953 a draft, which was agreed in principle by the six Governments in the summer of 1953. The project was finally laid to rest with the failure of the EDC in August 1954, although many of its ideas were to reappear, and Article 82 became a starting point for the conclusion of the Treaty establishing the European Economic Community.

'Draft Treaty Embodying the Statute of the European Community Adopted by the Ad Hoc Assembly', 11 March 1953

We . . . [h]ave decided to create a European Community . . .

Article 1

The present Treaty sets up a European Community of a supranational character. The Community is founded upon a union of peoples and States, upon a respect for their personality and upon equal rights and duties for all. It shall be indissoluble.

Article 2

The Community has the following mission and general aims:

- to contribute towards the protection of human rights and fundamental freedoms in member States;

- to cooperate with the other free nations in ensuring the security of member States against all aggression;

- to ensure the coordination of the foreign policy of member States in questions likely to involve the existence, the security or the prosperity of the Community;

- to promote, in harmony with the general economy of member States, the economic expansion, the development of employment and the improvement of the standard of living in member States, by means, in particular, of the progressive establishment of a common market, . . .

[. . .]

Article 5

The Community, together with the European Coal and Steel Community, and the European Defence Community, shall constitute a single legal entity . . .
[. . .]

Article 9

The institutions of the Community shall be:

- Parliament

- the European Executive Council

- the Council of National Ministers

- the Court of Justice . . .

- the Economic and Social Council

Article 10

Parliament shall enact legislation and make recommendations and proposals. It shall also approve the budget . . . It shall exercise such powers of supervision as are conferred upon it by the present Statute.

Article 11

Parliament shall be composed of two Chambers which, unless the present Statute otherwise provides, shall have identical powers and competence.

The first Chamber, entitled the People's Chamber, shall be composed of deputies representing the peoples united in the Community.

The second Chamber, entitled the Senate, shall be composed of senators representing the people of each State.

Article 12

Deputies and senators shall vote as individuals . . . They may not accept any mandate as to the way in which they shall cast their votes.

Article 13

Deputies shall be elected by universal, equal and direct suffrage . . . The Community shall enact legislation defining the principles of the electoral system.

[. . .]

Article 23

1. Members of Parliament and of the European Executive Council shall have the right to initiate legislation.

2. Members of Parliament shall have the right of amendment and interpellation. They may put oral or written questions to the European Executive Council, which shall be required to answer them . . .

[. . .]

Article 27

The European Executive Council shall undertake the general administration of the Community. It shall have no powers other than those conferred upon it by the present Statute.

Article 28

The Senate shall elect the President of the European Executive Council in secret ballot, by majority of its members.

[. . .]

2. The President shall appoint the other members of the European Executive Council.

3. The European Executive Council shall not include more than two members of the same nationality.

4. The members of the European Executive Council shall have the title of Ministers of the European Community.

[. . .]

Article 31

1. The European Executive Council . . . shall . . . request the People's Chamber and the Senate for their vote of confidence, which shall be given by each Chamber by majority vote of its members.

2. The European Executive Council shall remain in office until the end of the life of the current People's Chamber. It shall resign from office notwithstanding, if a vote of no confidence is passed against it by the People's Chamber or the Senate. It shall also be required to resign if the People's Chamber or the Senate refuses to grant its request for a vote of confidence . . .

[. . .]

Article 33

In order to fulfil the tasks entrusted to it, and in accordance with the conditions laid down in the present Statute, the European Executive Council shall take decisions, make recommendations or express opinions.

Decisions shall be binding in all aspects.

Recommendations shall have binding effect as regards the aims specified therein, but shall leave the means of implementation to the Authorities to whom the recommendation is addressed.

Opinions shall not be binding.

[. . .]

Article 36

The Council of National Ministers shall be composed of representatives of the member States. Each State shall delegate a member of its Government as a representative . . .

[. . .]

Article 52

1. The passing of legislation shall require the assent of each of the two Chambers in succession by simple majority . . .

Article 53

The European Executive Council may issue regulations to ensure the implementation of the laws of the Community.

The European Executive Council and the Authorities of each member State shall be charged, as they are each and severally affected, with the execution of the Community's legislation and of the regulations of the European Executive Council . . .

[. . .]

Article 69

In order to achieve the general aims laid down in Article 2, the Community shall ensure that the foreign policies of member States are coordinated. For this purpose the European Executive Council may be empowered, by unanimous decision of the Council of National Ministers, to act as common representative of the member States.

[. . .]

Article 82

The Community, while upholding the principles defined in Articles 2, 3 and 4 of the Treaty instituting the European Coal and Steel Community, shall establish progressively a common market of goods, capital and persons.

In order to achieve the aim mentioned in the preceding paragraph, the Community shall foster the coordination of the policy of the member States in monetary, credit and financial matters . . .

Document 19

When the Assemblée Nationale buried the European Defence Community and the European Political Community in 1954, the other member States of the ECSC declined to accept that European integration had suffered irreparable harm. The Dutch picked up the declaration of intention in Article 82 of the EPC Treaty concerning a European customs union (See Document 18). Working with M. Paul-Henri Spaak, Belgium's Foreign Minister, they called for a conference of Foreign Ministers to make a fresh start.

A Belgian draft became the basis of the declaration adopted at Messina on 1 and 2 June 1955. It looked to the establishment of a tariff-free European market; and invited the UK, as a member of the Western European Union and an associate of the ECSC to participate in the next stage of work.

The UK agreed to attend, but in the person of a Board of Trade official, Mr Russell Bretherton, who had European experience in the OEEC and in

Marshall Aid administration. *The other participants in a complex of groups collectively called the Spaak Committee were of Ministerial rank.*

In the discussions, speakers for the Six advocated a Customs Union, which appeared to them to be the sense of the Messina Declaration. Mr Bretherton spoke in favour of a free trade area. In November 1955, M. Spaak began to force the pace towards a final report. There is some difference of interpretation or recollection over whether Britain was pushed out, or withdrew.

The Spaak Report was presented to the Foreign Ministers of the Six meeting in Venice in May 1956. The meeting was brief. Expected French reservations were not uttered. The meeting accepted that the Report should be the basis for the drafting of a Common Market Treaty (and a customs union) and a Euratom Treaty. The only substantial matter not raised in the Spaak Report but negotiated during Treaty drafting was the French demand, almost in the form of an ultimatum, that overseas territories of the member States should be included in the Treaty.

'Resolution Adopted by the Ministers of Foreign Affairs of the Member States of the ECSC', Messina, June 1955

The Governments . . . believe the moment has come to go a step further towards the construction of Europe. In their opinion this step should first of all be taken in the economic field.

They consider that the further progress must be towards the setting up of a united Europe by the development of common institutions, the gradual merging of national economies, the creation of a common market, and the gradual harmonization of their social policies.

Such a policy appears to them to be indispensable if Europe's position in the world is to be maintained, her influence restored, and the standard of living of her population progressively raised.

I

To this end, the six Ministers have agreed on the following objectives:

1. The expansion of trade and the movement of persons call for the common development of large-scale communication facilities.

With this end in view, a joint study will be undertaken of a European network of canals, motor-highways, electric railway-lines, and the standardization of equipment, as well as on efforts to achieve a better coordination of air transport.

2. More and cheaper energy placed at the disposal of the European

economies is a fundamental necessity for economic progress. All measures should, therefore, be taken to develop the exchange of gas and electric current in order to raise the profitability of investments and reduce the cost of supplies. A study will also be made of the methods coordinating the common prospects for the development of energy production and consumption and establishing the broad outlines of an overall policy.

3. Before long, the development of nuclear energy for peaceful purposes will open up prospects of a new industrial revolution far beyond anything achieved during the past hundred years.

The six signatory States consider that it is essential to examine ways and means for creating a common organization which would have the responsibility and the facilities for ensuring the peaceful development of nuclear energy, taking into consideration the special arrangements made by certain Governments with third parties . . .

The six Governments agree that the setting up of a common European market, free from all customs duties and all quantitative restrictions, is the aim of their work in the field of economic policy.

They consider that such a market must be established by stages. Its introduction will necessitate a study of the following questions:

(a) procedure and rhythm required for the gradual elimination of impediments to trade between the participating countries, as well as appropriate measures for the gradual unification of custom systems in regard to third countries;

(b) steps to be taken for the harmonization of the general policy of the participating countries in the financial, economic and social fields;

(c) adoption of methods which will ensure a degree of coordination between the monetary policies of the member States which will enable the creation and development of a common market;

(d) a system of saving clauses;

(e) establishment and operation of a readaptation fund;

(f) gradual introduction of freedom of movement for workers;

(g) setting up of rules ensuring the full play of competition in the common market, in such a way as to exclude in particular all forms of national discrimination;

(h) the appropriate institutional means for the realization and operation of the common market.

The creation of a European investment fund will be examined. This fund would be used for the common development of Europe's inherent economic potentialities and, in particular for the development of the less favoured regions of the participating countries.

As far as the social field is concerned, the six Governments consider it imperative to study the progressive harmonization of the regulations now in force in the various countries, especially those relating to working hours, payment for over-time (night-work, work on Sundays and public holidays), length of statutory holidays and holiday pay.

II

The six Governments have decided to adopt the following procedure:

1. A conference or conferences will be convened for the purpose of drafting the relevant Treaties or arrangements.

2. These conferences will be prepared by a Committee of Government delegates assisted by experts under the chairmanship of a leading political figure whose task it will be to coordinate the work to be undertaken.

3. The Committee will call on the High Authority of the ECSC and on the Secretariats-General of the OEEC, the Council of Europe and the European Conference of Ministers of Transport for any cooperation it may require.

4. The general report of the Committee will be submitted to the Foreign Ministers not later than 1 October 1955.

5. The Foreign Ministers will meet before that date in order to examine the interim reports prepared by the Committee and to give the necessary directives.

6. The Government of the United Kingdom, as a State belonging to WEU and associated with ECSC will be invited to participate in this work.

7. The Foreign Ministers will decide in due time which other States are to be invited to participate in the conference or conferences mentioned in para. 1 above.

Documents 20

*Having withdrawn or been excluded from the Spaak Committee and from
the preparation of the new Treaties, the British Government sought to
enlist the US as an opponent of the closed circle developing in Europe.*

*The US answer was forthright. How the Europeans integrated them-
selves was for them to decide. But the US supported the 'six nation grouping
approach', even if it might tend towards protectionism and even if it could
make Europe more independent (i.e. less likely to accept US political leadership).*

'Memorandum of a Conversation', Department of State, Washington, November 1955

Subject: European Integration; Common Market and EURATOM

Sir Roger Makins, Ambassador, British Embassy
J. E. Coulson, Minister, British Embassy
Livingston T. Merchant, Assistant Secretary
Outerbridge Horsey, Director, BNA

The Ambassador said that he had been asked to discuss these questions informally with us. The British Government felt that it would
conflict with the interests of the Commonwealth association and with
their policy of freeing trade and payments for them to be associated
with the common market of the six Messina countries. The Government had, therefore, made the decision not to join . . .

The enterprise seemed, he said, to have an air of unreality since
the real French position seemed very questionable. There was no
question of the convictions of people like Spaak and Mayer, but the
Ambassador doubted very much whether, when the chips were down,
the French would be prepared to make the internal adjustments
which would be necessary for progress towards a common market.

More importantly, the British were concerned with the protectionist
and exclusive consequences of the six countries trying to move
towards a common market. The British recognized the political
advantages of integration but the inevitable economic effects would
seem to them to go contrary to our broader trade objectives as embodied, for example, in GATT. They wondered if we had thought
through this aspect of the question.

Mr Merchant said we felt very strongly that progress towards further integration was more important now than ever and that we hoped the Messina group would form a basis for such progress. We also thought that the peaceful uses of atomic energy might be the most practical immediate means of moving along this line. We would discuss the question further with interested officers in the Department, particularly in the economic area . . .

The Secretary of State, 'Letter to Foreign Minister Macmillan', Washington, December 1955

I am impressed with the necessity of strengthening in every way possible the unity and purpose of the West. I believe we can derive comfort from the fact that the Soviets seem unlikely to resort to general war to achieve their objectives in Europe. At the same time, . . . [T]heir tactics will inevitably be to try to divide us and, through so-called 'peaceful competition', to step up the battle for men's minds. I am confident of our ability to compete on any basis with the Soviet system. Our ability to do so, however, will depend upon the degree to which we are successful in preserving our unity and strength.

There is also the related question of Germany. I have no doubt about the present devotion of the Adenauer Government to full co-operation with the West. There is, however, the danger that the appeal of reunification will, over a period of time, become so strong in Germany as to give rise to temptation to discard the associations with the West in an effort to advance reunification on terms which would at best result in a neutral Germany and at worst in an Eastern-oriented Germany. Our problem is to prevent this possibility arising. The best means of doing this . . . is to so tie Germany into the whole complex of Western institutions – military, political and economic – and to so command her loyalties that neutrality or orientation to the East will be commonly accepted as unthinkable. This is a large order, I know, but I see no other alternative.

The form European unity takes is, of course, for the Europeans themselves to decide. We should not prescribe. Anything other than objective advice and cooperation could well be self-defeating. Europe can only unite effectively if it sees the advantages of uniting and wants to unite. Only in such a development can the required strength be built . . .

[I]t seems to me that the closer community of interests that Europe can build, the more hope Europe will have of realizing its potential for security, prosperity and influence in world affairs. To my mind, the six-nation grouping approach gives the greatest hope of achieving this end because of the closer unity which is inherent in that Community and because of the contribution which it will make to the strength and cohesion of the wider European grouping. It may well be that a six-nation community will evolve protectionist tendencies. It may be that it will show a trend towards greater independence. In the long run, however, I cannot but feel that the resultant increased unity would bring in its wake greater responsibility and devotion to the common welfare of Western Europe.

It is for these reasons, . . . [We] have been anxious to encourage in every appropriate way the current revival of initiative by the six nations in their search for new forms of integration in the fields of nuclear and conventional energy, a common market and transportation. We hope that progress will be swift, but we should be satisfied if there is sustained and real advance towards the practical ideal inherent in the supranational principle . . .

Document 21

The British were unhappy about the nature and direction of developments on the continent. In the summer of 1958 Prime Minister Macmillan gave vent to his growing exasperation in an internal memorandum to his Foreign Secretary (Selwyn Lloyd) and Chancellor (Heathcoat-Amory). A few days later Macmillan told President de Gaulle of France that failure to reach a free trade agreement between the EEC States and Britain could spell the end of NATO. In the end it was Britain that had to adjust (See Documents 23, 31 and 34).

Prime Minister, Harold Macmillan, 'Personal Minute to Selwyn Lloyd and D. Heathcoat-Amory', June 1958

I think sometimes our difficulties with our friends abroad result from our natural good manners and reticence. We are apt to press our points too strongly in the early stages of a negotiation, and then when a crisis arises and we have to take a definite position we are accused of perfidy. I feel we ought to make it quite clear to our European friends that if Little Europe is formed without a parallel development of a Free Trade Area we shall have to reconsider the whole of our political and economic attitude towards Europe. I doubt if we could remain in NATO. We should certainly put on highly protective tariffs and quotas to counteract what Little Europe was doing to us. In other words, we should not allow ourselves to be destroyed little by little. We would fight back with every weapon in our armoury. We would take our troops out of Europe. We would withdraw from NATO. We would adopt a policy of isolationism. We would surround ourselves with rockets and we would say to the Germans, the French and all the rest of them: 'Look after yourselves with your own forces. Look after yourselves when the Russians overrun your countries'. I would be inclined to make this position quite clear both to de Gaulle and to Adenauer [the West German Chancellor], so that they may be under no illusion.

Document 22

Having excluded itself from the Customs Union, Britain faced the prospect of 'reverse preferences', as the tariffs began to come down inside the EEC. One possible solution, which would secure all other British requirements, would be the setting up of a free trade area in which the European Community Customs Union would be a partner. A free trade area had already been much discussed within the OEEC and the mechanisms were well understood. So far as Britain was concerned agriculture could not come under free trade.

With the support of the Six, the OEEC set up a Ministerial Committee to pursue the various proposals for free trade in Europe. The chairman was Mr Reginald Maudling of Britain.

The Maudling Committee began work in October 1957. In November 1958 the French Government announced, outside the Committee, that it would not be possible to reach agreement on an industrial free trade area. The British then issued the following report.

British Government, 'Report on the Course of Negotiations up to December 1958'

1. This Command Paper describes the history up to the end of 1958 of the negotiations to establish a European free trade area.
[. . .]

4. The Council of the OEEC . . . in July 1956, decided to 'study the possible forms and methods of association, on a multilateral basis, between the proposed Customs Union and member countries not taking part therein' and set up a working party under the chairmanship of Baron Snoy (Belgium) to do this.

5. This working party, on which all the seventeen Member countries of OEEC were represented, concluded in its report published in January 1957 that it was technically possible to operate a free trade area in Europe which would include the customs and economic union of the Six.

[. . .]

8. The OEEC Council met at Ministerial level on 12/13 February 1957, to consider the report of Baron Snoy's working party. A resolution was unanimously adopted stating that the Council:

'Decides to enter into negotiations in order to determine ways and means on the basis of which there could be brought into being a European Free Trade Area, which would, on a multilateral basis, associate the European Common Market with other member countries of the Organization, and to prepare the necessary instruments. It draws special attention to the objective of finding ways to ensure the expansion of trade in agricultural products on a non- discriminatory basis between all member countries of the Organization. It also draws attention to the need to deal with the special situation of member countries in the course of economic development'.

[. . .]

17. The Council also decided [on 17 October 1957] to establish an Inter-Governmental Committee at Ministerial level, on which all seventeen member countries of OEEC were represented, to carry on the negotiations. There was agreement that the negotiations should be pressed forward so that the free trade area could be established in time for the first steps in the removal of tariffs and quotas to be taken on 1 January 1959, simultaneously with the first measures to reduce tariffs and quantitative restrictions in the European Economic Community.

[. . .]

20. The range of subjects under discussion had . . . been greatly enlarged beyond the original concept, which had been related primarily to the elimination of tariffs and quantitative restrictions. Throughout the second half of 1957, including the period when negotiations at the political level were suspended, experts had

continued to examine the technical and trade policy aspects of the free trade area. Several important documents emerged from these discussions, in particular a comprehensive report to the Inter-Governmental Committee on the problems of defining the origin of the goods to benefit from the tariff reductions and of avoiding trade deflections resulting from differences in external tariffs. Other subjects which were discussed up till March 1958 either in the Inter-Governmental Committee or in working parties or groups reporting to it included: the length and stages of the transitional period, the removal of quantitative import restrictions, rules for the reduction of tariffs, rules for administering the definition of origin, rules of competition, agriculture and fisheries, coordination of economic policy, harmonization of legislation, payments questions, coal and steel, nuclear materials, invisibles and capital movements, movement of workers, freedom of establishment, inland transport and transport charges, and the problems of the less developed countries . . .

[. . .]

23. On 15 January 1958, the French Government who had already indicated the difficulties which they feared in a free trade area of the type under discussion, announced their intention of preparing an alternative approach. The members of the European Economic Community subsequently agreed that any proposals to the Inter-Governmental Committee arising from this plan should take the form of a joint memorandum by the Community.

[. . .]

27. The Memorandum setting out the agreed views of the European Economic Community (paragraph 23 above) was circulated on 20 October. In this Memorandum the Community reaffirmed that it was determined, both for economic and political reasons, to arrive at an agreement which would make it possible to associate with the Community, on a multilateral basis, the other members of the OEEC in a European Economic Association to come into force on 1 January 1959 . . .

28. The latest meeting of the Inter-Governmental Committee was held on 13–14 November 1958. On 14 November an announcement was made to the Press on behalf of the French Government that it did not seem possible to them to establish the free trade area as it had been proposed and that they were looking for a new solution. As the Paymaster General informed Parliament on 17 November 1958, the further meetings in Paris which had been arranged could not take

place in these circumstances, because the whole basis on which the
Inter-Governmental Committee had been operating, namely the
unanimous determination of all Governments to secure the establishment of a free trade area, seemed to have been brought into
question.

Documents 23

*With the failure of the Maudling negotiations (See Document 22), Britain
began to realize the depth of commitment of the Six, and that a wider free
trade arrangement was unattainable. With one last throw of the dice,
Britain played a leading role in the creation of the European Free Trade
Area (EFTA) in 1960, involving Austria, Denmark, Norway, Portugal,
Sweden, and Switzerland. Meanwhile, the decision of the Six to accelerate
tariff reductions gave fresh edge to British concerns.*

*Very slowly a policy shift began to emerge, accelerated by a report
prepared under the chairmanship of Sir Frank Lee of the Treasury. By the
summer of 1960 political arguments suggested British membership might
contribute to European stability and that there was a danger that the Six
would replace Britain as the prime interlocutor of the United States. Economically, membership was seen as a way of stimulating competition and
bringing economies of scale. None of these arguments were clear cut or
decisive, and there was still much hesitation. Eventually Macmillan made
his announcement on 31 July 1961.*

*The brief extract from the speech of Hugh Gaitskell, the leader of the
Labour opposition, illustrates that hesitation was widespread, and gives a
hint of future Labour policy.*

*Despite the hesitations and the frequent assertions that the United King-
dom was only applying to join an 'economic' Community, there was
awareness of the wider political agenda of the Six. This awareness is still
disputed by Eurosceptics, but in 1962 Harold Macmillan made clear that
the UK did accept the ultimate political goal of the founding Six, although
there is a clear undercurrent that this acceptance was not so much with
enthusiasm, but as a sign of a lack of perceived alternatives. This acceptance
was, of course, later made a requirement of entrance negotiations by the
decisions flowing from The Hague summit in 1969 (See Document 33).*

*This British attempt was vetoed by President de Gaulle of France in
January 1963, although (or because?) some progress had been made in
the negotiations (See Document 29).*

The Prime Minister Mr Harold Macmillan and the Leader of the Opposition, Mr Hugh Gaitskell, 'Speeches in the House of Commons', August 1961

The Prime Minister (Mr Harold Macmillan)

I beg to move:

That this House supports the decision of Her Majesty's Government to make formal application under Article 237 of the Treaty of Rome in order to initiate negotiations to see if satisfactory arrangements can be made to meet the special interests of the United Kingdom, of the Commonwealth and of the European Free Trade Association; and further accepts the undertaking of Her Majesty's Government that no agreement affecting these special interests or involving British sovereignty will be entered into until it has been approved by this House after full consultation with other Commonwealth countries, by whatever procedure they may generally agree.
[. . .]

The underlying issues, European unity, the future of the Commonwealth, the strength of the free world are all of capital importance, and it is because we firmly believe that the United Kingdom has a positive part to play in their development – for they are all related – that we ask the House to approve what we are doing.
[. . .]

Meanwhile, there has grown up the practical application of the aspirations towards unity in continental Europe by the formation of the European Economic Community. I ask Hon. Members to note the word 'economic'. The Treaty of Rome does not deal with defence. It does not deal with foreign policy. It deals with trade and some of the social aspects of human life which are most connected with trade and production . . .

In this country, of course, there is a long tradition of isolation . . . a certain suspicion of foreigners . . . [and] the additional division . . . of a wholly different development of our legal, administrative and, to some extent, political systems. If we are basically united by our religious faith, even here great divisions have grown up.

Nevertheless, it is perhaps worth recording that in every period when the world has been in danger of tyrants of aggression, Britain has abandoned isolationism. It is true that when the immediate danger was removed, we have sometimes tried to return to an insular policy. In due course we have abandoned it. In any case, who can say today that our present danger had been removed, or will soon disappear? Who doubts that we have to face a long and exhausting struggle over more than one generation if the forces of Communistic expansion are to be contained?

[. . .]

There is also a feeling, and I share it, and it is a serious danger felt by many people, that it would be very dangerous if the United Kingdom, by helping to create a truly united Europe, united in every aspect of its life, were to join in a movement tending to isolate Europe from the world and turn its back on the world and look inwards only upon itself. It may, of course, be that there are some people in Europe who believe that this small but uniquely endowed continent can lead a rich, fruitful and prosperous life almost cut off from contact with the rest of the world.

But I do not believe that such people, if they exist, are to be found among the leading men or the Governments of Europe. Certainly, this island could never join an association which believed in such medieval dreams, but if there are little Europeans, and perhaps there are, is it not the duty of this country, with its world-wide ties, to lend weight to the majority of Europeans who see the true prospective of events? I believe that our right place is in the vanguard of the movement towards greater unity of the free world, and that we can lead better from within than outside. At any rate, I am persuaded that we ought to try . . . It is, of course, argued . . . that by associating more closely with Europe in this new economic grouping we should injure the strength of the Commonwealth . . . I ask myself the question: how can we best serve the Commonwealth? . . . Britain in isolation would be of little value to our Commonwealth partners, and I think that the Commonwealth understand it. It would, therefore, be wrong in my view to regard our Commonwealth and our European interests as conflicting. Basically they must be complementary.

If it is vital not to destroy the influence of the Commonwealth in the political field, . . . it is equally vital to do nothing that would damage it economically . . .

The system of free entry and preferences has been of great advantage to all the partners . . .

Our aim in these negotiations is to make satisfactory arrangements to meet the special interests of the Commonwealth, particularly, of course, in the economic field . . .

[A]gricultural industry . . . I frankly admit that if the structure of

the European Economic Community had been going on for a generation or more this task [meeting special interests] would be not only
difficult, but well-nigh impossible. But it has not. It is very new. The
Treaty lays down a number of principles, but the working out of
detailed policies, especially so far as agriculture is concerned, is only
just beginning . . .

Arrangements which will meet satisfactorily the legitimate concerns of our fellow-members of EFTA must be among the conditions
for our own entry into the EEC . . .

Our own agricultural industry . . . any decision to join . . .
depend[s] upon satisfactory arrangements being made . . . Our objective is to have a prosperous, stable and efficient agricultural industry,
organized to provide a good life for those who live and work in the
countryside . . .

Our system of agricultural support is basically different from the
methods which are being employed on the Continent, and which
seem likely to give the pattern of the common agricultural policy
when it is decided . . . Such a development would mean much more
substantial adaptations in our methods than we have been accus-
tomed to, at any rate in recent years – although our methods have
never been static.

I believe that there is a growing recognition that with changing
world conditions we are faced with the possibility of changes anyway
. . . But . . . we shall have to be satisfied that the actual policies
adopted can successively achieve what is desired . . . Our view that
we cannot carry matters further without formal negotiation applies
with special force to agriculture . . .

The development of the European Economic Community, the
opportunity of the mass market which this has created for European
industrialists, and the spur that this has given them to competitiveness and efficiency, present the British economy with great challenge.
Whether or not we go into the Common Market we shall have to face
the competition of very efficient industries throughout Western
Europe . . . in the long run an island placed as ours is, where our
need to export to other people which will always be greater than their
need to export to us, cannot maintain the high standards of life that
we want for our people in an isolated protective system . . .

With some modern industries . . . the economic scale of production
and the capital expenditure involved are so large that the industries
can be established and developed economically only with a mass
market . . . which can bring great savings in unit costs . . .

At present, the countries of the Six are only beginning what we might call the harmonization of their social policies . . . so if we join at a formative stage, as it were, we should be able to bring our own ideas into the common pool . . .

These apprehensions about the social implications of joining the Treaty are really aspects of a wider constitutional anxiety about what has often been called 'sovereignty'.

I must remind the House that the EEC is an economic community, not a defence alliance, or a foreign policy community, or a cultural community. It is an economic community, and the region where collective decisions are taken is related to the sphere covered by the Treaty, economic tariffs, markets and all the rest. Of course, every treaty limits a nation's freedom of action to some extent . . . Since the war this tendency has grown and our freedom of action is obviously affected by our obligations in NATO, WEU, OEEC and all the rest.

A number of years have passed since the movement began which culminated in the Treaty of Rome and I am bound to say that I do not see any signs of the members of the Community losing their national identity because they have delegated a measure of their sovereignty. This problem of sovereignty, to which we must, of course, attach the highest importance is, in the end, perhaps a matter of degree. I fully accept that there are some forces in Europe which would like a genuine federalist system . . . They would like Europe to turn itself into a sort of United States, but I believe this to be a completely false analogy.

The United States of America was originally born out of colonists with only a few generations of history behind them. They were of broadly the same national origins and spoke the same language. Europe is too old, too diverse in tradition, language and history to find itself united by such means. Although the federalist movement exists in Europe it is not one favoured by the leading figures and certainly not by the leading Governments of Europe today. Certainly not by the French Government.

The alternative concept, the only practical concept, would be a confederation, a commonwealth if Hon. Members would like to call it that – what I think General de Gaulle has called *Europe des patries* – which would retain the great traditions and the pride of individual nations while working together in clearly defined spheres for their common interest. This seems to me a concept more in tune with the national traditions of European countries and, in particular, of our own. It is one with which we could associate willingly and wholeheartedly. At any rate, there is nothing in the Treaty of Rome which commits the members of the EEC to any kind of federalist solution, nor could such a system be imposed on member countries.

Here again, unless we are in the negotiations, unless we can bring our influence to bear, we shall not be able to play our part in deciding the future structure of Europe . . .

To sum up, there are . . . some to whom the whole concept of Britain working closely in this field with other European nations is instinctively disagreeable. I am bound to say that I find it hard to understand this when they have accepted close collaboration in even more critical spheres. Others feel that our whole and sole duty lies with the Commonwealth. If I thought that our entry into Europe would injure our relations with and influence in the Commonwealth, or be against the true interest of the Commonwealth, I would not ask the House to support this step.

I think, however, that most of us recognize that in a changing world, if we are not to be left behind and to drop out of the mainstream of the world's life, we must be prepared to change and adapt our methods. All through history this has been one of the main sources of our strength.

I therefore ask the House to give Ministers the authority – not to sign a treaty – but to find out on what honourable basis such a treaty could be put forward for the decision of the House . . .

Leader of the Opposition (Mr Gaitskell)

I think that there is no question whatever of Britain entering into a federal Europe now. British opinion simply is not ripe for this, and in any event it is surely incompatible with all the pledges and promises which have been made about the Commonwealth. I am not saying that we have to commit ourselves for all time . . . But . . . there is no commitment at all, even to eventual federation. That must be left open.

Prime Minister, Harold Macmillan, Conservative Political Centre Booklet, 1962

By joining this vigorous and expanding community and becoming one of its leading members . . . This country would . . . increase its standing and influence in the councils of the world.

If we remain outside . . . the realities of power would compel our American friends to attach increasing weight to the views and

interests of the Six . . . and to pay less attention to our own . . . To
lose influence both in Europe and Washington, as this would mean,
would seriously undermine our international position.

It is true, of course, that political unity is the central aim of these
European countries and we would naturally accept that ultimate
goal . . . The form which that political unity should take is now under
active discussion in Europe, where opinions on it are strongly divided.

One thing is certain. As a member of the Community, Britain would
have a strong voice in deciding the nature and timing of political
unity. By remaining outside, we could be faced with a political solution in Europe which went counter to our views and interests, but
which we could do nothing to influence . . .

Document 24

*In both major British parties there was opposition to the application. Tory
opponents tended to focus on the federal objectives of the Six, which they
believed should be taken seriously and the damage to the 'old' Commonwealth. Labour critics, in opposition, were somewhat freer to express their
reservations, which focused on the Commonwealth and EFTA. The Labour
Party conference of October 1961 showed great hostility to EEC membership, although a resolution unconditionally opposing entry was rejected.
The adopted resolution was negative in tone and most speakers showed a
preference for the Commonwealth over Europe, and a fear of loss of independence. In the Labour National Executive's statement of September 1962
the basis of Labour's opposition became clearer, and set the tone for subsequent debates.*

'Statement by the Labour National Executive Committee',
September 1962

The Labour Party regards the European Community as a great and
imaginative conception. It believes that the coming together of the
six nations which have in the past so often been torn by war and
economic rivalry is, in the context of Western Europe, a step of great
significance. It is aware that the influence of this new Community on
the world will grow and that it will be able to play – for good or for
ill – a far larger part in the shaping of events in the 1960s and the
1970s than its individual member States could hope to play alone.

It is these considerations, together with the influence that Britain as a member could exercise upon the Community – and not the uncertain balance of economic advantage – that constitute the real case for Britain's entry.

The Labour Party, however, is also aware that membership of the Common Market would involve commitments to the nations of the Six which, in their scope and depth, go far beyond our relationships with any other group of nations. For the central purpose of the Common Market is not just the removal of trade barriers between its member States, but the conscious merging of their separate national economies into a single unit. Within this single Community the power of national Governments over commercial, industrial, financial, agricultural, fiscal and social policies will progressively wither away. In their place, common policies, arrived at by majority decisions, will emerge.

Moreover the Rome Treaty is itself only one expression of the will of the Six to closer political unity. The aim is to build on the foundations of the Common Market a single political Community, with a Common Parliament and, eventually, a Common Government. Powerful and ardent voices have indeed long urged the creation of a West European Federal State.

For Britain, such wide commitments present special and serious difficulties. Full membership of the Common Market is limited to European States. Although there is provision for associated status for some territories, many important members of the Commonwealth will be totally excluded. Moreover our situation is not the same as that of the other countries of the Community. While our histories have certainly overlapped, they have also diverged, and this has shaped our separate institutions and policies. Our connections and interests, both political and economic, lie as much outside Europe as within it. Membership of the Common Market could, therefore, decisively change our political and economic relations with the rest of the world. Unlike the Six, Britain is the centre and founder member of a much larger and still more important group, the Commonwealth. As such we have access to the largest single trading area in the world and political influence within a world-wide, multi-racial association of 700 million people.

Finally, although the unification of Western Europe is in itself a great historic objective, it has to be considered in the light of the effect it has on the two transcendent issues of our times: the Cold War, with its immense threat of global destruction, and the ever increasing division of the world into the affluent nations of Europe and North America and the poverty-stricken nations elsewhere . . .

The essential conditions

While deliberately refraining from hobbling the Brussels negotiations by laying down in advance a series of rigid and detailed terms, the Labour Party clearly stated the five broad conditions that would be required:

1. Strong and binding safeguards for the trade and other interests of our friends and partners in the Commonwealth.

2. Freedom as at present to pursue our own foreign policy.

3. Fulfilment of the Government's pledge to our associates in the European Free Trade Area.

4. The right to plan our own economy.

5. Guarantees to safeguard the position of British agriculture.

The acceptance by the Six of these five conditions . . . would mean a conscious decision to liberalize their commercial policy and to become an outward-looking rather than an inward-looking Community – one that recognizes, in deeds as well as words, that it has obligations not only to the 170 million people within the Common Market, but to the hundreds of millions outside.

Document 25

Ireland was a founder member of the OEEC and the Council of Europe. But given its neutrality, pre-occupation with Partition, irredentism and relative recent independence, it remained outside the mainstream of European developments. There was a strong emphasis upon protectionism and a belief that sovereignty was everything. Despite this, Irish policy on economic integration was decisively linked to that of Britain, since between 1948 and 1960 over 75 per cent of its exports went to Britain.

However, in 1958 an economic re-appraisal in the White Paper 'Economic Development' concluded that previous policies had not produced a viable economy.

Ireland was excluded from EFTA by the British who believed that the Irish economy was not developed enough, and who also were determined to exclude agriculture from the new arrangement.

The whole environment changed with the British decision of 1961. As Mr Lemass, the Irish Prime Minister admitted, Ireland could not afford to be on the wrong side of an agricultural and industrial tariff wall between itself and Britain and the continent. The Irish came to believe that only membership offered an equal voice and participation in the Common Agricultural Policy. Membership would be no panacea, but the alternative was worse.

Such was Irish concern with the potential negative consequences of exclusion, that they began to fudge their traditionally independent foreign policy and especially their attitude to neutrality.

Mr Sean Lemass, Irish Prime Minister, and Mr Brendan Corish, Leader of the Irish Labour Party, 'Speeches in Dail Eireann', July 1961

Sean Lemass

Government's conviction [had been] that the national interest would not be served by our seeking to join the European Economic Community unless and until Britain decided to do so . . .

[E]ach member of the Community must apply the common external tariff to all non-member countries; and it is unnecessary to elaborate on the fundamental change which our being obliged to do this *vis à vis* Britain would cause in the special trading relations we have long had with her. For these reasons, the question of our establishing a link with the Common Market while Britain should remain outside is not a practical one. If, however, Britain should join the Community, the reasons which, in the alternative case – namely, her not joining – militate against our being linked with it, constitute arguments in favour of that course and are reinforced by other considerations . . .

If Britain and other EFTA countries join the Common Market, the special position which our exports at present enjoy in the British market will be shared not only with these EFTA countries for industrial goods, but with the members of the Community for both industrial and agricultural products. Thus, Britain's entry to the Common Market would have as a consequence a potentially very serious dilution of the export advantages we now have in Britain. But she would be obliged, at the same time, to apply the common external tariff of the Community to imports from this country, subject to whatever exceptional treatment she might secure in respect of imports at present enjoying preferential treatment . . .

The Government have taken steps to inform each of the Six Governments of the European Economic Community and the Commission of the Community in Brussels that, in the event of the United Kingdom applying for membership of the EEC, we also will so apply, while at the same time informing them of our difficulty in accepting, in the present stage of our development, the full obligations of membership and of our desire to explore the modifications of these obligations that might be negotiated having regard to our circumstances . . .

Brendan Corish

There is no necessity for me to say that a decision as to whether we should join or not join is of the greatest importance to this country. I suppose it is the greatest challenge which this country has ever been called upon to meet. The fortunate or unfortunate thing about it is that when Britain makes her decision, it will be more or less Hobson's choice for us . . .

Document 26

Sweden had not suffered military occupation or defeat in modern times, and given its geographic position had greater opportunities than most States to choose to go its own way. For over 150 years that had included the path of neutrality, and despite some problems that policy had served Sweden well in both world wars. Given that legacy, in the Cold War period Swedish policy routinely became described as 'non-participation in alliances in peacetime, aiming at neutrality in the event of war'.

In 1961 Sweden emphasized the so-called neutrality reservations and particular clauses in the Treaty of Rome which intrude upon its freedom of decision and action, which it believed to be sine qua nons *of neutrality.*

Many of Sweden's arguments in 1961 and 1972 were echoed by Austria and Switzerland.

Mr Erlander, Swedish Prime Minister, 'Speech at the Congress of the Swedish Steel and Metalworkers' Union', August 1961

A new situation has arisen now that the United Kingdom and Denmark have applied to join the Common Market on the proviso that certain conditions are fulfilled. At the same time, in a joint communiqué, all the EFTA countries have declared themselves ready to negotiate with the Six . . .

The reasons that have been decisive for the United Kingdom and Denmark do not have the same force in the case of Sweden.

In the first place our economic situation does not provide a reason for replanning our trade policy. It is not boasting to say that the economic development of this country has been very favourable . . .

[. . .]

Furthermore, the political aim of strengthening the Atlantic Alliance is no inducement for us to participate in European cooperation. On the contrary, in view of the fundamental line of our foreign policy, a political aim of this kind gives us very definite cause for restraint . . .

Nor, as in the case of Denmark with its agriculture, is our own foreign trade associated particularly with only one group of commodities . . .

Our main line of policy will therefore continue to be an attempt to promote a united European market without any political strings for its individual members, with low external tariffs and without any new protectionist measures. This was our hope when we participated in the OEEC and in attempts to create a European free trade area. The leading part we took in the creation of EFTA was but one step in our endeavours . . .

In the position which has now arisen the Government has decided not to follow the example of Denmark and the United Kingdom and apply for membership of the Economic Community. The same line has been adopted by the other neutral EFTA countries – Austria, Switzerland and of course Finland . . .

The central question is of course foreign policy.

It has been customary to describe Swedish foreign policy as freedom from alliances in peace with the aim of neutrality in the event of war . . .

I am able to assert that the Swedish policy of neutrality has earned respect during recent years from the Great Powers . . .

For us to be able to satisfy as far as we possibly can our foreign policy interests, we need a certain degree of freedom of movement both in practice and as laid down by formal agreements. Freedom from alliances is an important and substantial part of this freedom of movement but it must be supplemented by a persistent effort to avoid any commitment, even outside the sphere of military policy, which would make it difficult or impossible for Sweden, in the event of a conflict, to choose a neutral course and which would make the world around us no longer confident that Sweden really wanted to choose such a course.

It is in this light that our attitude towards the work of integrating Western Europe must be examined . . .

The Government came to the conclusion that membership of the European Economic Community set up in accordance with the Treaty of Rome, in its present form, would not be compatible with the Swedish policy of neutrality . . .

The rules on trade with outside countries are considered to be most characteristic of the political restrictions imposed upon its members by the Treaty of Rome . . .

Documents 27

European integration as embodied by the Six was never simply about coal and steel, atomic energy or a Common Market. The Six were committed as it said in the Treaty of Rome to 'ever closer union', a political enterprise, even a federal union in some eyes. They were also committed to restoring European influence in the world, a belief reflected in the Messina memorandum (See Document 19).

After the abortive EDC and EPC (See Documents 17 and 18) the Six shied away from such questions, but at his first meeting with Chancellor Adenauer of Germany, President de Gaulle of France proposed regular meetings of Foreign Ministers, assisted by a small secretariat. President de Gaulle who had assumed the French Presidency in May 1958, had a clear vision of the future of Europe as a concert of sovereign powers with no independent body to superimpose the wider interest.

In November 1959 the Foreign Ministers of the Six began to discuss the question of foreign policy coordination in this context. De Gaulle's five partners were wary, but mostly welcomed the idea.

In February 1961 a European 'summit' of Heads of State and Government and Foreign Ministers agreed to establish a committee under the chairmanship of M. Christian Fouchet, a French official, to examine the problem of political cooperation, and in Bonn in July they agreed to meet at regular intervals to compare views on foreign policy, to concert policies and 'to reach common positions in order to further the political union of Europe'.

An Inter-Governmental Committee on Political Union was set up. It was to submit proposals on 'the means which will, as soon as possible, enable statutory character to be given to the union of their peoples'.

It became apparent that there were different ideas about the nature of 'union'. The Dutch and Belgians were wary of the potential down-grading of the Commission, and the Germans and Dutch worried over de Gaulle's hostility to NATO. On 2 November 1961 Fouchet put forward proposals bearing the full imprint of de Gaulle's views. The proposed Union was of 'States' not 'peoples'.

On 18 January 1962 the French Government submitted a second draft, which the five generally regarded as less acceptable than the first. The second draft maintained all of the disputed provisions of the first draft and added that the Union was also to act in the economic field. The talks faltered over the perennially disputed issues of whether to move away from supra-nationalism and how far, whether to circumvent the EEC Commission, and whether to deal with defence outside of NATO. The Dutch and Belgians were also concerned that there should be no commitment to political union until Britain, which had applied for membership in July 1961 (See Document 23) as a member of the EEC could take part in the discussions.

At a press conference on 15 May 1962 de Gaulle poured scorn on his opponents and their 'Europe of the stateless'. The project was dead.

'Draft Treaty submitted by M. C. Fouchet to the Committee set up by the Bonn Conference in July 1961', November 1961

The High Contracting Parties, . . . [r]esolved . . . to give statutory form to the union of their peoples . . . have agreed as follows.

Title I – Union of the European peoples

Article 1

By the present Treaty, a union of States, hereafter called 'the Union' is established.

The Union is based on respect for the individuality of the peoples and of the member States and for equality of rights and obligations. It is indissoluble.

Article 2

It shall be the aim of the Union:

- to bring about the adoption of a common foreign policy in matters that are of common interest to member States;

- to ensure, through close cooperation between member States in the scientific and cultural field, the continued development of their common heritage and the protection of the values on which their civilization rests;

- to contribute thus in the member States to the defence of human rights, the fundamental freedoms and democracy;

- to strengthen, in cooperation with the other free nations, the security of member States against any aggression by adopting a common defence policy.

[. . .]

Article 4

The Institutions of the Union shall be as follows:

- the Council
- the European Parliament
- the European Political Commission

Article 5

The Council shall meet every four months at Head of State or Government level, and at least once in the intervening period at Foreign Minister level. It may, moreover, at any time hold extraordinary sessions at either level at the request of one or more member States . . .

Article 6

The Council shall deliberate on all questions whose inclusion on its agenda is requested by one or more member States. It shall adopt decisions necessary for achieving the aims of the Union unanimously. The absence or abstention of one or more members shall not prevent a decision from being taken.

The decisions of the Council shall be binding on member States that have participated in their adoption. Member States on which a decision is not binding, by reason of their absence or abstention, may endorse it at any time. From the moment they endorse it, the decision will be binding upon them.

Article 7

The European Parliament . . . [set up by the Treaty of Rome] shall deliberate on matters concerning the aims of the Union.

It may address oral or written questions to the Council.

It may submit recommendations to the Council.

[. . .]

Article 9

The European Political Commission shall consist of senior officials of the Foreign Affairs departments of each member State. Its seat shall be in Paris. It shall be presided over by the representative of the member State that presides over the Council, and for the same period . . .

Article 10

The European Political Commission shall assist the Council. It shall prepare its deliberations and carry out its decisions. It shall perform the duties that the Council decides to entrust to it.

Title III – Obligations of member States

Article 11

There shall be solidarity, mutual confidence and reciprocal assistance as between member States. They undertake to abstain from any step or decision that might hinder or delay the achievement of the aims of the Union. They shall loyally cooperate in any consultations proposed to them and respond to requests for information addressed to them from the Council or, in compliance with the instructions of the Council, by the European Political Commission.

[. . .]

'Second Draft submitted by M. Fouchet', January 1962

Article 2 [New]

It shall be the aim of the Union to reconcile, coordinate and unify the policy of member States in spheres of common interest: foreign policy, economics, cultural affairs and defence.

Document 28

Professor Walter Hallstein (1901–82), German academic and statesman, was the first President of the European Commission (1958–67). Significantly, the title of the first (German) edition of his memoirs (Econ Verlag;

1969) was 'The Uncompleted Federation' and of the second (French) edition (Laffont) 'Europe incomplete'.

President Hallstein never had any doubt that the European Community was a stage on the way to European political union and that, as he put it, the Commission was in the business of politics. He made an immense contribution to the founding of the Commission and left on it his mark in its blend of 'German thoroughness and French juridicism'.

In the internal document which was an introduction to the Commission's action programme for the second stage (1 January 1963), President Hallstein set out his interpretation of the aims of the EEC Treaty. It could only be a question of time before he would collide with another European leader with a different agenda – President de Gaulle.

Mr Walter Hallstein, President of the Commission, 'Introduction to the Commission's Action Programme for the Second Stage', October 1962

1. The so-called economic integration of Europe is essentially a political phenomenon. The EEC is, together with the ECSC and Euratom, a European economico – and socio-political union.

2. In conformity with the inclusive character of integration in accordance with the wishes of the Contracting Parties, and in view of the economic conditions for the establishment of a single economic space, the Treaty envisages the blending of the six economies of the member States into an overall economic union.

To understand the task which the Community has undertaken in the development of common policies, i.e. in the economic union, it has to be kept in view that the modern liberal economic system cannot exist without the constant presence of the State in the economy.

The presence of the State is twofold. First, the State fixes a legal framework for all areas of the economy and for all areas which touch on the economy. Secondly, the State intervenes through a constant change of factors, through day-by-day actions of economic policy in countless measures, in short, through a 'policy' in the true sense of the word. The presence of the State in these two roles is particularly illustrated when we speak of economic union. It is a matter of making the influences of the six member States on the economy so mutually compatible that from the separate member States there emerges a new single economic space in which the six States present themselves in a common economic system and with a common policy.

This fusion or coordination of the individual economic policy measures of the States and the legal framework is in the logic of the matter. When the economy is integrated into the greater European economic space by the lifting of trade barriers, national economic policies of the six member States must also be integrated.

3. This is the first reason to make us move from the opening of markets to the blending of economically relevant national activity into a community system. There is a second reason. The integration of that part of national policy which concerns the economy and social life is called for in the Treaty of Rome as a means to the establishment of the political unity of Europe. For what is being 'communitized', what is being put together, is the policy of the States. A union is being forged among the member States in the eminently political area of the economy, or rather in the area of the influence of the State on the economy, that is economic policy. That implies union for an important part of the internal policy of the member States and for part of the external policy, namely commercial policy.

For the EEC it is not a case of a purely economic undertaking, beside which a political undertaking must be put in place. It is much more that with the Community political integration has already begun in an important field – and as can be shown, successfully begun – whereas other fields – cultural policy, the remaining part of external policy, defence policy – remain in the hands of the individual member States.

4. The way upon which the EEC embarked on its foundation is correct in a double sense. It is firstly correct because we can only create a large European internal market if integration penetrates to the economically relevant parts of national policy and national regulation, and secondly because such integration offers an appropriate instrument to realize political unity in one area, the economy. In other words European integration was desired, and for it the Customs Union was desired, demanding in itself the completion of the union.

5. Whereas the prescriptions for the Customs Union are automatically being put into practice in accordance with a predetermined timetable, this procedure is not applicable to the wider and more complicated areas of the economic union. The making of European law and the approximation of national legal systems, the 'communitization' of policies and the coordination of national action are not operations which can be made to proceed in all their details under a pre-arranged plan.

Accordingly the authors of the Treaty drafted the chapter on economic union in the form of framework rules, to be implemented generally speaking during the transitional period by means of detailed legislation enacted by the organs of the Community and by individual policy measures.

6. It follows from what has been said about the political character of the EEC that the Commission has an unreservedly positive stance towards every extension of European unification into matters other than economic and social policy, notably defence, the non-economic aspects of external policy, that is to say, towards the efforts to secure what is called 'political union'. If this leads to the reflection that this extension might be achieved by the enlargement and strengthening of the existing Communities, the Commission understands that for such new matters the organizational solutions need not be identical with those displayed in the EEC. Certainly the Commission, drawing on its experience, must warn against solutions which do not include the incorporation of the Community interest as such. The Commission must also uphold the opinion which it has always emphatically expressed, that the extension of European integration to other subjects must not in any way jeopardize or weaken the existence, functioning and dynamic further development of the existing Communities – it must instead reinforce their effect.

Document 29

As seen above (Document 23) Britain applied for membership of the EEC on 31 July 1961. Ireland (See Document 25) beat the British by a day, applying on 30 July, while the Danes followed on 10 August 1961 and the Norwegians on 30 April 1962. The British negotiations to identify the terms on offer commenced on 10 October 1961.

On 14 January 1963, the day before two scheduled marathon negotiating sessions were due to take place, de Gaulle announced at a press conference that in the French view Britain was not ready to accept the conditions of EEC membership. His five partners were unconsulted, and the negotiations petered out on 29 January 1963, both for Britain and the other applicants.

After de Gaulle's veto in January 1963, the Commission issued a report which suggested that substantial progress had been made in the negotiations and that contrary to French assertions, Britain had demonstrated a willingness to accept the Treaty of Rome. The report implied that the negotiations might have eventually succeeded, and that it was possible to envisage solutions to the major unresolved issues.

A decisive point for de Gaulle seems to have been his belief that Britain had not grasped that Community membership was incompatible with and indeed even precluded, in his view, any 'special relationship' with the United States. Another explanation of the veto was given by a Gaullist minister privately as: 'Now, with six members, there are five hens and a rooster. If you join [with the other countries], there will perhaps be seven or eight hens. But there will be two roosters. That isn't as agreeable'.

These matters were crystallized by the Nassau meeting between the British Prime Minister Harold Macmillan and President Kennedy of the United States on 18 December 1962, just three days after de Gaulle and Macmillan had met at Rambouillet to discuss defence and the EEC negotiations. At Nassau Kennedy offered Britain Polaris missiles for British built launchers (submarines) and warheads, in order to allow Britain to maintain its strategic nuclear force. He made the same offer to Paris, but this was declined, The offer was seen in Paris as an American attempt to dominate the European nuclear weapon capability. The British acceptance of the offer was seen as confirmation that Britain's heart lay elsewhere than Europe.

President de Gaulle, 'Press Conference', January 1963

The Treaty of Rome was concluded between six continental States – States which are, economically speaking, one may say, of the same nature. Indeed, whether it be a matter of their industrial or agricultural production, their external exchanges, their habits or their commercial clientele, their living or working conditions, there is between them much more resemblance than difference. Moreover, they are adjacent, they inter-penetrate, they are an extension of each other through their communications.

The fact of grouping and linking them in such a way that what they have to produce, buy, sell and consume is produced, bought, sold, and consumed in preference among themselves is therefore in conformity with realities. Moreover, it must be added that from the point of view of their economic development, their social progress, their technical capacity, they are keeping pace. They are marching in similar fashion . . .

Then, finally, they are in solidarity through the fact that not one among them is bound abroad by any special political or military agreement.

Thus it was psychologically and materially possible to create an economic community of the Six, though not without difficulties. When the Treaty of Rome was signed in 1957, it was after long discussions; and when it was concluded, it was necessary – in order to achieve something – that we French put in order our economic, financial, and monetary affairs . . . and that was done in 1959. From that moment the Community was in principle viable . . .

However, this Treaty, which was precise and complete enough concerning industry, was not at all so on the subject of agriculture, and for our country this had to be settled. Indeed, it is obvious that agriculture is an essential element in our national activity as a whole. We cannot conceive of a Common Market in which French agriculture would not find outlets in keeping with its production. And we agree further that, of the Six, we are the country on which this necessity is imposed in the most imperative manner.

This is why when, last January, consideration was given to the setting in motion of the second phase of the Treaty – in other words a practical start in its application – we were led to pose the entry of agriculture into the Common Market as a formal condition. This was finally accepted by our partners, but very difficult and very complex arrangements were needed and some rulings are still outstanding.

Thereupon Great Britain posed her candidature to the Common Market. She did it after having earlier refused to participate in the Communities which we were building, as well as after creating a sort of Free Trade Area with six other States, and finally – I may well say it as the negotiations held at such length on this subject will be recalled – after having put some pressure on the Six to prevent a real beginning being made in the application of the Common Market.

England thus asked in turn to enter, but on her own conditions. This poses without doubt to each of the six States, and poses to England, problems of a very great dimension. England in effect is insular, she is maritime, she is linked through her exchanges, her markets, her supply lines to the most diverse and often the most distant countries; she pursues essentially industrial and commercial activities, and only slight agricultural ones. She has in all her doings very marked and very original habits and traditions. In short, the nature, the structure, the very situation that are England's differ profoundly from those of the continentals . . .

The system of the Six consists of making a whole of the agricultural products of the entire Community, strictly fixing their prices, prohibiting subsidies, organizing their consumption between all the participants, and imposing on each participant the payment to the Community of any saving which they would achieve in fetching their food from outside instead of eating what the Common Market has to offer. Once again, what is to be done to bring England, as she is, into this system?

One might sometimes have believed that our English friends, in posing their candidature to the Common Market, were agreeing to transform themselves to the point of applying all the conditions which were accepted and practised by the Six . . . But the question is to know whether Great Britain can now place herself, like the Continent and with it, inside a tariff which is genuinely common, to renounce all Commonwealth preferences, to cease any pretence that her agriculture be privileged, and, more, than that, to treat her engagements with other countries of the Free Trade Area as null and void. That question is the whole question. It cannot be said that it is yet resolved. Will it be so one day? Obviously only England can answer.

The question is even further complicated, since after England other States which are linked to her through the Free Trade Area, would like or wish to enter the Common Market for the same reasons as Britain. It must be agreed that first the entry of Great Britain, and then of these States, will completely change the whole of the adjustments, the agreements, the compensation, the rules which have already been established between the Six, because all these States, like Britain, have very important peculiarities. It will then be another Common Market whose construction ought to be envisaged. But this Market, which would be increased to eleven and then thirteen and then perhaps eighteen, would without any doubt no longer resemble the one which the Six built.

Further, this Community, expanding in such fashion, would see itself faced with problems of economic relations with all kinds of other States, and first with the United States. It can be foreseen that the cohesion of its members, who would be very numerous and diverse, would not endure for long, and that finally it would appear as a colossal Atlantic community under American domination and direction which would quickly have absorbed the European Community. It is a hypothesis which in the eyes of some can be perfectly justified, but it is not at all what France wanted to do or is doing – and which is a properly European construction.

Yet it is possible that one day England might be able to transform herself sufficiently to become part of the European Community, without restrictions, without reserve, and in preference to anything else, and in that event the Six would open the door to her and France would raise no obstacle, although obviously the very fact of England's participation in the Community would considerably change its nature and its volume.

It is possible, too, that England might not yet be so disposed, and this is certainly what seems to emanate from the long, long Brussels conversations. But if that is the case, there is nothing dramatic about it. First, whatever decision England takes in this matter there is no reason, as far as we are concerned, for the relations we have with her to be changed. The consideration and the respect which are due to this great country, this great people, will not thereby be in the slightest impaired . . .

Moreover, I repeat, even if the Brussels negotiations were shortly not to succeed, nothing would prevent the conclusion between the Common Market and Great Britain of an agreement of association designed to safeguard exchanges and nothing would prevent close relations between England and France being maintained, nor the pursuit and development of their direct cooperation in all kinds of fields, notably the scientific, technical, and industrial – as the two countries have just proved by deciding to build together the supersonic aircraft *Concorde*.

Lastly, it is very possible that Britain's own evolution, and the evolution of the universe, might bring the English towards the Continent, whatever delays this achievement might demand . . .

Documents 30

The Empty Chair crisis of 1965–66 grew out of the development of the common agricultural policy, but went much wider. It became an attempt by the Government of President de Gaulle to uphold the authority of a member State at the expense of the Community.

The Community had entered into two commitments. One was to fix common cereal prices. This was an important French objective. The second commitment was to agree on permanent Community arrangements to finance expenditure incurred under the CAP in place of national contributions under Article 200 of the EEC Treaty.

It had been agreed among the member States that a decision on a permanent system to finance the CAP would be taken by 30 June 1965. On 13 December 1964 the Council asked the Commission to bring forward proposals by 1 April. The Commission complied on 31 March 1965. The proposals envisaged that from 1 July 1967 the CAP would be fully financed by the Community and that the Community should have its 'own resources' in the form of the agricultural levies (which bring the price of imports up to Community price levels) and customs duties. Since the monies concerned would no longer be subject to national budgetary control, being the Community's 'own resources', the Commission proposed – as especially the Dutch had asked – that the European Parliament, then called the Assembly, should have budgetary powers and that the Council should adopt the budget by qualified majority, rather than unanimity.

The Commission decided not to engage in a round of consultations with the member States about them. Some information leaked to members of the Assembly and the President of the Commission made a statement to that body before the proposal reached the Council. This set the scene for an all-out French attack, which had only a little to do with the nominal issue of agricultural financing.

Discussions were pursued until France abruptly broke off, accusing its partners of reneging on their promise to settle the financing question by 30 June 1965. France withdrew from the work of the Council and (most) official committee meetings, in the episode known as the 'empty chair'.

At his press conference on 9 September 1965, and later in his memoirs, General de Gaulle revealed that the target of his attack went far beyond CAP finances. He was opposing the strengthening of the power of Community institutions – the Commission which he saw behaving with all the pomp of a government which it was not; the Assembly which could, if the Commission's proposals were followed, oppose itself to the will of the member States; the Council, where majority voting, due to be extended under the EEC Treaty on 1 January 1966, could oblige France to knuckle down under policies and legislation it did not agree with. None of it squared with 'l'Europe des etats'.

The Belgian Foreign Minister, M. Paul-Henri Spaak, pressed for a meeting of the Six to resolve the crisis. It was agreed late in the year that there should be such a meeting in Luxembourg and without the Commission, both peculiarities to mark that this was not a run of the mill Council meeting.

The Five, who held together, noted that France was not seeking Treaty revision. They saw great difficulty with the French idea of a veto right on 'important matters'. M. Spaak, however, saw room for compromise.

The meeting adjourned to 28 January, also in Luxembourg. In the meantime the Permanent Representatives had met and they produced two texts, one on majority voting and one on relations between the Council and Commission in response to a series of proposals (known as 'the Decalogue'), which France had made at the previous meeting.

On the first the Germans nearly accepted the French position, especially on agriculture, but the solidarity of the Five held, agreeing that there should be a period of conciliation but that it could not go on indefinitely. Spaak felt the matter was academic, since it was unlikely that on a matter one State felt was crucial, it would be outvoted by the others.

It was decided not to conceal the divergence of view which had underlain the discussion.

The second text with only slight modifications was adopted. It gave France satisfaction on all the points it had raised in the Decalogue.

[Commission] 'Proposal for Provisions to be Adopted by the Council by Virtue of Article 201 of the Treaty Concerning the Replacement of the Financial Contributions of Member States by Independent Community Revenues', March 1965

Whereas from 1 July 1967 there will be a uniform agricultural price system and common prices for the various agricultural products will be in effect; and whereas, therefore, the single market stage will have been reached in this sector;

[. . .]

Whereas, as a result of the elimination of customs duties and agricultural levies in trade between member States, the place where the import charges are imposed and that where the goods are consumed will be less and less likely to lie within the territory of the same State, so as it is no longer reasonable for the proceeds of customs duties and levies to go to the member States that had collected them;

Whereas Article 2(1) of Regulation No. 25 on the financing of the common agricultural policy stipulates that, as soon as the single agricultural market comes into effect, the proceeds of agricultural levies shall accrue to the Community and shall be appropriated to Community expenditure;

Whereas Article 201 of the Treaty expressly provides for the possibility of allocating to the Community, as independent revenue, the proceeds of the common customs tariff when the latter has been finally introduced;

Whereas the procedure provided for in Article 201 of the Treaty should now be initiated, in order that the proceeds of the common customs duties and agricultural levies may accrue to the Community from 1 July 1967;

[. . .]

Has adopted the present provisions:

Article 1

From 1 July 1967, the proceeds, in trade with non-member countries, of

   i)   . . . 'agricultural levies', and

   ii)   . . . 'customs duties' . . .

Shall accrue, by the arrangements set out in Articles 2 and 3 below, to the Community as independent revenue . . .

[. . .]

Article 4

Without prejudice to other receipts, those arising from the implementation of Articles 1–3 shall form part of the budget of the Community and shall be used to finance without distinction any expenditure provided for therein . . .

[Commission] 'Draft Treaty Amending Articles 201 and 203 of the Treaty Establishing the European Economic Community'

Article 201

The Commission shall study the conditions under which the financial contributions of member States provided for in Article 200 may be replaced by independent Community revenue.

For this purpose, the Commission shall submit proposals to the Council, which shall refer them to the Assembly.

The Council, acting by unanimous vote, shall adopt the necessary provisions. Nevertheless, it may decide such provisions by qualified majority if the Assembly has rendered an opinion supporting the Commission's proposals by a two-thirds majority of the votes cast constituting an absolute majority of its members.

[. . .]

Article 203

[. . .]

2. [. . . Commission to draw up draft budget which] shall be laid before the Council by the Commission not later than 15 September of the year preceding that to which it refers . . .

3. The Council acting by qualified majority shall establish the draft budget and shall then transmit it to the Assembly . . .

The Assembly shall have the power to amend the draft budget by an absolute majority of its members . . .

'The Luxembourg Compromise: Voting and Vetoing', January 1966

1. Where in the case of decisions which may be taken by a majority vote on a proposal from the Commission very important interests of one or more partners are at stake, the members of the Council will endeavour, within a reasonable time, to reach solutions which can be adopted by all the members of the Council, while respecting their mutual interests and those of the Communities, in accordance with Article 2 of the Treaty.

2. With regard to the preceding paragraph, the French delegation considers that where very important interests are at stake the discussion must be continued until unanimous agreement is reached.

3. The six delegations note that there is a divergence of views on what should be done in the event of a failure to reach complete agreement.

4. The six delegations nevertheless consider that this divergence does not prevent the Community's work being resumed in accordance with the normal procedure.

[Luxembourg, 29 January 1966.]

'Relations between the Council and the Commission', January 1966

Close collaboration between the Council and the Commission is an essential element for the functioning and development of the Community.

In order to improve and intensify further this collaboration at all levels, the Council considers it right to apply the following practical methods of collaboration, to be settled by common agreement on the basis of Article 162 of the EEC Treaty, in no way damaging the competencies and attributions of the two institutions:

1. Before adopting a proposal of special importance, it is desirable that

the Commission should make appropriate contact with the Governments of the member States, through the Permanent Representatives, without damaging the right of initiative which the Treaty confers on the Commission.

2. Proposals and all other official acts which the Commission addresses to the Council and to the member States can be made public only after the latter have been informed and have the texts.

The Official Journal should be designed to bring out distinctively acts which are obligatory. The methods for publishing texts for which publication is obligatory will be settled in the framework of the work in hand on the reorganization of the Official Journal.

3. Credentials of the heads of mission of third countries accredited to the Community will be presented to the President of the Council and the President of the Commission, meeting for the occasion.

4. Representations on matters of substance made to the Council or to the Commission by Representatives of third countries will be conveyed to the other party rapidly and comprehensively.

5. Under Article 162 the Council and the Commission will hold consultations on the appropriateness, method and nature of the links which the Commission might establish under Article 229 of the Treaty with international organizations.

6. Cooperation between the Council and the Commission in the field of information about the Community, which the Council discussed on 24 September 1963 will be reinforced so that the programme of the Press and Information Service will be defined and its implementation monitored jointly, in accordance with procedures which will be specified later and which could include the creation of an ad hoc body.

7. The Council and the Commission will define in the context of the financial regulations concerning the establishment and execution of Community budgets, means of increasing the effectiveness of the control of the commitment, authorization and execution of Community expenditure.

Document 31

After de Gaulle's veto in 1963 there was a lull in Britain's European policy. On 2 May 1967 a Labour Prime Minister, Mr Wilson announced that Britain would again apply for EEC membership, and the new application was lodged on 11 May 1967.

There was again in 1967 a strong sense of a lack of viable alternatives to membership. A detailed civil service analysis had concluded that the arguments were finely balanced, with the political arguments the more compelling.

By the spring of 1967 familiar problems with the British economy were reappearing: growth was less than that of the members of the Six; there was a 'stop-go' economic policy; and a substantial Sterling crisis in July 1967. The Pound was devalued in November 1967.

Politically, Britain's standing was reduced by the Soviet mediation to bring peace between two Commonwealth States, India and Pakistan, in September 1965; November 1965 saw the Rhodesian Unilateral Declaration of Independence; and more generally it was clear that in a post Cuban missile crisis (1962) environment the world had become bipolar.

In February 1967 one-third of the Parliamentary Labour Party had tabled a motion recalling the 1961–62 stiff terms and in the May debate over 80 Labour MPs either abstained or voted against the Government motion on seeking to negotiate. The Conservatives were also split. The Commons voted 488 to 62 in favour of applying.

The second application, however, met the same fate as the first, with de Gaulle exercising another unilateral veto (See Document 32). It was only after he left office in April 1969, that the application was re-opened.

Mr Harold Wilson, Prime Minister, 'Speech to the House of Commons', May 1967

The Community today is already very different . . . from the Community . . . [we] sought to join four years ago . . . Once Britain is a member, we shall be able, as an equal partner, in our own interest and equally in the interest of the Community to help determine the direction, the pace and the developing institutional arrangements of the Community . . .

[Therefore] . . . some of the problems which we for our part shall wish to see settled can be better settled after Britain's entry than in negotiations . . .

I am not . . . one of those who see in British entry an automatic solution to our economic problems as a result of the sudden effect on our productivity and competitiveness of a devastating cold blast of competition . . .

This is not to deny that the balance will be unfavourable . . . for some industries . . .

British entry is not indispensable to the hopes of future industrial expansion and growth, or to a sustained level of investment. I am confident that these are aims within our capacity and that they are dependent on our own effort . . .

[T]he problems . . .

[The] increase in the cost of food to the consumer in this country probably lies within the range of 10 to 14 per cent . . . equivalent to an increase of 2½ per cent to 3½ per cent in the cost of living . . .

[It would be wrong to suggest] this policy is negotiable. We have to come to terms with it . . . [and increase will be spread over a period] . . . acceptance of that policy would mean considerable adjustments . . . in the structure of British agriculture . . .

[British entry would involve] ending of Commonwealth industrial preferences in the British market, and, through the mechanism of the common external tariff, the institution of reverse preferences against Commonwealth manufacturers . . .

[W]e shall make special arrangements to keep in consultation with our EFTA partners . . .

[P]roblem of movement of capital . . . direct investment and portfolio investment . . .

[R]egional policies . . . Anxieties . . . particularly on the question as to how far Britain would be able to continue to take the necessary steps to ensure the economic and social development of our development areas and other areas needing special help . . . [danger of pull to East and South] . . .

[N]ot a problem of the strength of Sterling . . . But . . . that a currency such as Sterling which is not only a national currency serving our own trading needs, but is a reserve currency, a currency widely used in international trade and hence widely held in many countries of the free world, might present difficulty if we entered the Community . . .

[E]ffects on Britain's balance of payments . . . estimates . . . if no changes were made as a result of the negotiations – a burden on our

balance of payments is estimated to be between £175 million and
£250 million . . . British entry would have a profound effect on British
industry by creating a new confidence, a new upsurge in investments,
a new concentration on modernization, on productivity and reduced
costs, by creating new prospects of a higher and more soundly-based
growth-rate . . .

[O]ne of the main arguments for Britain seeking to join a wider
economic community is the development of this 'technological community' . . .

[M]arket of approaching 300 million people . . . dynamic which
the enlarged Community would be generating and the enormous and
growing market for our own more sophisticated technological products which would result . . .

[O]ur examination [of the constitutional and legal implications]
has greatly reassured us about possible implications for Britain . . .
By far the greater part of our domestic law would remain unchanged
. . . The main effect of Community law on our existing law is in the
realms of commerce, Customs, restrictive practices and immigration
and the operation of the steel, coal and nuclear energy industries . . .

I now turn much more briefly to the political issues, the political
implications and the political aspirations which lay behind the Government's decision . . . It has been widely commented . . . that the
federal momentum towards a supranational Europe in which all
issues of foreign policy, for example, would be settled by majority
voting, for the time being at least, has died away.

The Government's decision, and I suggest Parliament's decision,
must be based not so much on what might ultimately evolve, but
upon the existing working of the Community and of modern Europe
. . . for the immediately foreseeable future, British public opinion
would not contemplate any rapid move to a federal Europe . . .

That does not imply any difference in approach by Britain from
that of the Six . . .

We are talking about Britain's joining the Community and joining
in the great drive towards European unity . . . It does not involve any
fundamental change or commitment to fundamental change in European defence arrangements, conventional or nuclear, particularly
changes which, in my view, would be destructive of the Western
Alliance and inimical equally to hopes of constructive moves for an
East–West detente . . .

The creation of a Community which would have the effect of ending
a thousand years of European warfare enabled supporters of European

unity to turn their minds to a far broader concept, the concept of strong Europe, strong economically, strong technologically, and – because it is strong and united – an independent Europe able to exert far more influence in world affairs than at any time in our generation . . . We do not see European unity as something narrow or inward-looking . . .

These applications will be made from strength, in a spirit of resolve, not as one who seeks favours, resolved, above all, to contribute in full measure what this country has to contribute in terms of skill and inventiveness, of industry, of technology, of science, and of political will to the creation of a more powerful Europe, and, therefore, of a more peaceful world . . .

But let no one think . . . that there is no other course for Britain except entry . . . There is no question of Britain's power to survive and develop outside the Communities, though no one will be in any doubt that the determination that would be needed, the efforts our people would have to make . . .

Document 32

At another press conference in May 1967 de Gaulle administered another 'veto', based upon a detailed comparision of British policies and those of the Six. The rejection was a shock. The British Prime Minister and his Foreign Secretary (George Brown) had toured the capitals of the Six early in 1967 and thought that an application would be welcomed, even by France.

But throughout 1967 France maintained the position that there could be no substantive negotiations until the UK took the necessary steps to repair its economic weakness, as France had been forced to do before the entry into force of the Treaty of Rome.

On 20 December Britain announced the shelving of its application, and it, the other applicants and the Five waited for the political demise of de Gaulle.

President de Gaulle, 'Press Conference', May 1967

Great Britain and the Common Market

The movement which now seems to be leading Great Britain to join up with Europe instead of staying outside, can cause nothing but satisfaction to France. This is why we have taken sympathetic note of the progress in this direction to which the intention declared by the British Government and the step taken by it seem to point. For our part, there cannot be, nor has there ever been, any question of a veto. The issue is merely one of knowing whether success is possible in the framework and under the conditions of today's Common Market, without involving it in destructive disturbances, or, otherwise, in what alternative framework and under what alternative conditions such success could come about, unless one wants to safeguard what has just been built up until such time as it may conceivably appear possible to receive a Great Britain which, for her part and on her own account, would have transformed herself fundamentally.

I have spoken of destructive disturbances inside the Common Market: we all know that it took ten years of gestation to bring it into full operation . . . And the Six still have to agree on the highly arduous problems of energy, taxes, social costs, transport, etc . . . And once they have finished building the structure in theory, they will have to live together in it, that is to say, year after year, to submit to the regulations, the compromises, the sanctions which have been and will be evolved. In short, the Common Market is a kind of prodigy. To introduce new and massive factors now in the midst of those which have been reconciled with such difficulty would obviously mean bringing both the structure as a whole and the details back into question and setting the problem of an entirely different nature; all the more so since, if we have succeeded in building this structure, it is because the parties involved were continental countries which were immediate neighbours, which admittedly differed in size but were complementary in their economic structures. Besides, the territories of the Six form a compact geographic and strategic whole. It should be added that, despite – and perhaps because of – their great battles of former times (I am speaking, of course especially of France and Germany) they tend now to support rather than oppose each other. Finally, conscious also of the potential of their material resources and human values, they all hope, whether openly or in secret, that together they will one day form a whole capable of balancing any power in the world.

In comparison with the motives which induced the Six to organize themselves together, one can well understand why Great Britain, which is not continental, which, because of her Commonwealth and her own insularity, has commitments far across the seas and which is tied to the United States by all kinds of special agreements, should not have merged into a Community with specific dimensions and strict rules. Whilst this Community built up its organization, Great Britain began by refusing to take part in it and even adopted a hostile attitude towards it, as though she thought it represented an economic and political threat. Then, she tried to negotiate entry into the Community, but in conditions such that the latter would have been stifled by her membership. This attempt having failed, the British Government then stated that it no longer wished to join the Community and directed its efforts towards tightening its ties with the Commonwealth and other European countries grouped around it in a Free Trade Area.

And now, Great Britain seems to have adopted a new state of mind and is declaring herself prepared to subscribe to the Treaty of Rome if she can be granted an exceptional and very long time limit and if, as far as she is concerned, essential changes can be made in the application of the Treaty. At the same time, she recognizes that, in order to attain this goal, obstacles would have to be overcome which the British Prime Minister, speaking from his vast experience and very great clear-sightedness, has described as formidable.

This is the case, for instance, with the agricultural regulations: it is well-known that these regulations are designed to enable the Community to feed itself from its own produce and to compensate, by means of what are known as financial levies, for any advantage which the various States might derive from imports of cheaper commodities from elsewhere. Great Britain is very largely fed by produce purchased at low cost all over the world and, in particular, in the Commonwealth. If she submits to the rules of the Six, her balance of payments will be crushed by the levies and she will, on the other hand, be forced at home to bring the price of food up to the level adopted by the Six, to raise her workers' wages correspondingly and to charge correspondingly more for her manufactured goods which will be that much more difficult to sell. She clearly cannot do this. But, on the other hand, to bring Britain into the Community without her being really bound by the agricultural regulations of the Six would amount automatically to disrupting the system and therefore to upsetting completely the balance of the whole Common Market and robbing France of one of her chief reasons for being a member.

Another essential difficulty lies in the fact that, among the Six, the rule is for capital to flow freely in order to promote expansion, while in Great Britain, although capital can enter the country, it may not leave, in order to limit her balance of payments deficit which is still threatening, despite praiseworthy efforts and some recent progress.

How can this problem be resolved? For it would be too great a risk for Great Britain to do away with the locks preventing capital from flowing out, and it would be unbearable for the Six to bring into their organization a partner that would be isolated in this respect in so exorbitant a system.

How, also, can one fail to see that the peculiar position of Sterling prevents the Common Market from including Great Britain? Indeed, the fact that the organization of the Six is bringing down all trade barriers between them necessarily entails that their currencies must have a constant relative value and that, if one of these were to be shaken, the Community would put it right. But this is only possible because the Mark, the Lira, the Florin, the Belgian Franc and the French Franc are in a thoroughly strong position. On the other hand, although we need not despair of seeing the Pound maintain itself, the fact is that we cannot be certain for a long time to come that it will succeed in this. We shall be all the less certain since, in relation to the currencies of the Six, Sterling has the special character of what is known as a reserve currency, which means that a great many States in the world, and particularly in the Commonwealth, hold enormous Sterling balances. Of course, one may attempt to draw a distinction between the fate of the Pound as a national currency and as an international one; it may also be claimed that, once Great Britain would be inside the organization, the Community would not be obliged to answer for what might happen to Sterling. But these are purely exercises of the mind.

When all is said and done, monetary parity and solidarity are essential rules and conditions of the Common Market and can assuredly not be extended to our neighbours across the Channel unless Sterling presents itself one day in a new position, with its future value seemingly secure, freed, like the others, from its reserve currency role and with the burden of Great Britain's debit balances inside the Sterling Area having been eliminated. When and how will this come about?

What is already true now in the economic sphere could also become true in the political one. The idea, the hope which, from the beginning, led the Six continental countries to unite was undoubtedly to form an entity that would be European in all respects, that is to say, that it would not only carry its own weight in trade and production, but that it would be capable one day of dealing politically with anyone, for its own sake and on its own. In view of the special relations of the British with America, together with the advantages as well as the liabilities arising for them out of these relations, in view of the existence of the Commonwealth and of the privileged relations they have with it, in view of the fact that the British are still assuming special commitments in various parts of the world, which set them fundamentally apart from the continental peoples, it is easy to see how the policy of the Six, providing that they have one, could, in many cases, be associated with that of the British. But it is not possible to see how the two policies could merge, unless the British resumed complete freedom of action, particularly with regard to defence, or unless the peoples of the Continent gave up the idea of ever building a European Europe.

It is true that the British quite naturally consider that their membership of the Community would automatically turn the latter into something quite different from what it is at present. Indeed, once their representatives had established themselves in the ruling bodies – the Council of Ministers, the Council of Deputies, the Commissions, the Assembly – once the very considerable and very special mass of their economic and political interests and obligations were represented within these bodies, where they would have an importance commensurate with their numbers and audience and where they would immediately be joined by the delegations of a number of other European countries that are in the Free Trade Area with them, it goes without saying that the inspiration, dimensions and decisions of the Community of the Six as it is today would give way to an inspiration, to dimensions and decisions that would be entirely different. Indeed, the British do not hide the fact that, once they were inside the Community, they would set out to obtain many modifications.

Where France is concerned, the industrial, agricultural, commercial, monetary and, lastly, political conditions in which she would then find herself would certainly no longer bear any relation to those she accepts inside the Common Market.

It truly seems that if, by general agreement, one wished to bring about a change in the position of the British in relation to the Six, a choice might have to be made between three solutions:

- Either it could be recognized that, in the present state of things, their entry into the Common Market with all the exceptions that would necessarily accompany it, the inrush of factors entirely new in both kind and quantity which it would inevitably entail, the participation of several other States which would certainly follow as a corollary, would amount to imposing the building of a completely new structure which would virtually wipe out everything that has just been built. What, then, would we end up with, other than the creation, perhaps, of a Western European free trade area, pending the Atlantic area which would deprive our continent of all real personality?

- Or a system of association, such as is provided for by the Treaty of Rome and which could increase and facilitate the contracting parties' economic relations without causing any upheavals, could be set up between the Community on the one hand and Great Britain and certain other States of the little Free Trade Area on the other.

- Or, lastly, before changing what exists, the third solution would be to wait until a certain internal and external evolution of which Great Britain seems to begin to show signs may possibly have been carried to its conclusion: that is to say, until this great people, so magnificently gifted in ability and courage, has first and for itself carried out the fundamental economic and political transformation needed to enable it to link up with the six continental countries. I really believe that this is the wish of many people who want to see the emergence of a Europe that would have its natural dimensions, and who have a great admiration and sincere friendship for Great Britain. If, one day, Britain reached this stage, how wholeheartedly France would welcome such a historic conversion.

Documents 33

De Gaulle's departure transformed the political environment, and his successor, Georges Pompidou quickly moved to obtain a meeting of Heads of State and Government. French standing was diminished by the events of 1968, when the regime came close to collapse. In Germany, in the autumn of 1969, the Christian Democrats were ousted from office, for the first time since the foundation of the German State. The new German Government, with the Social Democrats as the senior partner, was less willing to be subservient to the French.

The message from the meeting of the Heads of State and Government in

The Hague rang out for many years in the three words (drafted by M. Jean-Pierre Brunet, Head of the Economic Department of the French Foreign Office actually during the meeting) – completing, deepening, widening. They were not at the time seen as working against each other, as 'deepening' and 'widening' came to be seen twenty-five years later.

'Completing' came to mean the single market programme. From The Hague there came two reports on 'deepening'. The Davignon Report on the problems of political unification (whose author was then the Political Director of the Belgian Foreign Office, later a charismatic Commissioner) delicately picked up some of the aims of earlier and abortive ventures towards cooperation among the member States on foreign policy, such as the Fouchet Plan (See Document 27). It was a 'light' regime, without Treaty basis and without the entanglement of the classical Community method (Commission proposes, Parliament advises, Council decides, Court upholds the law). It took fifteen years for European Political Cooperation to find its way into a Treaty, in the 'Single European Act'.

The Werner Report (Chairman, Pierre Werner, Prime Minister of Luxembourg) concerned economic and monetary union, a concomitant to a Common Market. At the request of his colleagues, M. Werner brought out a plan to reach EMU in ten years. But he was well ahead of his time. His report was never endorsed. It was initially a casualty of disagreements between the oil price shocks which disrupted member States' economies in the 1970s. At their meeting in Paris in June 1972, the Heads of State and Government called for EMU by 1980, later restated, notably by M. Francois-Xavier Ortoli, President of the Commission 1973–76 and a member of it until 1984, as happening 'in the 1980s'.

'Widening' is strictly the process of acquiring more members, although some commentators also use it to describe the enlarging network of agreements of different kinds between the Community and other European States. The Hague meeting of 1969 removed the primary obstacles which the Government of President de Gaulle had placed in the way of British negotiation for membership.

'The European Communities: Text of the Communiqué issued by the Heads of State or of Government at their Meeting in The Hague', December 1969

[. . .]

4. The Heads of State or Government therefore wish to reaffirm their belief in the political objectives which give the Community its full meaning and scope,

[. . .]

The European Communities remain the original nucleus from which European unity sprang and developed. The entry of other countries of this continent into the Communities – in accordance with the provisions of the Treaties of Rome – would undoubtedly help the Communities to grow to dimensions, still more in conformity with the present state of economy and technology. The creation of special links with other European States which have expressed a desire to that effect would also contribute to this end. A development such as this would enable Europe to keep up its traditions of an open attitude to the world and increase its efforts on behalf of developing countries.

5. As regards the completion of the Communities, the Heads of State or Government have reaffirmed the will of their Governments to pass from the transitional period to the final stage of the European Community and accordingly, to lay down a definitive financial arrangement for the common agricultural policy by the end of 1969.

They agree to replace gradually, within the framework of this financial arrangement, the contributions of member countries by the Community's own resources, taking into account all the interests concerned, with the object of achieving in due course the integral financing of the Communities' budgets in accordance with the procedure provided for in Article 201 of the Treaty establishing the EEC and of strengthening the budgetary powers of the European Parliament.

The problem of direct elections will continue to be studied by the Council of Ministers.

6. They have asked the Governments to continue without delay, within the Council, the efforts already made to ensure a better control of the market by a policy of agricultural production making it possible to limit the burden on budgets.

7. The acceptance of a financial arrangement for the final stage does not exclude its adaptation by unanimous vote in an enlarged Community, on condition that the principles of this arrangement are not watered down.

8. They have reaffirmed their readiness to expedite the further action needed to strengthen the Community and promote its development into an economic union. They are of the opinion that the integration process should result in a Community of stability and growth. To this end they agreed that, within the Council, on the basis of the

memorandum presented by the Commission of 12 February 1969, and in close collaboration with the latter, a plan in stages will be worked out during 1970 with a view to the creation of an economic and monetary union.

The development of monetary cooperation should be based on the harmonization of economic policies.

They agreed to arrange for the investigation of the possibility of setting up a European reserve fund which should be the outcome of a joint economic and monetary policy . . .

[. . .]

13. They reaffirmed their agreement on the principle of the enlargement of the Community, in accordance with Article 237 of the Treaty of Rome.

In so far as the applicant States accept the Treaties and their political aims, the decisions taken since the entry into force of the Treaties and the options adopted in the sphere of development, the Heads of State or Government have indicated their agreement to the opening of negotiations between the Community on the one hand and the applicant States on the other.

They agreed that the essential preparatory work for establishing a basis of negotiation could be undertaken as soon as practically possible. By common consent, the preparations are to take place in the most positive spirit.

14. As soon as negotiations with the applicant countries have been opened, discussions on their position in relation to the EEC will be started with such other EFTA members as may request them.

15. They instructed the Ministers for Foreign Affairs to study the best way of achieving progress in the matter of political unification, within the context of enlargement. The Ministers are to make proposals to this effect by the end of July 1970.

'Report by the Foreign Ministers of the Member States on the Problems of Political Unification' [Davignon Report], July 1970

Part one

[. . .]

5. A united Europe should be based on a common heritage of respect for the liberty and rights of man and bring together democratic States

with freely elected parliaments. This united Europe remains the fundamental aim, to be attained as soon as possible, thanks to the political will of the peoples and the decisions of their Governments.

6. The Ministers therefore considered that their proposals should be based on three facts, in order to ensure consistency with the continuity and political purpose of the European design which were emphasized so forcefully by the Hague Conference.

7. The first fact is that, in line with the spirit of the Preambles to the Treaties of Paris and Rome, tangible form should be given to the will for a political union which has always been a force for the progress of the European Communities.

8. The second fact is that implementation of the common policies being introduced or already in force requires corresponding developments in the specifically political sphere, so as to bring nearer the day when Europe can speak with one voice. Hence the importance of Europe being built by successive stages and the gradual development of the method and instruments best calculated to allow a common political course of action.

9. The third and final fact is that Europe must prepare itself to discharge the imperative world duties entailed by its greater cohesion and increasing role.

[. . .]

Part two

The Ministers propose that:

Being concerned to achieve progress towards political unification, the Governments should decide to cooperate in the field of foreign policy.

Objectives

This cooperation has two objectives:

(a) To ensure greater mutual understanding with respect to the major issues of international politics, by exchanging information and consulting regularly;

(b) To increase their solidarity by working for a harmonization of views, concertation of attitudes and joint action when it appears feasible and desirable.

Ministerial meetings

1. (a) The Foreign Ministers will meet at least once every six months, at the initiative of the President-in-office.

    (b) A conference of Heads of State or Government may be held instead if the Foreign Ministers consider that the situation is serious enough or the subjects to be discussed are sufficiently important to warrant this.

    (c) In the event of a serious crisis or special urgency, an extraordinary consultation will be arranged between the Governments of the member States. The President-in-office will get in touch with his colleagues to determine how such consultation can best be arranged.

2. The meetings shall be chaired by the Foreign Minister of the country providing the President of the Council of the European Communities.

3. The ministerial meetings shall be prepared by a Committee of the heads of political departments.

Political Committee

1. This Committee, comprising the heads of the political departments, will meet at least four times a year to do the groundwork for the ministerial meetings and to carry out any tasks entrusted to it by the Ministers.
[. . .]

4. Any other form of consultation may be envisaged if the need arises.

Matters within the scope of the consultations

The Governments will consult each other on all major questions of foreign policy.

The member States will be free to propose any subjects they wish for political consultation.

Commission of the European Communities

The Commission will be consulted if the activities of the European Communities are affected by the work of the Ministers.

European Parliament

Public opinion and its spokesmen must be associated with the construction of the political union, so as to ensure that it is a demo-cratic process.

The Ministers and the members of the Political Affairs Committee of the European Parliament will hold six-monthly meetings to discuss questions which are the subject of consultations in the framework of foreign policy cooperation. These meetings will be informal, to ensure that the parliamentarians and Ministers can express their views freely.

General

1. The meetings will normally be held in the country of their chairman.

2. The host State will take all due steps to provide a secretarial service and for the practical organization of the meetings.

3. Each State will appoint one of its foreign affairs officials as the correspondent of his counterparts in the other countries.

Part three

1. To ensure continuity in the task embarked on, the Ministers propose to pursue their work on the best way to achieve progress towards political unification and intend to submit a second report.

2. The work in question will also cover improvement of foreign policy cooperation and a search for new fields in which progress can be made. It will have to allow for any studies undertaken in the context of the European Communities, more particularly with a view to strengthening structures so as to ensure that they can, if necessary, cope satisfactorily with the extension and growth of their tasks.

3. To this end, the Ministers shall instruct the Political Committee to arrange its work in such a way that it can discharge this task and to report back at each of their half-yearly meetings.

4. Once a year, the President-in-office of the Council will provide the European Parliament with a progress report on the work in question. [. . .]

'Report to the Council and the Commission on the Realization by Stages of Economic and Monetary Union in the Community' [Werner Report], October 1970

Starting point

Since the signature of the Treaty of Rome, the European Economic

Community has taken several steps of prime importance towards economic integration. The completion of the customs union and the definition of the common agricultural policy are the most significant landmarks.

However, the advances towards integration will have the result that general economic disequilibrium in the member countries will have direct and rapid repercussions on the global evolution of the Community. The experience of recent years has clearly shown that such disequilibrium is likely to compromise seriously the integration realized in the liberation of the movement of goods, services and capital. This is particularly true of the agricultural Common Market. Having regard to the marked differences existing between the member countries in the realization of the objectives of growth and stability, there is a grave danger of disequilibria arising if economic policy cannot be harmonized effectively.

The increasing interpenetration of the economies has entailed a weakening of autonomy for national economic policies. The control of economic policy has become all the more difficult because the loss of autonomy at the national level has not been compensated by the inauguration of Community policies. The inadequacies and disequilibrium that have occurred in the process of realization of the Common Market are thus thrown into relief. The efforts expended have made it possible to achieve partial progress but they have not in fact led to the coordination or effective harmonization of economic policies in the Community . . .

Quantitative objectives sufficiently harmonized, which are one of the important conditions for effective coordination, have not been achieved in the first two medium-term programmes. Investigations that have been made into the economic situation in the Community have often not had any other result than recommendations formulated in altogether general terms . . .

The extension of the liberation of movements of capital and the realization of the right of establishment and of the free rendering of services by banking and financial undertakings have not progressed far enough. The delay has been caused by the absence of sufficient coordination of economic and monetary policies and by local peculiarities of law or of fact.

The freedom of persons to circulate is not yet assured in an entirely satisfactory manner and real progress has not yet been accomplished as regards the harmonization of social policies.

In the matter of regional policy, policies for particular sectors, and transport policy the progress realized has so far been fairly modest.

In foreign relations, and more particularly in international monetary relations, the Community has not succeeded in making its personality felt by the adoption of common positions, by reason as the case may be of divergencies of policy or concept.

While these gaps have been appearing, economic agents have been adapting themselves at least partially to the new conditions in the markets. Thus, multinational companies have been formed and the markets in Euro-currencies and Euro-currency issues have sprung up and developed . . . These developments . . . help nonetheless to make still more difficult the control of economic development by member States, while the constantly increasing interdependence of the industrialized economies throws into clearer and clearer relief the problem of the individuality of the Community . . .

The final objective

The Group had not sought to construct an ideal system in the abstract. It has set out rather to determine the elements that are indispensable to the existence of a complete economic and monetary union. The union as it is described here represents the minimum that must be done, and is a stage in a dynamic evolution which the pressure of events and political will can model in a different way.

Economic and monetary union will make it possible to realize an area within which goods and services, people and capital will circulate freely and without competitive distortions, without thereby giving rise to structural or regional disequilibrium.

The implementation of such a union will effect a lasting improvement in welfare in the Community and will reinforce the contribution of the Community to economic and monetary equilibrium in the world . . . A monetary union implies inside its boundaries the total and irreversible convertibility of currencies, the elimination of margins of fluctuation in exchange rates, the irrevocable fixing of parity and the complete liberation of movements of capital. It may be accompanied by the maintenance of national monetary symbols or the establishment of a sole Community currency. From a technical point of view the choice between these two solutions may seem immaterial, but considerations of a psychological and political nature militate in favour of the adoption of a sole currency which would confirm the irreversibility of the venture.

For such a union only the global balance of payments of the

Community *vis à vis* the outside world is of any importance. Equilibrium within the Community would be realized at this stage in the same way as within a nation's frontiers, thanks to the mobility of the factors of production and financial transfers by the public and private sectors.

To ensure the cohesion of economic and monetary union, transfers of responsibility from the national to the Community plane will be essential. These transfers will be kept within the limits necessary for the effective operation of the Community and will concern essentially the whole body of policies determining the realization of general equilibrium. In addition, it will be necessary for the instruments of economic policy to be harmonized in the various sectors.

Quantitative objectives at medium term established in the form of projections compatible with one another and with the objects of the Common Market will be fixed at the Community level for growth, employment, prices and external equilibrium. These projections will be revised periodically.

Short-term economic policy will be decided in its broadest outlines at a Community level. For this purpose to appreciate and fix the conditions of operation of global supply and demand, especially by means of monetary and budgetary policy, it will be necessary to establish normative and compatible economic budgets each year and to control their realization.

It is indispensable that the principal decisions in the matter of *monetary policy* should be centralized, whether it is a question of liquidity, rates of interest, intervention in the foreign exchange market, the management of the reserves or the fixing of foreign exchange parities *vis à vis* the outside world. The Community must have at its disposal a complete range of necessary instruments, the utilization of which, however, may be different from country to country within certain limits. In addition, it will be necessary to ensure a Community policy and Community representation in monetary and financial relations with third countries and international organizations of an economic, financial and monetary nature.

For influencing the general development of the economy *budget policy* assumes great importance. The Community budget will undoubtedly be more important at the beginning of the final stage than it is today, but its economic significance will still be weak compared with that of the national budgets, the harmonized management of which will be an essential feature of cohesion in the union.

The margins within which the main budget aggregates must be held both for the annual budget and the multi-year projections will be decided at the Community level, taking account of the economic situation and the particular structural features of each country. A fundamental element will be the determination of variations in the volume of budgets, the size of the balance and the methods of financing deficits or utilizing any surpluses. In order to be able to influence the short term economic trend rapidly and effectively it will be useful to have at the national level budgetary and fiscal instruments that can be handled in accordance with Community directives.

In this field, it is necessary to guard against excessive centralization. The transfers of power to the Community organs must be effected to the extent necessary for the proper functioning of the union, and must allow for a differentiated budgetary structure operating at several levels, Community, national, etc.

To make possible the abolition of fiscal frontiers while safeguarding the elasticity necessary for fiscal policy to be able to exercise its functions at the various levels a sufficient degree of *fiscal harmonization* will be effected, notably as regards the value-added tax, taxes likely to have an influence on the movement of capital and certain excise duties.

The suppression of the obstacles of various kinds should make it possible to arrive at a true *Common Market for capital* free from distortions. The financial policy of the member States must be sufficiently unified to ensure the balanced operation of this market.

The realization of global economic equilibrium may be dangerously threatened by differences of structure. Cooperation between the partners in the Community in the matter of *structural and regional policies* will help to surmount these difficulties, just as it will make it possible to eliminate the distortions of competition. The solution of the big problems in this field will be facilitated by financial measures of compensation. In an economic and monetary union, structural and regional policies will not be exclusively a matter of national budgets. Furthermore, the problems of environment raised by industrial growth and urban development must be treated at the Community level under their various technical, financial and social aspects. Finally, the continuous development of intra-Community trade will find a new stimulus in a suitable transport policy . . .

A result of this is that on the plane of *institutional reforms* the realization of economic and monetary union demands the creation or the transformation of a certain number of Community organs to which powers until then exercised by the national authorities will have to be transferred. These transfers of responsibility represent a process of fundamental political significance which implies the progressive development of political cooperation. Economic and monetary union thus appears as a leaven for the development of political union, which in the long run it cannot do without.

The Group does not consider that it will have to formulate detailed proposals as to the institutional form to be given to the different Community organs; it nevertheless indicates the principal requirements to be observed by two organs that seem to it indispensable to the control of economic and monetary policy inside the union: a centre of decision for economic policy, and a Community system for the central banks.

The *centre of decision for economic policy* will exercise independently, in accordance with the Community interest, a decisive influence over the general economic policy of the Community. In view of the fact that the role of the Community budget as an economic instrument will be insufficient, the Community's centre of decision must be in a position to influence the national budgets, especially as regards the level and the direction of the balances and methods for financing the deficits or utilizing the surpluses. In addition, changes in the parity of the sole currency or the whole of the national currencies will be within the competence of this centre. Finally, in order to ensure the necessary links with the general economic policy its responsibility will extend to other domains of economic and social policy which will have been transferred to the Community level. It is essential that the centre of decision for economic policy should be in a position to take rapid and effective decisions by methods to be specified, especially as regards the way in which member States will participate.

The transfer to the Community level of the powers exercised hitherto by national authorities will go hand-in-hand with the transfer of a corresponding Parliamentary responsibility from the national plane to that of the Community's European Parliament. The latter will have to be furnished with a status corresponding to the extension of the Community missions . . .

The constitution of the Community system for the central banks could be based on organisms of the type of the Federal Reserve System operating in the United States. This Community institution will be empowered to take decisions, according to the requirements of the economic situation, in the matter of internal monetary policy as regards liquidity, rates of interest, and the granting of loans to public and private sectors. In the field of external monetary policy, it will be empowered to intervene in the foreign exchanges market and the management of the monetary reserves of the Community.

The transfer of powers to the Community level from the national centres of decision raises a certain number of political problems . . . [e.g.] it will be necessary to guarantee that the Community organ competent for economic policy and that dealing with monetary problems are aiming at the same objective . . .

The implementation of economic and monetary union demands institutional reforms which presuppose a modification of the Treaties of Rome . . .

The Group considers that economic and monetary union is an objective realizable in the course of the present decade, provided the political will . . . is present.

[. . .]

Conclusions

Economic and monetary union is an objective realizable in the course of the present decade provided only that the political will of the member States to realize this objective, as solemnly declared at the conference at The Hague, is present . . .

Document 34

With the path to membership re-opened by The Hague summit, the Labour Government published in February 1970 a White Paper on the economic aspects of membership. Little happened, however, before the June 1970 general election. In the election the Conservative position was that entry into the EEC would be the best solution, although there was a price that they would not be willing to pay.

The Conservatives won the election on other issues. The negotiations for membership were conducted, therefore, by the Heath Government but based on Labour preparations. Heath, a convinced European, had in his maiden House of Commons speech welcomed the Schuman Plan (See Document 15) and had been the British negotiator in 1961–63.

The main phase of the negotiations was concluded in June 1971, and in July the Government issued the White Paper, 'The United Kingdom and the European Communities'. It was debated on the 21–26 July 1971, but the decisive vote on the principle of membership was held 21–28 October 1971, and the motion received 356 votes in support to 244 against.

In February 1972 the European Communities Bill which gave domestic effect to the Treaty of Accession, signed in Brussels on 22 January 1972, was passed by eight votes.

Britain, Denmark and Ireland became members of the EEC on 1 January 1973.

Her Majesty's Government, 'Britain in Europe', July 1971

A short version of the Government's White Paper

The choice

Security

Will our security be better served by joining the European Community than by not doing so? No Government in these islands has been able to ignore for more than a short time, or without disastrous consequences, the course of events on the continent of Europe. Whatever the future holds, our security and that of Western Europe will remain interlocked.

Prosperity

Will we be able to manufacture and trade more favourably if we join the European Community than if we do not? The strength and prosperity of Britain depend partly on our efforts as a people and partly on economic conditions in the world outside. The conditions under which we manufacture and trade are of vital national interest to us.

If we say 'No'

A decision not to join would be a reversal of the whole direction of British policy under successive Governments, Conservative and Labour. No other grouping of countries which has been proposed is acceptable to the nations concerned. In a single generation we should have rejected an Imperial past and a European future, and we would have found nothing to put in their place.

The Government's decision

Her Majesty's Government is convinced that our country will be more secure and our people and our industries more prosperous if we join the European Community than if we remain outside. It will therefore seek the approval of Parliament in the autumn for a decision in principle that Britain should join the Community on 1 January 1973 on the terms which have been negotiated.

[. . .]

Our prospects

The Government believes that membership of the European Economic Community will enable Britain to achieve a higher standard of living. The Six have been able to do this themselves. Membership of the European Economic Community would provide the most favourable means of achieving the economic progress which we all desire and which has eluded us for so long.

Costs and benefits

Membership would not automatically improve our performance and we would be involved in costs as well as benefits. Prosperity in any country depends first and foremost upon the size and effective use of its resources and manpower, plant, equipment and managerial skill. For industry better opportunities once we are inside the Community will enable Britain to sell more and to produce more. As a result, we would increase our national wealth and so be able to improve our standard of living as well as meet the cost of entry. Given a minimum increase, by the end of five years our national income could be some £1,100 million a year higher. No firm estimate of the long-term industrial benefits can sensibly be made, but the Government is confident from the experience of the Six, that the effects of entry will be positive and substantial.

A larger market for trade and industry

Membership of the Community would mean that British manufacturers will be selling their products in a home market five times as large as at present. Trade amongst the Six has grown far faster than our exports to them. For advanced industrial countries like Britain large markets free from trade barriers can encourage a high level of investment in modern equipment and so offer the chance of new jobs.

[. . .]

The Community's farming policy

When adopted by us, this common agricultural policy will stimulate British farm output and open Community markets to our food exports. But at the same time it will raise the cost of our food imports. The extent of this increase in costs will depend on the difference between

Community and world food prices, which has been narrowing considerably in the last year or two. But if the present price gap were to continue the additional cost to our balance of payments on account of food imports is still not likely to be more than £5 million in the first year and £50 million a year by the end of five years.

Effect on food prices

On the same assumption about Community and world prices, it is expected that as a result of adopting the common agricultural policy, the average rise in the housewife's food bill over the first five years will be about 2.5p in the £ per year. This means the cost of living would increase by about 0.5p in the £ per year. Price increases would vary for different foods . . . The narrowing difference between world food prices and the Community's means that the effect on food prices in the shops after Britain joins the Community will not be as great as was once feared. In addition, tariff reductions should lead to lower prices for some manufactured goods.

Our standard of living

Wage earners will benefit from the increased prosperity of British industry and their real wages should rise as those of wage earners in the Six. Retirement pensioners and those on other social benefits will be protected from the effect of food price increases in the shops that may be due to British entry . . .

Our own identity

Our own vital interests

Britain, inside the Community, will have every opportunity to make its views heard and its influence felt. When a Government considers that vital national interests are involved, decisions are only made if all members agree.

No one nation can override another

There is no question of Britain losing essential national sovereignty; what is proposed is a sharing and an enlargement of individual national sovereignties in the common interest.

Our own way of life

The Six have not lost any of their national identities, national institutions and points of view. Nor will Britain . . .

Our own Queen and Parliament

They have kept their own Monarchs and Heads of State, their own Governments, their own Parliaments, Courts and local authorities. So will Britain.

Our own laws

The English and Welsh and Scottish legal systems will continue as before, except that there will be certain changes under the Treaties concerning economic and commercial matters. The British safeguards of *habeas corpus* and trial by jury will remain intact. So will the principle that a man is innocent until he has been proved guilty. Family law, nationality law, land law and the law of landlord and tenant will remain exactly the same. The common law will remain the basis of our legal system.

The negotiations

A successful outcome

All the main issues apart from fisheries were dealt with in the negotiations between Britain and the Communities.

Community institutions

An equal place and equal voting rights with France, Germany and Italy will be given to Britain. English will be one of the official languages . . .

Special arrangements

It has been agreed that we shall have five years in which to adjust ourselves to entry into the enlarged Community.
[. . .]

The Community budget

Only in 1977 will our share be broadly comparable to our economic size. Benefits from the budget which will be paid to Britain have to be offset against the payments that we make towards it. This means that Britain will pay about £100 million to the budget in the first year after entry, rising to some £200 million in 1977 . . .

New Zealand

New Zealand will be assured access to the Community market for a substantial quantity of its current dairy exports to Britain. This will decrease only gradually, so that by the end of 1977 New Zealand will still have a guaranteed market for at least 71 per cent of its butter and cheese exports to Europe. This should give New Zealand earnings equal to or higher than she gets in the British market now. Three years after our entry there will be a review of the arrangements for butter, and after that measures will be decided on to ensure the continuation of special arrangements beyond 1977. The New Zealand Government has described the arrangement as a whole as highly satisfactory.

Australia and Canada

[. . .]

Sugar

Britain's obligations to buy agreed quantities of sugar from the developing Commonwealth until the end of 1974 will be fulfilled. After that it is the firm declared purpose of the Community to safeguard the interests of these Commonwealth countries. The countries concerned have accepted this assurance.

Association

The Community has offered Association to the independent developing Commonwealth countries in Africa, the Caribbean, the Indian Ocean and the Pacific so that their exports will be protected and enjoy access to Europe.

[. . .]

The opportunity

The price we shall have to pay for the economic and political advantages of joining the Community has been set out in this short version of the Government White Paper. These advantages will more than outweigh the costs, provided we seize the opportunities of the far wider home market now open to us.

[. . .]

Britain and Europe

Together we could tackle the problems of technological development which would be far too big for any one of us.

Together we could compete more effectively overseas.

Together we could help the poorer countries of the world more generously than if we were working on our own.

For the first time since the war a Europe united would have the means of recovering the position in the world which Europe divided has lost.

Document 35

There was some progress on The Hague triptych (See Document 33); enlargement was negotiated, albeit with the loss of Norway. Cautious steps had been taken on foreign policy cooperation. Economic and monetary union proposals had not moved.

A new summit of the future enlarged Community was planned for October 1972. France aroused suspicion by re-launching their idea of a political secretariat (See Document 27). In June 1972 Pompidou warned the summit might have to be cancelled if no agreement seemed likely. Intensive negotiations took place, which led to the French dropping their secretariat proposal, and some agreement on key agenda items: economic and monetary union, political cooperation and institutional questions.

Against this background the communiqué seemed to mark a new phase in the evolution of the Community, launching an impressive array of new initiatives. However, real progress was left to be hammered out later.

However, the aspirations of the Paris summit were rapidly overtaken by events in 1973, notable by the Yom Kippur War between Israel and its neighbours in October 1973 which sparked first an oil and energy crisis in the winter of 1973–74, and then economic recession.

'The European Communities: Text of the Communiqué issued by the Heads of State of Government of the Countries of the Enlarged Community at their Meeting in Paris', October 1972

The Heads of State or of Government of the countries of the enlarged Community, meeting for the first time on the 19 and the 20 of October 1972, in Paris, at the invitation of the President of the French Republic solemnly declare:

[. . .]

2. The member States are determined to strengthen the Community

by establishing an economic and monetary union, the guarantee of stability and growth, the foundation of their solidarity and the indispensable basis for social progress and by ending disparities between the regions:

3. Economic expansion is not an end in itself. Its first aim should be to enable disparities in living conditions to be reduced. It must take place with the participation of all the social partners. It should result in an improvement in the quality of life as well as in standards of living. As befits the genius of Europe, particular attention will be given to intangible values and to protecting the environment, so that progress may really be put at the service of mankind:
[. . .]

7. The construction of Europe will allow it, in conformity with its ultimate political objectives, to affirm its personality while remaining faithful to its traditional friendships and to the alliances of the member States, and to establish its position in world affairs as a distinct entity determined to promote a better international equilibrium, respecting the principles of the Charter of the United Nations. The member States of the Community, the driving force of European construction, affirm their intention to transform before the end of the present decade the whole complex of their relations into a European Union.

Economic and monetary questions

1. The Heads of State or of Government reaffirm the determination of the member States of the enlarged European Communities irreversibly to achieve the economic and monetary union, confirming all the elements of the instruments adopted by the Council and by the representatives of member States on 22 March 1971 and 21 March 1972.

The necessary decisions should be taken in the course of 1973 so as to allow the transition to the second stage of the economic and monetary union on 1 January 1974 and with a view to its completion not later than 31 December 1980.

The Heads of State or Government reaffirmed the principle of parallel progress in the different fields of the economic and monetary union.
[. . .]

3. The Heads of State or of Government stressed the need to coordinate more closely the economic policies of the Community and for this purpose to introduce more effective Community procedures. Under

existing economic conditions they consider that priority should be
given to the fight against inflation and to a return to price stability . . .
[. . .]

Regional policy

5. The Heads of State or of Government agreed that a high priority
should be given to the aim of correcting, in the Community, the
structural and regional imbalances which might affect the realization
of economic and monetary union.

The Heads of State or of Government invite the Commission to prepare without delay a report analysing the regional problems which arise
in the enlarged Community and to put forward appropriate proposals.

From now on they undertake to coordinate their regional policies.
Desirous of directing that effort towards finding a Community solution
to regional problems, they invite the Community Institutions to create
a regional Development Fund. This will be set up before 31 December
1973, and will be financed, from the beginning of the second phase
of economic and monetary union, from the Community's own resources. Intervention by the fund in coordination with national aids
should permit, progressively with the realization of economic and
monetary union, the correction of the main regional imbalances in
the enlarged Community and particularly those resulting from the
preponderance of agriculture and from industrial change and structural underemployment.

Social policy

6. The Heads of State or of Government emphasized that they attached
as much importance to vigorous action in the social field as to the
achievement of the economic and monetary union. They thought it
essential to ensure the increasing involvement of labour and management in the economic and social decisions of the Community. They
invited the Institutions, after consulting labour and management, to
draw up, between now and 1 January 1974, a programme of action
providing for concrete measures and the corresponding resources
particularly in the framework of the Social Fund, based on the sug-
gestions made in the course of the Conference by Heads of State or
of Government and by the Commission.

This programme should aim, in particular, at carrying out a coordinated policy for employment and vocational training, at improving
working conditions and conditions of life, at closely involving workers
in the progress of firms, at facilitating on the basis of the situation in

the different countries the conclusion of collective agreements at European level in appropriate fields and at strengthening and coordinating measures of consumer protection.
[. . .]

Environmental policy

8. The Heads of State or of Government emphasized the importance of a Community environmental policy. To this end they invited the Community Institutions to establish, before 31 July 1973, a programme of action responsibilities incumbent on Europe.
[. . .]

External relations

14. The Heads of State or of Government agreed that political cooperation between the member States of the Community on foreign policy matters had begun well and should be still further improved. They agreed that consultations should be intensified at all levels and that the Foreign Ministers should in future meet four times a year instead of twice for this purpose. They considered that the aim of their cooperation was to deal with problems of current interest and, where possible, to formulate common medium and long-term positions, keeping in mind, *inter alia*, the international political implications for and effects of Community policies under construction. On matters which have a direct bearing on Community activities, close contact will be maintained with the Institutions of the Community. They agreed that the Foreign Ministers should produce, not later than 30 June 1973, a second report on methods of improving political cooperation in accordance with the Luxembourg Report.

Document 36

The Paris summit called for Foreign Ministers to report on improving political cooperation (See Documents 33 and 35). Despite the fact that since Paris in October 1972, the Community had experienced a number of problems, the report, in July 1973, proposed that Europe needed to establish its position in the world as a distinct entity. The problems related partly to the problems of adjusting to the 1973 enlargement, but were also related to international developments.

One of these was a deteriorating relationship with the United States. This was partly caused by the international monetary crises, and by long-standing American complaints about the Common Agricultural Policy and other trade matters. The Americans had alarmed the Europeans when Secretary of State Kissinger launched his 'Year of Europe' and proposed a new 'Atlantic Charter' with little consultation. In September 1972 Kissinger had asked 'Who speaks for Europe?'.

These and other developments prompted the French call for another summit, but between that and the Copenhagen summit the Yom Kippur War broke out between Israel and its neighbours, leading to a huge price rise in oil and an embargo against Holland by the Arabs. In a variety of ways the Nine showed an inability to work together in a crisis. The 'Declaration on European Identity' was, therefore, something of a damp squib, and the Community drifted towards sclerosis.

'Final Communiqué issued by the Conference Chairman', Copenhagen, December 1973

Declaration on European identity

1. The Nine member countries of the European Communities have decided that the time has come to draw up a document on the European Identity. This will enable them to achieve a better definition of their relations with other countries and of their responsibilities and the place which they occupy in world affairs. They have decided to define the European Identity with the dynamic nature of the Community in mind. They have the intention of carrying the work further in the future in the light of the progress made in the construction of a united Europe . . .

2. The Nine have the political will to succeed in the construction of a united Europe. On the basis of the Treaties of Paris and Rome setting up the European Communities and of subsequent decisions, they have created a Common Market, based on a customs union, and have established institutions, common policies and machinery for cooperation. All these are an essential part of the European Identity. The Nine are determined to safeguard the elements which make up the unity they have achieved so far and the fundamental objectives laid down for future development at the summit conferences in The Hague and Paris. On the basis of the Luxembourg and Copenhagen Reports, the Nine Governments have established a system of political cooperation with a view to determining common attitudes and, where possible

and desirable, common action. They propose to develop this further. In accordance with the decision taken at the Paris conference, the Nine reaffirm their intention of transforming the whole complex of their relations into a European Union before the end of the present decade.

[. . .]

6. Although in the past the European countries were individually able to play a major role on the international scene, present international problems are difficult for any of the Nine to solve alone. International developments and the growing concentration of power and responsibility in the hands of a very small number of great powers mean that Europe must unite and speak increasingly with a single voice if it wants to make itself heard and play its proper role in the world.

7. The Community, the world's largest trading group, could not be a closed economic entity. It has close links with the rest of the world as regards its supplies and market outlets . . .

8. The Nine, one of whose essential aims is to maintain peace, will never succeed in doing so if they neglect their own security. Those of them who are members of the Atlantic Alliance consider that in present circumstances there is no alternative to the security provided by the nuclear weapons of the United States and by the presence of North American forces in Europe: and they agree that in the light of the relative military vulnerability of Europe, the Europeans should, if they wish to preserve their independence, hold to their commitments and make constant efforts to ensure that they have adequate means of defence at their disposal.

The European identity in relation to the world

9. The Europe of the Nine is aware that, as it unites, it takes on new international obligations. European unification is not directed against anyone, nor is it inspired by a desire for power. On the contrary, the Nine are convinced that their union will benefit the whole international community since it will constitute an element of equilibrium and a basis for cooperation with all countries, whatever their size, culture or social system. The Nine intend to play an active role in world affairs and thus to contribute, in accordance with the purposes and principles of the United Nations Charter, to ensuring that international relations have a more just basis; that the independence and equality of States are better preserved; that prosperity is more equitably shared; and that the security of each country is more effectively

guaranteed. In pursuit of these objectives the Nine should progressively define common positions in the sphere of foreign policy.

10. As the Community progresses towards a common policy in relation to third countries, it will act in accordance with the following principles:

(a) The Nine, acting as a single entity, will strive to promote harmonious and constructive relations with these countries. This should not however jeopardize, hold back or affect the will of the Nine to progress towards European Union within the time limits laid down.

(b) In future when the Nine negotiate collectively with other countries, the institutions and procedures chosen should enable the distinct character of the European entity to be respected.

(c) In bilateral contacts with other countries the member States of the Community will increasingly act on the basis of agreed common positions.

[. . .]

Documents 37

The legacy of the 1972 debates on the outcome of the negotiations for British accession was a Labour Party divided on the terms of entry, with a faction opposed to membership on any terms, and a commitment by the party leadership to the renegotiation of the terms and to a referendum on membership or a new election to be fought on the issue.

Labour took office as a minority Government in February 1974 and presented a demand for renegotiation at a meeting of the General Affairs Council in Luxembourg on 1 April 1974.

Serious discussion did not begin until the Labour Government had strengthened itself at home by winning a new election in October 1974 with a majority of three. The negotiating team consisted of Mr Callaghan, Mr Peter Shore, the Trade Minister, a harsh critic of the EEC and Mr Roy Hattersley, a junior Minister at the Foreign Office, and a pro-European. Although the British regarded themselves as renegotiating, the word was unwelcome among the others, to whom it suggested an attempt to renege on a deal. Changes in the wording of the Accession Treaty were out. It therefore became a matter of the British obtaining assurances, on some of which they could put their own interpretations.

By March 1975 the Government judged that it had secured sufficient satisfaction from the other members of the EEC to enable it to recommend the new terms of membership to the electorate.

Public support for membership, as renegotiated, was to be tested in a referendum. The Government recommended acceptance, but allowed its supporters, including members of the Cabinet, to campaign against. Two main cross-party campaigning groups formed, pro and anti, with public funds contributing (along with private subscriptions) to their costs. Each produced a pamphlet paid for by the Government, and the Government produced its own on 'Britain's New Deal in Europe'.

The National Referendum Campaign, authors of the NO pamphlet, was an umbrella organization, chaired by the Conservative MP Neil Marten, but also comprising Welsh and Scottish Nationalists, as well as Labour, Conservative and Liberal anti-marketeers.

In a two-thirds turn-out, 67.2 per cent voted in favour of continuing membership. The Prime Minister, Mr Wilson, declared that the 'debate was over' and that normal party discipline and collective ministerial responsibility were restored. The debate, however, continued.

Her Majesty's Government, 'Membership of the European Community: Report on Renegotiation', March 1975

Introduction

[. . .]

7. This chapter describes the outcome of renegotiations on each of the seven objectives in the Labour Party Manifesto of February 1974.

Food and agriculture

Renegotiation objectives

8. The February Manifesto undertook to secure: 'major changes in the common agricultural policy so that it ceases to be a threat to world trade in food products, and so that low cost producers outside Europe can continue to have access to the British food market'.

Outcome

9. To secure the supply of food at fair prices, Common Agricultural Policy (CAP) price levels have been held down in real terms; progress has been made towards relating them more closely to the needs of

efficient producers, and towards securing a better balance between supply and demand.

[. . .]

15. As a result of changes in the world food situation and the progress achieved in renegotiation the Government believe that the CAP can be operated flexibly in the enlarged Community and in a way which meets the needs of consumers and producers. Further improvements in the CAP are foreshadowed and it should be possible to contain the net cost within reasonable limits . . .

[. . .]

The Community budget

Renegotiation objective

33. The February Manifesto stated that one object of the renegotiation would be 'new and fairer methods' of financing the Community budget. It said: 'Neither the taxes that form the so-called "own resources" of the Communities, nor the purposes, mainly agricultural support, on which the funds are mainly to be spent, are acceptable to us. We would be ready to contribute to Community finances only such sums as were fair in relation to what is paid and received by other countries'.

Outcome

34. (a) At the meeting of Community Heads of Government in Dublin on 10–11 March, the Government secured agreement on a budget correcting mechanism which will provide a refund to the United Kingdom if in any year our contribution to the Community budget goes significantly beyond what is fair in relation to our share of Community GNP.

(b) Much has already been achieved, and further progress can be expected, in containing Community expenditure on agricultural support and in the development of expenditure policies more beneficial to the United Kingdom.

[. . .]

Economic and Monetary Union

Renegotiation objective

46. The February Manifesto said: 'We would reject any kind of international agreement which compelled us to accept increased

unemployment for the sake of maintaining a fixed parity, as is required by current proposals for a European Economic and Monetary Union (EMU). We believe that the monetary problems of the European countries can be resolved only in a world-wide framework'.

Outcome

47. (a) Events have shown that the programme for movement towards full EMU by 1980, which was laid down in 1972 at the Community Heads of Government meeting in Paris, was over-ambitious and unattainable. In practice other members of the Community accept this.

(b) Closer cooperation between Community countries in the economic and monetary fields is valuable and presents no threat to employment in the United Kingdom.

[. . .]

Regional, industrial and fiscal policies

Renegotiation objective

52. The Government's objective, as set out in the February 1974 Manifesto, was to ensure the 'retention by Parliament of those powers over the British economy needed to pursue effective regional, industrial and fiscal policies'.

Outcome

53. (a) *Regional policy.* New principles for the coordination of regional aids within the Community will allow the United Kingdom to continue to pursue effective regional policies adjusted to the particular needs of individual areas of the country. The Communication setting out these principles acknowledges that national governments are the best judges of what is required in their own countries, and that changes in national aid systems will not be regarded as incompatible with the Common Market when they are justified by problems of unemployment, migration or other valid requirements, subject to the condition that a member State's actions do not damage the interests of other member States.

(b) *Industrial policy.* The Government are satisfied that their policies for aid to industry generally, their nationalization proposals, and the establishment of the National Enterprise

Board and of Planning Agreements will not be hampered by Treaty obligations.

(c) *Steel.* In the particular case of steel, it has been established that neither the Commission nor the United Kingdom now has powers to control private sector investment . . .

(d) *Fiscal policy.* The Government are satisfied that membership of the Community does not limit their powers to pursue effective fiscal policies.

(e) The Government are satisfied that subject to the question of steel, which cannot be resolved yet, their renegotiation requirements have been met.

[. . .]

Capital movements

Renegotiation objective

69. The February Manifesto said: 'We need an agreement on capital movements which protects our balance of payments policies'.

Outcome

70. Experience, including the experience of other member States, confirms that in practice the Government can act to control capital movements when necessary. This has already been done, under the terms of the Treaties, without any special agreement.
[. . .]

The Commonwealth and the developing countries: trade and aid

[. . .]

Renegotiation objective

76. The February Manifesto said: 'The economic interests of the Commonwealth and the developing countries must be better safeguarded. This involves securing continued access to the British market and, more generally, the adoption by an enlarged Community of trade and aid policies designed to benefit not just "associated overseas territories" in Africa, but developing countries throughout the world'.

Outcome

77. Substantial changes have been secured in Community policies on a number of fronts:

(a) Continued access on fair terms has been secured for sugar from the developing countries of the Caribbean and elsewhere and improvements have been obtained in the arrangements for dairy products from New Zealand.

(b) Reductions in Community tariffs have been secured on a range of items of particular interest to Commonwealth countries, . . . The detailed mandate for the multilateral trade negotiations agreed by the Community in February 1975 provides for the negotiation of further reductions in agricultural tariffs as well as for wide ranging negotiations on agricultural products in general; for substantial reductions in industrial tariffs; and for particular attention to be paid to the needs of the developing countries.

(c) In relation to the developing countries a major step forward was taken with the conclusion of the Lomé Convention between the enlarged Community and forty-six developing countries including twenty-two Commonwealth countries in Africa, the Caribbean and the Pacific. Under the Convention the developing countries are guaranteed free entry into the Community for their industrial exports, almost completely free entry for their agricultural exports, and also substantial aid.

(d) In addition major improvements, which will benefit the trade of other developing countries, particularly the Commonwealth countries of Asia, have been secured in the Community's Scheme of Generalized Preferences for 1975 . . .

(e) A start has been made in securing a more balanced distribution of Community aid; in particular the principle has been accepted of providing financial and technical aid for developing countries without special relationships with the Community.

[. . .]

Value Added Tax (VAT)

Renegotiation objective

92. The February Manifesto said that there should be 'no harmonization of Value Added Tax which would require us to tax necessities'.

Outcome

93. The Government have established that they can resist any proposals for such harmonization which are unacceptable.
[. . .]

Sovereignty and membership of the Community

115. No country nowadays has unqualified freedom of action . . .

116. Countries are increasingly coming together in interdependent groupings in order to defend and advance their interests. Since 1945 we have found it necessary to combine with others to organize our trade relations, our defence, our monetary interests and economic policies . . .

117. Each of these organizations imposes rights and duties on its members which match the purposes of the organization . . .
[. . .]

123. It is clear that the power of political decision in the Community rests with the member States. Decisions on major policy questions are taken by the Council of Ministers, on which each of the member States is equally represented. At each stage in discussions in the Council and its subordinate machinery, efforts are made to accommodate the views of the member States and to narrow the differences between them. The final decision is the responsibility of the Council itself . . .

124. The importance of accommodating the interests of individual member States is recognized in the Council's general practice of taking decisions by consensus, so that each member State is in a position to block agreement unless interests to which it attaches importance are met. This has been the practice in the Community since the conclusions reached in Luxembourg on 28 January 1966 . . . It remains the unchallenged right of each member State to decide which issues it does regard as sufficiently important to require unanimous decision.
[. . .]

132. The Government do not accept any commitment to any sort of federal structure in Europe. No member Government has asked us for any such commitment in the course of renegotiation. All member States agree that future institutional developments must conform to political decisions of the Governments and Parliaments of member States – the consent of the United Kingdom Parliament would be sought before any institutional development of major importance.
[. . .]

The role of Parliament

134. Thus membership of the Community raises for us the problem of reconciling this system of directly applicable law made by

the Community with our constitutional principle that Parliament is the sovereign legislator and can make or unmake any law whatsoever. That principle remains unaltered by our membership of the Community: Parliament retains its ultimate right to legislate on any matter ...

135. The problem therefore has to be considered from two aspects: first, the general issue of whether the ultimate sovereignty of Parliament has been weakened, and secondly, whether Parliament can play an effective role in the making of any particular new Community law. On the general issue, Parliament by the European Communities Act 1972 authorized the application in this country of directly applicable Community law and to that extent has delegated its powers. Parliament has however the undoubted power to repeal that Act, on which our ability to fulfil our Treaty obligations still depends. Thus our membership of the Community in the future depends on the continuing assent of Parliament.

136. At the level of the day-to-day legislative activity of the Community there is a range of legislative instruments, from the purely technical and regulatory to items of major policy significance. Apart from the instruments made by the Commission in specific areas, ... all items of Community law are contained in instruments adopted by the Council, in whose discussions and decisions United Kingdom Ministers necessarily take part. Parliament, by passing the 1972 Act, in effect remitted to the Government responsibility for safeguarding United Kingdom interests in the Council deliberations which result in directly applicable Community law. United Kingdom Ministers remain directly answerable to Parliament, since the continuance of any Government depends on Parliament's support. Parliament thus operates in the Community law-making process by exercising its traditional role of controlling and restraining the Government against the background of the ultimate sanction of withdrawal of confidence. This applies to Ministers when they are sitting in the Council in Brussels as much as when they are taking decisions solely as members of the Government of the United Kingdom.

137. For Parliament to exercise this control and restraint it is essential that it should have sufficient information and the opportunity to make its views known to Ministers. The Government have been concerned since they took office in 1974 to ensure that these requirements are met.
[. . .]

Wider considerations

146. In the Government's view the consequences of Britain's withdrawal from the Community would be adverse – and would result in uncertainty. This uncertainty could be protracted and would itself be damaging.

147. There could be a significant effect on confidence, affecting both investment in the United Kingdom and our ability to finance our balance of payments deficit. There would be a risk of a deterioration, for a time at least, both in the level of employment and in the rate of inflation.

148. The United Kingdom would have to engage in the negotiation of a new trading relationship with the Community and with the rest of the world; this would be bound to be difficult. If it were not possible to secure special trading arrangements with the Community, British exports would face a high Community tariff on such products as chemicals, commercial vehicles and textiles. Even if an acceptable free trade arrangement could be negotiated, this would be accompanied by conditions which would be likely to limit the Government's freedom to give assistance to British industry.

[. . .]

150. The Government have always believed that, provided the terms of membership were right and fair, it is in the interests of Britain and of Europe that we should be a member of the Community. The wider considerations set out in this Chapter confirm the Government's judgement that continued membership of the Community is in Britain's interest on the basis of the renegotiated terms.

151. Through membership of the Community we are better able to advance and protect our national interests – this is the essence of sovereignty. We are only at the start of our relationship with the Community: we can now begin to play a full part in its construction and development. The Community has shown that it is a flexible organization, which is ready to adapt to the changing circumstances of the world and to respond to the differing needs of member States.

[. . .]

The decision

153. If our membership of the Community is confirmed, the Government will be ready to play a full part in developing a new and wider

Europe. The decision is now for the British people. The Government will accept their verdict.

'Referendum on the European Community (Common Market): Why You Should Vote NO'

This is a statement by the National Referendum Campaign NOT by HM Government.

Renegotiation. The present Government, though it tried, has on its own admission failed to achieve the 'fundamental renegotiation' it promised at the last two general elections. All it has gained are a few concessions for Britain, some of them only temporary. The real choice before the British peoples has been scarcely altered by renegotiation.

What did the pro-Marketeers say? Before we joined the Common Market the Government forecast that we should enjoy:

- A rapid rise in our living standards

- A trade surplus with the Common Market

- Better productivity

- Higher investment

- More employment

- Faster industrial growth

In every case the opposite is now happening, according to the Government's figures. Can we rely upon the pro-Marketeers' prophecies this time?

The anti-Marketeers' forecasts have turned out to be all too correct. When you are considering the pro-Marketeers' arguments, you should remember this.

Remember also that before the referendum in Norway, the pro-Marketeers predicted, if Norway came out, just the same imaginary evils as our own pro-Marketeers are predicting now. The Norwegian people voted NO. And none of these evil results occurred.

Our legal right to come out. It was agreed during the debates which took us into the Common Market that the British Parliament had the absolute right to repeal the European Communities Act and take us out. There is nothing in the Treaty of Rome which says a country cannot come out.

The right to rule ourselves

The fundamental question is whether or not we remain free to rule ourselves in our own way.

For the British people, membership of the Common Market has already been a bad bargain. What is worse, it sets out by stages to merge Britain with France, Germany, Italy and other countries into a single nation. This will take away from us the right to rule ourselves which we have enjoyed for centuries.

The Common Market increasingly does this by making our laws and by deciding our policies on food, prices, trade and employment – all matters which affect the lives of us all.

Already, under the Treaty of Rome, policies are being decided, rules made, laws enacted and taxes raised, not by our own Parliament elected by the British people, but by the Common Market – often by the unelected Commissioners in Brussels.

As this system tightens – and it will – our right, by our votes, to change policies and laws in Britain will steadily dwindle. Unlike British laws, those of the Common Market which will take precedence over our own laws – can only be changed if all the other members of the Common Market agree.

Your vote affects the future of your country.

This is wholly contrary to the wishes of ordinary people who everywhere want more, not less, control over their own lives.

Those who want Britain in the Common Market are defeatists; they see no independent future for our country.

Your vote will affect the future of your country for generations to come.

We say: Let's rule ourselves, while trading and remaining friendly with other nations. We say: No rule from Brussels. We say: Vote NO.

Your food, Your jobs, Our trade

We cannot afford to remain in the Common Market because:

It must mean still higher food prices. Before we joined, we could buy our food at the lowest cost from the most efficient producers in the world. Since we joined, we are no longer allowed to buy all our food where it suits us best. Inside the Common Market, taxes are imposed on food imported from outside countries. For instance, we now have to pay a tax of over £300 a ton on butter imported from outside the Market and over £350 a ton on cheese.

Our food is still cheaper than in the rest of the Common Market. But if we stay in, we will be forced by Common Market rules to bring our food prices up to Common Market levels. All of us, young and old alike, will have to pay. For example, the price of butter has to be almost doubled by 1978 if we stay in.

Food destroyed – or sold to Russia. If the vote is Yes, your food must cost you more. Not merely do the Common Market authorities tax food imports or shut them out, but they also buy up home-produced food (through Intervention Boards) purely to keep the prices up. Then they store it in warehouses, thus creating mountains of beef, butter, grain, etc. Some of this food is deliberately made unfit for human consumption or even destroyed, and some is sold to countries like Russia, at prices well below what the housewife in the Common Market has to pay.

The Common Market has already stored up a beef mountain of over 300,000 tons, and all beef imports from outside have been banned.

Food price increases due to the Market. If we come out of the Market, we could buy beef, veal, mutton, lamb, butter, cheese and other foods more cheaply than if we stay in. World food prices outside the Market are now falling.

There is no doubt that the rise in food prices in Britain in the last three years has been partly due to joining the Common Market. For example, between 1971 and 1974, food prices rose in Britain and Ireland (which joined) by over 40%. In Norway and Sweden (which stayed out) they rose only by about 20%.

Your jobs at risk. If we stay in the Common Market, a British Government can no longer prevent the drift of industry southwards and increasingly to the Continent. This is already happening.

If it went on, it would be particularly damaging to Scotland, Wales, Northern Ireland and much of the North and West of England, which have suffered so much from unemployment already.

If we stay in the Common Market, our Government must increasingly abandon to them control over this drift of industry and employment.

Their threat to iron, steel and our oil. Far-reaching powers of interference in the control of British industry, particularly iron and steel, are possessed by the Market authorities.

Interference with the oil around our shores has already been threatened by the Brussels Commission.

Huge trade deficit with the Common Market. The Common Market pattern of trade was never designed to suit Britain. According to our Department of Trade, our trade deficit with the Common Market was running, in the early months of 1975, at nearly £2,600 million a year – a staggering figure, compared with a very small deficit in 1970 when we were free to trade in accordance with our own policies.

What they said was wrong. Yet before entry, the pro-Marketeers said that the 'effect upon our balance of trade would be positive and substantial'. If you don't want this dangerous trade deficit to continue, vote NO.

Taxes to keep prices up. The Common Market's dear food policy is designed to prop up inefficient farmers on the Continent by keeping food prices high. If we stay in the Market, the British housewife will not only be paying more for her food but the British taxpayer will soon be paying many hundreds of millions of pounds a year to the Brussels budget, largely to subsidize Continental farmers. We are already paying into the Budget much more than we get out. This is entirely unreasonable and we cannot afford it.

Agriculture. It would be far better for us if we had our own national agricultural policy suited to our own country, as we had before we joined. We could then guarantee prices for our farmers, and, at the same time, allow consumers to buy much more cheaply.

In the Common Market, the British taxpayer is paying as much to keep food prices up as we used to pay under our own policy to keep them down.

The Market also have their eyes on British fishing grounds because they have over-fished their own waters.

Commonwealth links. Our Commonwealth links are bound to be weakened much further if we stay in the Common Market. We are being forced to tax imported Commonwealth goods. And as we lose our national independence, we shall cease, in practice, to be a member of the Commonwealth.

Britain a mere province of the Common Market? The real aim of the Market is, of course, to become one single country in which Britain would be reduced to a mere province. The plan is to have a Common Market Parliament by 1978 or shortly thereafter. Laws would be passed by that Parliament which would be binding on our country. No Parliament elected by the British people could change those laws.

This may be acceptable to some Continental countries. In recent times, they have been ruled by dictators, or defeated or occupied. They are more used to abandoning their political institutions than we are.

Unless you want to be ruled more and more by a Continental

Parliament in which Britain would be in a small minority, you should vote NO.

What is the alternative?

A far better course is open to us. If we withdraw from the Market, we could and should remain members of the wider Free Trade Area which now exists between the Common Market and the countries of the European Free Trade Association (EFTA) – Norway, Sweden, Finland, Austria, Switzerland, Portugal and Iceland.

These countries are now to enjoy free entry for their industrial exports into the Common Market without having to carry the burden of the Market's dear food policy or suffer rule from Brussels.

Britain already enjoys industrial free trade with these countries. If we withdrew from the Common Market, we should remain members of the wider group and enjoy, as the EFTA countries do, free or low tariff entry into the Common Market countries without the burden of dear food or the loss of the British people's democratic rights.

The Common Market countries would be most unlikely to oppose this arrangement, since this would neither be sensible nor in their own interests. They may well demand a free trade area with us. But even if they did not do so, their tariffs on British exports would be very low.

Scare-mongering of the pro-Marketeers. It is scare-mongering to pretend that withdrawal from the Common Market would mean heavy unemployment or loss of trade. In a very few years we shall enjoy in North Sea oil a precious asset possessed by none of the Common Market countries. Our freedom to use this oil, and our vast coal reserves, unhampered by any threatened Brussels restrictions, will strengthen our national economy powerfully.

For peace, stability and independence

Some say that the Common Market is a strong united group of countries, working closely together, and that membership would give us protection against an unfriendly world.

There is no truth in this assertion.

The defence of Britain and Western Europe depends not on the Common Market at all, but on the North Atlantic Treaty Organization (NATO), which includes other countries like the United States, Canada, and Norway, which are not members of the Common Market.

Any attempt to substitute the Common Market for NATO as a defence shield would be highly dangerous for Britain. Most anti-

Marketeers rightly believe that we should remain members of NATO,
the Organization for Economic Cooperation and Development, EFTA,
and the Council of Europe, as well as of the UN and its agencies.

In all these, we can work actively together as good internationalists,
while preserving our own democratic rights.

The choice is yours.

It will be your decision that counts.

Remember: you may never have the chance to decide this great
issue again.

If you want a rich and secure future for the British peoples, a free
and democratic society, living in friendship with all nations – but
governing ourselves,

VOTE NO

Document 38

*After the disappointments of 1973 the political environment was changed
again in the spring of 1974. In both France and Germany new leaders
emerged. In France Valery Giscard d'Estaing took over from the deceased
Pompidou, and in Germany Helmut Schmidt replaced a dispirited Willy
Brandt.*

*The two new leaders grew increasingly close politically and breathed
new life into both the Franco-German relationship and the leadership of
the Community. Under that leadership another Paris summit in December
1974 commissioned the Prime Minister of Belgium, Leo Tindemans, to
produce a report on how political union might realistically be achieved.
Realism was the order of the day, and concern was as much with crisis
management as rejuvenation.*

*On the eve of 1976 Tindemans produced his Report, which was relatively
unambitious. One reason was Tindemans' own awareness of the contemporary mood, another was the realization that after the rhetoric of Paris
in 1972 a more practical approach was required, and a third was an
appreciation of the hesitations over the balance of powers between Brussels
and national capitals.*

*One suggestion attracted a great deal of criticism, namely the idea of a
possible 'two-tier' or 'two-speed' Europe. This was viewed with deep suspicion by those who feared being in the second tier or slower lane, like
Britain, Denmark and Ireland. More broadly, there was little enthusiasm*

for Tindemans' plans, although despite nothing coming of the Tindemans Report immediately, several of its ideas reappeared later.

'European Union: Report by Mr Leo Tindemans to the European Council', December 1975

European Union

I propose that the European Council should define the different components of European Union as follows:

1. European Union implies that we present a united front to the outside world. We must tend to act in common in all the main fields of our external relations whether in foreign policy, security, economic relations or development aid. Our action is aimed at defending our interests but also at using our collective strength in support of law and justice in world discussions.

2. European Union recognizes the interdependence of the economic prosperity of our States and accepts the consequences of this: a common economic and monetary policy to manage this prosperity, common policies in the industrial and agricultural sectors and on energy and research to safeguard the future.

3. European Union requires the solidarity of our peoples to be effective and adequate. Regional policy will correct inequalities in development and counteract the centralizing effects of industrial societies. Social action will mitigate inequalities of income and encourage society to organize itself in a fairer and more humane fashion.

4. European Union makes itself felt in people's daily lives. It helps to protect their rights and to improve their life style.

5. In order to achieve these tasks European Union is given institutions with the necessary powers to determine a common, coherent and all-inclusive political view, the efficiency needed for action, the legitimacy needed for democratic control. The principle of the equality of all our States continues to be respected within the Union by each State's right to participate in political decision-making.

6. Like the Community whose objectives it pursues and whose attainments it protects, European Union will be built gradually. So as to restart the construction of Europe straight away and increase its credibility its initial basis is the political commitment of the States to carry out in different fields specific actions selected according to their importance and the chances of success.

Europe in the world

A single decision-making centre

I propose that the European Council should now decide:

(a) To put an end to the distinction which still exists today between ministerial meetings which deal with political cooperation and those which deal with the subjects covered by the Treaties: in order to decide on a policy the Ministers must be able to consider all aspects of the problems within the Council.

(b) That the institutions of the Union can discuss all problems if they are relevant to European interests and consequently come within the ambit of the Union . . .

I propose changing the political commitment of the member States which is the basis of political cooperation into a legal obligation.

Towards a common foreign policy

[. . .]

Security: I therefore propose that we should decide:

(a) regularly to hold exchanges of views on our specific problems in defence matters and on European aspects of multilateral negotiations on security. Exchanges of views of this kind will one day enable member States to reach a common analysis of defence problems and, meanwhile, to take account of their respective positions in any action they take;

(b) to cooperate in the manufacture of armaments with a view to reducing defence costs, and increasing European independence and the competitiveness of its industry. The efforts undertaken at present to provide the European countries of the Alliance with an organization for the standardization of armaments, on the basis of joint programmes, will have important consequences for industrial production. This strengthens the need to initiate a common industrial policy on the manufacture of armaments within the framework of the European Union. Setting up a European armaments agency for that purpose must be given consideration.

[. . .]

European economic and social policies

A new approach

It is impossible at the present time to submit a credible programme of action if it is deemed absolutely necessary that in every case all stages should be reached by all the States at the same time. The divergence of their economic and financial situations is such that, were we to insist on this, progress would be impossible and Europe would continue to crumble away. It must be possible to allow that:

- within the Community framework of an over-all concept of European Union . . .

- and on the basis of an action programme drawn up in a field decided upon by the common institutions, whose principles are accepted by all:

  (a) those States which are able to progress have a duty to forge ahead

  (b) those States which have reasons for not progressing which the Council, on a proposal from the Commission, acknowledges as valid do not so

- but will at the same time receive from other States any aid and assistance that can be given to enable them to catch the others up,

- and will take part, within the joint institutions, in assessing the results obtained in the field in question.

This does not mean Europe *a la carte*: each country will be bound by the agreement of all as to the final objective to be achieved in common; it is only the timescales for achievement which vary . . .

I therefore propose that the European Council should adopt the following guidelines:

- bearing in mind the objective difficulties of certain States, progress as regards economic and monetary policy may be sought initially between certain States in accordance with the Community practices and the limitations mentioned above;

[. . .]

Social policy

Security. Supplementing measures already in force within the Community, the Union must lay down standards applicable in all our

States as regards wages, pensions, social security and working conditions, laying particular emphasis on the problems of women at work.

The Union must afford particular protection to certain categories of workers: migrants, the handicapped . . .

Concertation. The gradual transfer to the European level of some powers of decision in economic policy matters reflects a step which large firms took long ago. This parallel development means that the practice of concertation between employers, workers and public authorities which exists to some extent in all our States, must also be introduced at European level.

Framework agreements or collective European settlements must be reached by means of concertation in individual sectors.

This means considerably increasing the activity of the Standing Committee on Employment. This body will have to be consulted during preparation of the Union's social policy, and it must be associated with its implementation. It must have a right of initiative *vis-à-vis* the European institutions so that, along with the Parliament and the Economic and Social Committee, it can act as a spur to the development of the social side of the Union.

Worker participation. The problem of the place of workers in an enterprise arises perhaps in differing degrees but along similar lines, in all our countries. In view of the increasing integration of economic units this problem should be solved at the European level by increasing worker participation in the management, control or profits of businesses. This policy fits in with the search for a more humane and just society which lies at the heart of the European effort.

[. . .]

A citizen's Europe

We should adopt:

• the protection of the rights of Europeans, where this can no longer be guaranteed solely by individual States;

• concrete manifestation of European solidarity by means of external signs discernible in everyday life.

Protection of rights

Fundamental rights

[. . .]

External signs of our solidarity

1. As regards movement of persons, measures leading to uniformity of passports and later to a passport union are currently under discussion.

I propose that in addition the European Union should set as its aim:

- the gradual disappearance of frontier controls on persons moving between member countries, as a corollary of passport union;

- improved transport and communication, if necessary by harmonizing rules, and by abolishing tariffs which discriminate between national transport and telecommunications and those taking place within the Union;

- the simplification of procedures for refunding medical expenses incurred by Union citizens in another country of the Union . . .

I propose that a pragmatic solution should be found to the delicate matter of the equivalence of diplomas and studies, this being the main obstacle in the way of integration of educational systems.
[. . .]

3. I propose that a serious effort should be made to promote collaboration between information media, in particular radio and television, to encourage the spread of information and better knowledge of each other.
[. . .]

Strengthening the institutions

The powers of the Parliament

I propose that:

- the Council should immediately allow the Parliament to take initiatives by undertaking to consider the resolutions which Parliament addresses to it. This will permit the Assembly to make an effective contribution towards defining common policies.

- in the course of the progressive development of the European Union this practice should be given legal value through a Treaty amendment which would accord to the Parliament a real right of initiative.

- Parliament should be able, from now on, to consider all questions within the competence of the Union, whether or not they are covered by the Treaties.

[. . .]

The European Council

I submit to it the following propositions defining its role and its method of working:

1. The European Council is to give coherent general policy guidelines, based on a comprehensive vision of problems. This is an indispensable precondition for an attempt to produce a common policy.

2. Within this framework the Heads of Government will collectively use the authority which they have at the national level to give from within the European Council the impetus which is needed for the construction of Europe, and to search together for that political agreement which will allow dynamic progress to be maintained, in spite of difficulties . . .

The Council

1. *Coherence.*

(a) The Council of Ministers (Foreign Affairs) should be entrusted by a decision of the European Council with coordinating in the most appropriate manner the activities of the specialist Councils.

(b) The distinction between ministerial meetings devoted to political cooperation and meetings of the Council should be abolished. The abolition of this distinction would not however affect the current procedures for preparing the diplomatic discussions of the Ministers.

2. *Speed.* Speeding up the decision-making process requires greater use of majority mechanisms.

(a) Recourse to majority voting in the Council should become normal practice in the Community field.

(b) In those sectors of external relations where the member States have undertaken to pursue a common policy, they must be able speedily to reach decisions and to act when faced with a crisis. This implies that by analogy with the institutional mechanism of the Treaties, minority opinion should, in these sectors, rally to the view of the majority at the end of the discussion.

3. *Continuity.*

(a) A Treaty amendment should extend to a whole year the term of the Presidency of the European Council and the Council in order to:

- strengthen the authority of the Presidency,

- permit a more coherent dialogue between the Parliament and the Council,

- lend more continuity to its activity.

(b) The European Council and the Council should entrust special or temporary tasks, like a negotiation or study, to the Commission, to a single country or to one or more persons independently of changes in the Presidency. This should in no way diminish the powers which the Commission derives from the Treaties.

The Commission

1. *Role of the Commission.* I propose that:

- for the execution and administration of common policies within the Community greater use should be made of Article 155 of the Treaty which makes provision for such powers to be conferred on the Commission.

[. . .]

2. *The cohesion of the Commission.* In order to give the European Commission increased authority and cohesion I propose that the Treaties be amended as follows:

(a) The President of the Commission will be appointed by the European Council.

(b) The President when appointed will have to appear before the Parliament to make a statement and have his appointment confirmed by vote.

(c) The President of the Commission will then appoint his colleagues in consultation with the Council and bearing in mind the number of Commissioners allocated to each country.

[. . .]

The Court of Justice

The Court of Justice stressed in its report on European Union that the Community constitutes a 'state of law' and that this characteristic must be maintained within the Union. This is an essential factor

conferring legitimacy upon our undertaking which leads me to formulate the following:

1. In the new sectors covered by the Union, the Court must have
powers identical to those which it has at present, so as to be able to
interpret the law of the Union, to annul the acts of the institutions
not in accordance with the Treaties and to point out when the member States fail to comply with their obligations;

2. Individuals must also be able to appeal directly to the Court of
Justice against an act of one of the institutions of the Union infringing
their basic rights.

[. . .]

Document 39

*After the 1973 enlargements (See Documents 33 and 34), the next
enlargements were the 'southern' or 'Mediterranean' enlargements of
1981 (Greece) and 1986 (Spain and Portugal). In many ways the Greek
enlargement raised both specific and general issues. The three had many
experiences in common, especially recent experience of dictatorship and
levels of economic development well below the Community average. The
Community felt a political obligation to consolidate democracy in these
States, but their accession posed new issues for the Community.*

*Given its geographical position, chequered political history, and relatively
low levels of socio-economic development, Greece had not been involved in
the mainstream of European developments, although it was a founder
member of the OEEC. It joined the Council of Europe just after its foundation (See Document 14) and NATO in 1952. In 1959 Greece requested
an association with the Six, and in 1961 the 'Athens Agreement' was
signed. This was seen by both the Greeks and the Six as a first step towards
membership.*

*The development of relations was disrupted by the Colonels' Coup in
April 1967, which led to the agreement being frozen. It was reactivated
in July 1974 after the fall of the Colonels and the return to democracy in
Greece.*

*The new Government applied to join the Community in June 1975. Both
sides hoped membership would consolidate stability, but economically both
had doubts. The political position led to the Council sweeping aside the Commission's reservations. Following protracted negotiations, when specific*

interests almost interfered with the perceived general interest (as it did in negotiations with Spain and Portugal), the Treaty of Accession was signed in May 1979.

'Commission Opinion on Greek Application for Membership', 1976

[. . .]

4. It is the first time that the European Community has been presented with an application for full membership from a country with which it already has close contractual links. This relationship is defined in the Association which was created between the EEC and Greece in 1962, covering not just trade policy but a whole series of steps that were to be undertaken to ensure Greece's progressive integration into the entire fabric of Community life. In particular, the Athens Agreement was explicitly aimed at paving the way for eventual full membership.

Fourteen years later, in the aftermath of fundamental changes in its political and economic situation, Greece has decided that it is now in a position to move on to this final stage in its relations with the Community.

Given the avowed aims of the Community in establishing the Association, and Greece's return to a democratic form of government, there can be no doubt, in the view of the Commission that the Community must now give a clear positive answer to the Greek request.

5. The Greek application for membership in the timescale currently envisaged, that is without first waiting for the full implementation of the present Association, necessarily raises a complex of issues which need to be identified for they entail important consequences for both Greece and the Community, and taking a positive verdict on the principle of membership as the starting point, this paper proposes certain guidelines for approaching these problems.

Eastern Mediterranean

6. The prospect of Greek membership raises the problem of the disagreements between Greece and Turkey, an Associate country whose agreement with the Community also has full membership as its stated final objective.

The European Community is not and should not become a party to the disputes between Greece and Turkey . . .

[. . .]

Economic implications of Greek accession

8. Where the Community is concerned, the overall impact in macro-economic terms of Greek membership of the Community will be limited given the relative magnitudes involved, and the main economic implication of Greek membership for the Community is likely to be financial and budgetary.

9. The Greek economy at its present stage of development contains a number of structural features which limit its ability to combine homogeneously with the economies of the present member States. [. . .]

Development of the Community

13. A quite different issue raised by the prospect of Greek membership is that implied by any enlargement of the Community, namely its effect on the working methods and the future development of the Community.

The prospect of further enlargement at a time when the full consequences of the preceding one have not yet been absorbed must give rise to concern. The Commission considers therefore that any further enlargement must be accompanied by a substantial improvement in the efficiency of the Community's decision-making processes and strengthening of its common institutions.

14. Furthermore, in so far as its future development is concerned, the Community is preparing to take some important new steps on the road towards European Union comprising a whole range of political (e.g. direct elections to the European Parliament) and economic (e.g. economic and monetary union) questions. On some of these matters, decisions of principle have already been taken. This on-going integration process must not be delayed by further enlargement. Indeed further enlargement calls for an acceleration of this process. Therefore the Commission believes it essential for the Community to make significant progress in its own internal development in the period leading up to enlargement.

Conclusions

15. In preparing the present opinion the Commission has been deeply conscious of the obligation that lies on the Community to find a fitting and appropriate response to the Greek request for membership. This request, coming a few months only after the restoration of democracy in Greece and enjoying the support of almost every shade of Greek

political opinion, represents a remarkable affirmation by the Greek people and their leaders of the overriding importance they attach to their country being committed to the cause of European integration. It is clear that the consolidation of Greece's democracy which is a fundamental concern not only of the Greek people but also of the Community and its member States, is intimately related to the evolution of Greece's relationship with the Community. It is in the light of these considerations that the Commission recommends that a clear affirmative reply be given to the Greek request and that negotiations for Greek accession be opened.

16. The present opinion has examined a number of difficult political and economic issues which are raised by such a decision. In the view of the Commission these should not be regarded as obstacles in the path of Greek accession, but should serve rather as a stimulus to the search for solutions and to the Community's own internal development and reinforcement. They do, however, give rise to certain considerations on timing.

The Community's experience has already shown the need for a transitional period of some years even for countries with a highly developed industrial base and an agricultural structure comparable to the other member States. In the case of Greece, where structural changes of a considerable magnitude are needed, it would seem desirable to envisage a period of time before the obligations of membership, even subject to transitional arrangements, are undertaken. During this period, which will in any case need to be limited, it would be necessary to do much more than simply press ahead with the final stages of the development of the Association. In the Commission's view what is needed is on the one hand a substantial economic programme which would enable Greece to accelerate the necessary structural reforms, and on the other, measures to bring Greece into a closer working relationship with the Community's institutions. For example it would seem appropriate, in addition to the new financial protocol proposed under the Association, to envisage the use of certain of the Community's own existing financial instruments in Greece during this period; thus the Community could allocate in its budget special funds for Greece as an additional part of the Social, Regional and Agricultural Guidance Funds. The work of committing this expenditure could be so organized that Greece would herself participate actively in the process. In these fields, as well as possibly in others, Greece would thus be brought more and more into the working of the Community mechanisms.

Moreover, it would seem also appropriate that the member States of the Community should work out ways of bringing Greece into closer contact with the procedures of political cooperation on matters of foreign policy.

At the same time, and in parallel with the implementation of these measures, negotiations towards accession should begin with Greece, priority being given to those issues which experience in previous membership negotiations has shown to require a very considerable amount of time and effort.

[. . .]

Documents 40

Mr Roy Jenkins became the first British President of the Commission in January 1977. His first six months were hard going. Seeking an initiative, he decided to proclaim afresh the goal of monetary union; and to do so not by the traditional Brussels policy of 'little steps', but by advocating a quantum leap forward. In his speech in Florence in October 1977 he developed seven arguments in favour of monetary union. The thesis also includes an early presentation of what would later be called subsidiarity.

On 16 November 1977 the Commission sent a communication to the Council on the prospects for economic and monetary union. This stated that the project was stagnating and that this was in itself a reason for a fresh push. The communication did not contain concrete proposals, which were promised to follow.

At its meeting in Brussels on 5 and 6 December 1977 the European Council welcomed the Commission's communication and reaffirmed its attachment to the objective of EMU. It skipped over the subject at its next meeting in Copenhagen on 7–8 April 1978. Meanwhile the ball had been picked up by France and Germany (who invited Britain to work with them, a partnership which lasted only briefly).

The Bremen meeting of the European Council on 6–7 July 1978 discussed a scheme for a European Monetary System and the European Council adopted such a scheme at the meeting in Brussels on 5 December 1978 (still under the German Presidency). The mechanisms were a mixture of Council regulations and agreements and rules of the Central Banks of the member States.

Three States contended they needed help – Britain, Ireland and Italy – and after a delay, arrangements were made to compensate Ireland and Italy, who joined. Britain stayed aloof for over another decade. A two-tier Europe had begun.

'Jean Monnet Lecture Delivered by the Right Hon. Roy Jenkins, President of the Commission of the European Communities', Florence, October 1977

Europe's present challenge and future opportunity

Some commentators believe the time is unpropitious for adventurous ideas. I do not agree. The concept and indeed the politics of monetary union stand immobilized in scepticism, following the demise of the Werner Plan, whose initial exchange rate mechanism was shattered by the turbulent monetary events of the past few years . . .

We must now look afresh at the case for monetary union because there are new arguments, new needs and new approaches to be assessed, which go to the heart of our present apparently intractable problems of unemployment, inflation and international financing. There are no less than seven arguments that I would like to put forward for your consideration. The first and the seventh are classical, but none the less valid for that. The remaining five, however, are all practical points that need to be formulated differently from the way they were presented in the early 1970s.

Basic to the case is the ineluctable internationalization of Western economic life. This has been a long and gradual process, but one which has been unmatched by a comparable evolution in the economic institutions of the Community. The past four years have shown the limitations in Europe even of good national economic policies. This has been superimposed on the revolutionary effect of the oil crisis – that sharp confirmation of the end of the old international monetary order which added the hazard of a massive overhang of maldistributed and largely uncontrolled international liquidity to an already vulnerable European economy.

No proposition as radical as monetary union in Europe can be achieved at a stroke. My belief is that we should use the period immediately prior to the first direct elections of the European Parliament to relaunch a major public debate on what monetary union has to offer. In doing so, we have to reckon with the problems of how to get from where we are to where we want to go and what must necessarily accompany monetary union if it is to appeal equally to strong and weak economies, to the richer and poorer parts of the Community.

I wish today to outline the major criteria by which the case has to be judged. I expect no easy consensus on the problems it raises, several of which are either at the heart of what is most controversial in modern economic theory, or the most debatable – in the best sense – in political terms. The debate must now be re-opened and subsequently sustained. It will not be quickly foreclosed.

The first argument is that monetary union favours a more efficient and developed rationalization of industry and commerce than is possible under a customs union alone. This argument is as valid now as it has always been, and is reflected in the repeated attempts in European history to form monetary unions – for example the Austro-German monetary union of 1857, the Latin monetary union led by France in 1865, and the Scandinavian union of 1873. Somewhat later Sterling operated a different kind of imperial monetary union over large and disparate parts of the globe. But that is history, although relatively recent history. To return to the present day, discussion with businessmen across Europe produces a clear and consistent complaint that it is difficult, almost impossible, to plan a rational European dimension to their enterprises with the present exchange risks and inflation uncertainties as between member States. The same complaint is often heard from those outside who wish to increase their investment in, and trade with Europe. This means that the potential benefits of the Community as a Common Market are far from fully achieved.

The second argument is based on the advantages of creating a major new international currency backed by the economic spread and strength of the Community, which would be comparable to that of the United States, were it not for our monetary divisions and differences. The benefits of a European currency, as a joint and alternative pillar of the world monetary system, would be great, and made still more necessary by the current problems of the Dollar, with its possible de-stabilizing effects. By such a development the Community would be relieved of many short-run balance of payments preoccupations. It could live through patches of unfavourable trading results with a few points drop in the exchange rate and in relative equanimity. International capital would be more stable because there would be fewer exchange rate risks to play on, and Europe would stand to gain through being the issuer of a world currency. National balance of payments problems, in the sense that these are experienced today by the Community's member States, would be largely removed as an immediate constraint on economic management. There would still be major financial questions to be resolved, between regions, and between member States, and to these I will return in a moment; but the essential point is that economic welfare in Europe would be improved substantially if macro-economic policy was not subject to present exchange rate and external financial risks. They hang as a sword of Damocles over the heads of many of our countries in Europe today.

[. . .]

My third argument concerns inflation. It is fairly certain that monetary union would radically change the present landscape by leading to a common rate of price movement. But I would also like to argue, although I accept this to be more controversial, that monetary union could help establish a new era of price stability in Europe and achieve a decisive break with the present chronic inflationary disorder. Of course the sources of contemporary inflation are diverse, and prominent among these are what may seem to be essentially domestic and highly political struggles over income distribution. But let us suppose at some stage a currency reform: the issue of a new single currency by a European monetary authority; and adoption by this authority of a determined and relatively independent policy of controlling note issue and bank money creation. The authority would start by adopting target rates of growth of monetary expansion consistent with a new European standard of monetary stability, following the best traditions of our least inflationary member States. This would of course mean that national Governments lose some considerable control over some aspects of macro-economic policy. But Governments which do not discipline themselves already find themselves accepting very sharp surveillance from the International Monetary Fund, a body far further away from them and less susceptible to their individual views than is the Community.

[. . .]

The fourth argument concerns employment: no medium-term recipe for reducing inflation which does not have a beneficial effect upon employment is now acceptable. Present levels of unemployment are the most damaging and dangerous social ill that confront us. At best they produce a self-defeating nationalistic caution and immobilism. At worst they threaten the stability of our social and political systems. We now have six million unemployed in the Community . . .

There is already broad agreement on what we need for a fundamental turn in the tide of Europe's employment prospects:

- there has to be confidence in steady and more uniform economic
  policies favouring investment and expansions;
- there has to be a strengthening of demand with a wide geographical base;
- if inflation is to continue, it must be at lower and more even rates
  than Europe has known in recent years;
- we have to ensure that spasmodic, local economic difficulties will
  not be magnified by exchange rates and capital movements into
  general crises of confidence.

These four requirements may seem obvious enough. The challenge
is how to change radically and for the better the institutional weaknesses that have been hindering our ability to restore high
employment in conditions of price stability and a sound external
payments position. I believe that monetary union can open perspec-
tives of this kind.

My argument is not that the Community ought to make some new
choice on the combination of these three objectives, still less that we
should seek to impose a caricature of some country's traditional preference on the rest of the Community. Economists have now spent
years tracking the deteriorating inflation–employment relationship
and the deteriorating effectiveness of exchange rate changes in the
balance of payments adjustment process. The decisions now required
are political rather than simply economic; and I hope that these would
in years ahead come to be recognized by economists as a break-out
from their accepted systems and current models. In this process, we
need also to discard political argument based on obsolete, inadequate,
or irrelevant economic theory: that the objections to European integration are the differing preferences on inflation and unemployment
as between member States, and that floating exchange rates within
Europe allow each country to achieve on its own happily optimal
outcome of its own preference. This is not how the world really is,
and we all know it.

The fifth argument to which I now turn concerns the regional
distribution of employment and economic welfare in Europe. Monetary union will not of itself act as some invisible hand to ensure a

smooth regional distribution of the gains from increased economic integration and union. Those who have criticized a purely liberal model of the Community economy, one that aims to establish perfect competition and do no more, have strong arguments on their side.

But the Community of today bears no relation to the *laissez-faire* caricature of some of its critics. Nor does it correspond to the model I suggest we should now contemplate for monetary union. All our member States find themselves obliged to redistribute large sums of public money and to use less strong but more overt regional policy measures to secure a reasonable distribution of national wealth and employment.

In the Community of today, we have a battery of financial instruments, but all of them rather small guns: the Regional and Social Funds, the Coal and Steel Community's financial powers, the European Investment Bank and the Guidance Section of the Agricultural Fund. The Commission has recently made a number of decisions and proposals for the coordination and expansion of the logic of these operations. These are worthwhile developments in themselves, and they go in the right direction. But their scale is small in relation both to current needs and to the financial underpinning that would be required to support a full monetary union. This is an example of how short-term practical needs and the demands of a longer-term perspective march alongside each other. There is no contradiction in modern integrated economies.

[. . .]

The sixth argument concerns institutional questions, the level at which decisions have to be made, or the degree of decentralization that we should seek to maintain in the Community. Monetary union would imply a major new authority to manage the exchange rate, external reserves and the main lines of internal monetary policy.

The public finance underpinning of monetary union which I have just described would involve a substantial increase in the transfer of resources through the Community institutions. The question then is: can monetary union be reconciled with the profound pressures that are manifest in almost all our member States in favour of more, rather than less, decentralized government? I believe the answer can be and should be yes. But this requires us to envisage a very special and original model for the future division of functions between levels of government. This is not a subject that has been considered at all systematically in the Community in the two decades which have passed since the Treaties of Paris and Rome laid down certain sectors of Community competence. Monetary policy can only be decentralized to a very limited degree. But for most policies requiring public expenditure, the reverse is the case. The vast growth of public expenditure in the postwar period, now approaching half of GNP, has emphasized the need for multi-tiered government with various levels according to country, local, regional, state, national, etc. This is a natural and healthy development. It avoids a monolithic concentration of political and economic power and allows for more efficient specialization by level of government. It also associates people more closely with the decision-making process.

The federal model is clearly only one in a number of possibilities for multi-tiered government. Some support the federal model; others would prefer something confederal; others like neither. I for my part believe that the Community must devise its own arrangements and that these are unlikely to correspond to any existing prototype. We must build Europe upon the basis of our late twentieth-century nation States. We must only give to the Community functions which will, beyond reasonable doubt, deliver significantly better results because they are performed at the Community level. We must fashion a Community which gives to each member State the benefits of results which they cannot achieve alone. We must equally leave to them functions which they can do equally well or even better on their own.

[. . .]

On the seventh and final argument, I can be quite short since, like the first, it is a traditional one. It is the straight political argument that monetary union stands on offer as a vehicle for European political integration. Jacques Rueff said in 1949 'L'Europe se fera par la monnaie ou ne se fera pas'. I would not necessarily be quite so categorical. It should, however, be clear that the successful creation of a European monetary union would take Europe over a political threshold. It seems equally clear that Europe today is not prepared to pursue the objective of monetary union uniquely for ideological reasons. To move in this direction Europe also needs materially convincing arguments. I have tried to set out some of the economic arguments.

I summarize as follows. We must change the way we have been looking at monetary union. A few years ago we were looking at a mountain top through powerful binoculars. The summit seemed quite close, and a relatively accessible, smooth approach was marked out. But then an avalanche occurred and swept away this route. The shock was such that more recently it has even seemed as if we have been looking at the summit with the binoculars both the wrong way round and out of focus . . .

We must not only do what is best in the circumstances. We must give our people an aim beyond the immediately possible. Politics is not only the art of the possible, but as Jean Monnet said, it is also the art of making possible tomorrow what may seem impossible today.

'Conclusions of the Presidency of the European Council', Bremen, July 1978

Monetary policy

Following the discussion at Copenhagen on 7 April 1978 the European Council has discussed the . . . scheme for the creation of a closer monetary cooperation (European Monetary System) leading to a zone of monetary stability in Europe which has been introduced by members of the European Council. The European Council regards such a zone as a highly desirable objective. The European Council envisages a durable and effective scheme. It agreed to instruct the Finance Ministers at their meeting on 24 July 1978 to formulate the necessary guidelines for the competent Community bodies to elaborate by 31 October 1978 the provisions necessary for the functioning of such a scheme – if necessary by amendment. There will be concurrent studies of the action needed to be taken to strengthen the economies of the less prosperous member countries in the context of such a scheme: such measures will be essential if the zone of monetary stability is to succeed. Decisions can then be taken and commitments made at the European Council meeting on 4 and 5 December 1978.
[. . .]

'Resolution of the European Council of 5 December 1978 (Brussels) on the Establishment of the European Monetary System (EMS) and Related Matters'

The European Monetary System

Introduction

1. In Bremen we discussed a 'scheme for the creation of closer monetary cooperation leading to a zone of monetary stability in Europe'. We regarded such a zone 'as a highly desirable objective and envisaged a durable and effective scheme'.

2. Today, after careful examination of the preparatory work done by the Council and other Community bodies we are agreed as follows: A European Monetary System (EMS) will be set up on 1 January 1979.

3. We are firmly resolved to ensure the lasting success of the EMS by policies conducive to greater stability at home and abroad for both deficit and surplus countries.

4. The following chapters deal primarily with the initial phase of the EMS. We remain firmly resolved to consolidate, not later than two years after the start of the scheme, into a final system the provisions and procedures thus created.

This system will entail the creation of the European Monetary Fund as announced in the conclusions of the European Council meeting at Bremen on 6 and 7 July 1978, as well as the full utilization of the ECU as a reserve asset and a means of settlement. It will be based on adequate legislation at the Community as well as the national level.

The ECU and its functions

1. A European Currency Unit (ECU) will be at the centre of the EMS. The value and the composition of the ECU will be identical with the value of the EUA at the outset of the system.

2. The ECU will be used:

(a) as the denominator (numeraire) for the exchange rate mechanism;

(b) as the basis for a divergence indicator;

(c) as the denominator for operations in both the intervention and the credit mechanism;

(d) as a means of settlement between monetary authorities of the EC.

3. The weights of currencies in the ECU will be re-examined and if necessary revised within six months of the entry into force of the system and thereafter every five years or on request if the weight of any currency has changed by 25 per cent.

Revisions have to be mutually accepted, they will, by themselves, not modify the external value of the ECU. They will be made in line with underlying economic criteria . . .

[. . .]

The exchange rate and the intervention mechanism

5. An ECU basket formula will be used as an indicator to detect divergences between Community currencies. A 'threshold of divergence' will be fixed at 75 per cent of the maximum spread of divergence for each currency. It will be calculated in such a way as to eliminate the influence of weight on the probability to reach threshold. [. . .]

6. When a currency crosses its 'threshold of divergence', this results in a presumption that the authorities concerned will correct this situation by adequate measures, namely:

(a) Diversified intervention;

(b) Measures of domestic monetary policy;

(c) Changes in central rates;

(d) Other measures of economic policy.

In case such measures, on account of special circumstances, are not taken, the reasons for this shall be given to the other authorities, especially in the 'concertation between Central Banks'.

Consultations will, if necessary, then take place in the appropriate Community bodies, including the Council of Ministers.

After six months these provisions shall be reviewed in the light of experience. At that date the questions regarding imbalances accumulated by divergent creditor or debtor countries will be studied as well.

Third countries and international organizations

1. The durability of EMS and its international implications require cooperation of exchange rate policies *vis à vis* third countries and, as far as possible, a concertation with the monetary authorities of those countries.

2. European countries with particularly close economic and financial ties with the European Communities may participate in the exchange rate and intervention mechanism.

Participation will be based upon agreements between Central Banks; these agreements will be communicated to the Council and the Commission of the EC.

3. EMS is and will remain fully compatible with the relevant articles of the IMF Agreement. [. . .]

Document 41

*The French, despite having played a role in thwarting the Tindemans Report
(See Document 38), were still anxious about the lack of progress on political
cooperation, and proposed an investigation into Community reform, without treaty revision. Others were suspicious of French motives, fearing
renewed attempts to promote the French inter-governmentalism, and even
remembering the Fouchet debates (See Document 27), but after much
haggling about the composition of the group, it was agreed to invite Edmund
Dell (formerly UK Labour Treasury minister), Barend Bushevel (former
Dutch Prime Minister) and Robert Marjolin (a French former Vice-President of the Commission) to carry out the investigation.*

*The 'Three Wise Men' produced their Report quickly. Its conclusions
were not surprising, blaming the cumbersome nature of Community
decision-making for the lack of real progress. Their Report was discussed
at the November 1979 Dublin European Council meeting, but it was not
something that the member States were willing to accept.*

'Report on European Institutions: presented by the Committee of Three to the European Council', October 1979

The best institutional system in the world could not have saved the
Community of Nine (or one of Six) from the economic crisis of the
70s . . . What, then, can we hope to achieve by adaptations to
the machinery and procedures? The only problem we can tackle . . .
is . . . the extra handicaps imposed by inefficiency and dispersion of
effort within the machinery itself . . .

The European Council

[Key requirements are] . . . limited agendas, limited attendance,
coherent preparation and follow-up, early circulation of documents,
Presidency responsibility for conclusions and so on . . . [other
suggestions] strengthening the Commission in its collaboration with
Heads of Government [etc.] . . . are designed to integrate the European
Council so far as possible within the normal framework of inter-
institutional relations, with all the safeguards that implies . . .

Council of Ministers

[Need for] . . . identification of overall priorities, and a clear central authority to allocate resources in accordance with them and monitor the implementation . . . regular Presidency work programme, and improvements in vertical and horizontal coordination . . .

We have identified four main directions for improvements:

- Reinforcement of the Presidency in its authority to apply agreed rules, and in its ability to draw on the necessary resources.

- More use of normal voting procedures on matters not engaging very important interests.

- Greater use of COREPER's potential for supporting the Council and supervising lower levels of the machine.

- Extension of the Commission's delegated management powers, and their use on agreed terms in new areas . . .

The Commission

1. [17 plus membership] fatal for the organization's coherence and efficiency . . . All hope of collegiate operation would be lost. We therefore support the proposal that in future the Commission should be composed of one member per country . . . at the next re-appointment of the Commission . . . If the will cannot be found to act at this stage, it will certainly not be found at any later date . . .

2. The structure of the Commission must be slimmed down and rationalized at all levels. The number of Directorates-General should be reduced . . .

3. The college of Commissioners must be more homogeneous . . . The college should deliberate collectively on major policy questions . . .

4. Administrative coordination within the Commission must be strengthened. The Presidency of the Commission must be given both the means and the capacity to redeploy the institution's resources in accordance with policy priorities. The grouping of central services – budget, personnel, administration, etc. – directly under the Presidency is a logical step to this end . . .

5. There is a need for better personnel management, including more rational planning of the Commission's future staff requirements . . .

6. The authority of the Commission's President needs strengthening in every way possible . . . he must have the personal authority to play

a full part in the Community's affairs at the highest level, including
the meetings of the European Council which he attends as of right . . .

. . . a Government should not persist in offering a candidate to
whom the President has objected. But the President's standing could
be further enhanced in the matter of the distribution of portfolios . . .
the President must ultimately have the last word . . .

Enlargement

We have said there is no magic solution for the problems of the
Community . . .

One possible general approach has been mooted from time to time
. . . This would be to introduce a permanent and systematic differentiation in the position of various States within the Community,
resulting in an implicit or explicit two-tier system . . . We believe this
model of development, whether the two-tier effect be deliberate or
merely implicit, must be rejected outright. It goes without saying that
any limitations of States' institutional rights to participate in Community business, other than by the traditional system of 'weightings',
is quite out of the question for a Community that wishes to regard
itself as democratic. But a systematic limit on participation in the
substance of integration would, in our view, create serious threats of
its own to the cohesion of the Twelve . . .

Progress towards European Union

When we speak of European Union, . . . we are speaking not so much
of a definite goal as of a direction of movement. We wish to see more
and more united action in efforts to resolve the manifold problems
which now face the Community itself and its member States, problems
which may well become even more serious in the years to come.

One cannot speak of solidarity in the abstract. The concept needs
to be defined and measured in relation to the obstacles which will
have to be overcome.

[. . .]

Moreover, there are two unwritten Community rules which are of an
importance comparable with that of the Treaties themselves. Indeed
they express the profound solidarity which unites the Community's
member States. The first rule, which might be called the 'rule of active
solidarity', can take numerous forms . . . The rule may be defined as
follows: if a member State finds itself in serious difficulty, whether as
a result of circumstances, or of the application of certain Community
rules, or of its own mistakes, it is a question both of duty and of

self-interest for the other Community countries to help it find solutions or to give assistance, by all the means in their power, within a programme aimed at correcting the situation.

The second rule might be defined as the 'rule of passive solidarity'. Every member State should refrain, so far as is at all possible, from any act which might directly or indirectly make life more difficult for other member States and for the Community as a whole. We are aware that it is not always practicable to apply this rule . . .

[. . .]

European Union

We shall try now to list some of the imperatives which should dominate the actions of both States and Community in the course of the next few years. The first priority is the maintenance and consolidation of the Community's cohesion and that of its members, so that the Community acquis – notably the free movement of industrial and agricultural goods, of services, capital and labour and the common policies serving these goals – may be preserved . . . All the great problems facing a united Europe today whether we think of monetary stability, energy supplies or the new international division of labour – are world problems, . . . It is desirable that the Community and the Nine should, in these various relationships, act as a united body.

Economic problems and political problems are closely linked. Hence the importance which attaches to the maintenance and strengthening of political cooperation. Unity in economic negotiations with the outside world, and enhanced political cooperation, will give Europe greater weight in the world at large and offer her only chance of influencing the course of affairs.

[. . .]

Finally, the EMS has been found by eight member States to be the most effective means, if not of unifying their economic and monetary policies, at least of allowing them to converge towards joint objectives of stability. It is seen as a powerful factor for discipline. Without guaranteeing that Governments will effectively resist pressures which irresponsible political elements will constantly exert upon them, it does provide arguments for doing so as well as an objective measure of the divergences resulting from national economic behaviour or errors of policy.

[. . .]

The few thoughts set out above on progress towards European Union may appear to some to be insufficiently ambitious. Our answer to this is . . . [that] the present time seems to us ill-suited to futuristic visions which presuppose a profound and rapid transformation of attitudes within the Community. The chance of such a transformation in the next few years seems to us exceedingly slight. We have preferred to concentrate our reflections on a few more specific ideas, designed to protect the Community against the dangers which constantly threaten it in an uncertain world, while at the same time preparing the ground for further progress.

Document 42

Towards the end of a difficult year for the Community, in November 1981 the German Foreign Minister, with his State's Presidency just a year ahead, launched a new initiative for European Union. He was immediately joined by his Italian colleague. They gave their name to the Genscher–Colombo initiative. The European Council meeting in London in November 1981 took delivery, and discussions occupied some eighteen months until a docu-ment was signed under the German Presidency at the exceptionally long meeting of the European Council in Stuttgart on 17, 18 and 19 June 1983. By that time it had changed from being a Draft Act of European Union (which might have had treaty status and required national ratification) to a Solemn Declaration of European Union.

It is said often that the Solemn Declaration disappeared without trace. It certainly had no immediate effect, but its Preamble is regurgitated in the Preamble to the Single European Act and some of its clauses reappear in articles of the Treaty on European Union.

The negotiators spent a good deal of time trying to overhaul the situation which the Luxembourg compromise had left behind, but once again, a general statement on majority voting was doomed to disagreement.

'Draft European Act submitted by the Government of the Federal Republic of Germany and the Italian Republic', November 1981

The Heads of State and Government of the ten member States . . . reaffirm their political will to develop the whole complex of the rela-tions of their States and create a European Union. To this end they have formulated the following principles of a European Act as a further contribution to the establishment of the European Union:

Part one: principles

1. Our peoples expect the process of European unification to continue and to bring increasing solidarity and joint action. To this end the construction of a United Europe needs a firmer orientation to its political objective, more effective decision-making structures, as well as a comprehensive political and legal framework capable of development. The European Union to be created step by step will be an ever closer union of the European people and States based on genuine, effective solidarity and common interests, and on the equality of the rights and obligations of its members.

2. Desiring to consolidate the political and economic progress already achieved towards the European Union, the Heads of State and Government endorse the following aims:

(a) to strengthen and further develop the European Communities as the foundation of European unification, in accordance with the Treaties of Paris and Rome;

(b) to enable member States, through a common foreign policy, to assume joint positions and take joint action in world affairs so that Europe will be increasingly able to assume the international role devolving upon it by virtue of its economic and political importance;

(c) the coordination of security policy and the adoption of common European positions in this sphere in order to safeguard Europe's independence, protect its vital interests and strengthen its security;

(d) close cultural cooperation among the member States, in order to promote an awareness of common cultural origins as a facet of the European identity, while at the same time drawing on the existing variety of individual traditions and intensifying the mutual exchange of experiences, particularly among young people;

(e) the harmonization and standardization of further areas of the legislation of the member States in order to strengthen the common European legal consciousness and create a legal union;

(f) the strengthening and expansion of joint activities by the member States to cope; through coordinated action, with the international problems of the public order, major acts of violence, terrorism and transnational criminality in general.

[. . .]

Part two: institutions

The following measures shall serve to amalgamate the existing structures of the European Communities (EC), European Political Cooperation (EPC) and the European Parliament and to strengthen the political orientation of the work of European unification.

1. The structures for decision-making in the European Communities and European Political Cooperation shall be merged under the responsibility of the European Council. The European Council is the organ of political guidance of the European Community and European Political Cooperation. It is composed of the Heads of State and Government and the Foreign Ministers of the member States.

The European Council shall deliberate upon all matters concerning the European Community and European Political Cooperation. Its meetings shall be prepared on the special responsibility of the Foreign Ministers. The European Council may take decisions and lay down guidelines.

Matters concerning the European Communities shall continue to be governed by the provisions and procedures laid down in the Treaties of Paris and Rome and the supplementary agreements thereto.

The Heads of State and Government reaffirm that central importance attaches to the European Parliament in the development of the European Union, an importance which must be reflected in its participatory rights and control functions . . .

[. . .]

1.4. Before the appointment of the President of the Commission, the President of the Council shall consult the President of the European Parliament. After the appointment of the members of the Commission by the Governments of the member States, an investiture debate should be held in which the Parliament shall discuss the programme of the Commission.

[. . .]

1.6. Before the accession or association of further States and before the conclusion of international treaties by the European Communities the European Parliament shall be heard; its appropriate committees shall be informed on a continuous basis. In formulating the expanded hearing procedure, due regard shall be given to the requirements of confidentiality and urgency.

[. . .]

1.8. Continuous reciprocal contacts and consultations between the European Parliament and the national Parliaments should be developed further, with the latter defining the relevant procedures, with a view to enhancing public awareness of European unification and making the debates on aspects of European Union more fruitful.

(a) The Council of Foreign Ministers shall be responsible for European Political Cooperation.

This shall not affect the powers of the Council of the European Communities pursuant to the Treaties of Paris and Rome.

The coordination in matters of security should promote common action with a view to safeguarding the independence of Europe, protecting its vital interests and strengthening its security. For these discussions the Council may convene in a different composition if there is a need to deal with matters of common interest in more detail.

(b) In addition, a Council of Ministers responsible for cultural cooperation and a Council of Ministers of Justice shall be established.

(c) The European Council may decide on the establishment of further Councils of Ministers to coordinate the policy of the member States in areas not covered by the Treaties of Paris and Rome.

[. . .]

7. The European Council and the Council of Ministers shall, where matters pertaining to the European Communities are concerned, be assisted by the Secretariat of the Council and, in the fields of foreign policy, security policy and cultural cooperation, by an expandable Secretariat of European Political Cooperation.

8. (a) In view of the need to improve the decision-making processes and hence the European Communities' capacity for action, decisive importance attaches to the voting procedures provided in the Treaties of Paris and Rome. The member States will utilize every opportunity to facilitate decision-making.

(b) To this end greater use should be made of the possibility of abstaining from voting so as not to obstruct decisions. A member State which considers it necessary to prevent a decision by invoking its 'vital interests' in exceptional circumstances will be required to state in writing its specific reasons for doing so.

(c) The Council will take note of the stated reasons and defer its decision until its next meeting. If on that occasion the member State concerned once more invokes its 'vital interests' by the same procedure a decision will again not be taken.

(d) Within the scope of European Political Cooperation as well, the member States shall utilize every opportunity to facilitate decision-making, in order to arrive more quickly at a common position.

[. . .]

Draft statement on questions of economic integration

1. The achievement of the European Union requires further progress as regards the economic integration of Europe. Therefore the Heads of State and Government reaffirm in the European Act the primary goal of strengthening and developing the European Communities in accordance with the Treaties of Paris and Rome.

[. . .]

3. This implies, in the interest of all member States and the standard of living of their citizens, a functioning internal market, an adjustment of the common agricultural policy and an improvement in the budgetary structure. The Common Market must not only be maintained but brought to completion.

4. The EMS, which has led to the creation of a major zone of monetary stability, is a positive element. Beyond the monetary stability guaranteed by the EMS, the member States should strive to achieve an increasing convergence of their economies. In the perspective of economic and monetary union which, as a part of the European Union, is to consolidate the economic and financial solidarity of the Community, they should aim at a closer coordination of their economic policies, not least in view of the further development of the EMS.

The member States should examine how, within the framework of the means available, Community policies suitable for achieving the goal of integration might be developed.

[. . .]

Documents 43

The veteran Italian federalist, Altiero Spinelli (1907–86) stood as an 'independent Communist' in the first direct elections to the European Parliament in 1979.

He gathered together a group, who named themselves the 'Crocodile Club' from the restaurant in Strasbourg to which they repaired. They proposed the setting up of a Parliamentary Committee on Institutional Affairs. The Committee began its work – 'to prepare a draft of modifications of the Treaties' – in January 1982. Mr Spinelli himself was the coordinating rapporteur, with six other rapporteurs for individual chapters.

One of the members of the Committee, Mr Christopher Jackson, was responsible for drafting a clause dealing with competence. He devised the formula: 'The Union shall only act to carry out those tasks which may be undertaken more effectively in common than by the member States acting separately . . .'. His colleagues approved and told him that he had exactly described the principle of subsidiarity, of which Mr Jackson had not until then heard.

On 14 February 1984 the European Parliament adopted the text of the draft Treaty establishing the European Union by 237 votes for, 31 against, 43 abstentions. On Mr Spinelli's proposal, the Parliament decided to bypass the Council and send its handiwork direct to national parliaments.

The outcome was not at all what Mr Spinelli might have hoped for, but what he could have expected. Speaking on 16 January 1986 he dismissed the Single European Act as a 'dead duck'. If he had lived to see it he would perhaps have regarded the later Treaty on European Union as only a little less moribund.

Altiero Spinelli, 'Speech: Battling for the Union', September 1983

First, let us dwell briefly on the role of the Community in world politics. For decades we allowed the principal responsibility for our destiny in this regard to remain in the hands of our American ally, adopting an auxiliary role ourselves.

[. . .]

The course of events, which . . . has brought us to a point where not one or other of the Community countries but all of them together urgently need to assume new, great and serious responsibilities. These

responsibilities concern our contribution to peace, to security, to the
proper and productive management of alliances, to the freedom of
international trade, to monetary stability, to a new world economic
order which firmly binds the recovery of our more advanced economies to growth in the less advanced countries.

[. . .]

What we lack is an adequate European institutional system able
to mould the common feeling into a common political will through
a joint effort to find the necessary compromises; a system able to
create a broad and reliable consensus around the common will and
ensure the necessary continuity in international action.

[. . .]

One has only to consider these chaotic methods employed to deal
with the serious problems of the European presence on the world
scene to understand that it is impossible for us to be satisfied with
them much longer . . . there is a great danger that the very meaning
of our Community in the context of world politics will dissolve in the
face of these inconsistencies, and that each of our countries will return
to the pursuit of the delusion of anachronistic national sovereignty.

The picture is no different if we shift our gaze from the world scene
to the Community one. During the great development of the 1950s
and 1960s . . . thanks to the rules of the Common Market, an
unprecedented degree of interdependence and integration among the
countries of the Community was attained.

In the 1970s, however, and even more so in the early 1980s, the
picture changed completely. Unemployment, inflation, high energy
costs, structural inflexibility, decreasing competitiveness on the world
market and acute regional imbalances began to take their toll. The
ecological crisis, . . . [A]ll of these are the new ills now shared by all
the countries which make up the European Community. But these
ills strike to a different degree and in different ways in each of them.
In each country our Governments, and with them the political forces
– the Governmental ones no less than those of the opposition – are
desperately struggling against all these ills. I say 'desperately' because
in nearly every case coherent action at the national level alone is
either impossible – because it needs to be completed by converging
and compatible action by the other countries to which we are most
closely bound, that is, the other countries of the Community – or
possible only at the cost of destroying a greater or lesser degree of
interdependence with these other countries. The Community, which
should guarantee this convergence and compatibility and, when

necessary, assume direct responsibility for action on the European level, has neither the necessary authority nor the institutions suitable for dealing with these problems.

For this reason we have a Commission which promises great programmes and then does not even dare to elaborate them because it fears they will not be approved; we have a European Council which outlines great objectives and then allows the Councils of Ministers, prisoners all of ten different national ways of thinking, to obscure these objectives and let them melt away; we have a Parliament which solemnly approves great resolutions on hunger, on own resources, on the better functioning of the present institutions and so on, but must then resign itself to having its resolutions ignored and never put into effect.

These are the reasons which necessitate a reform of the Community and of the para-Community institutions of political cooperation and the EMS.

The brief summary just made of the great internal and external tasks facing the Community should be more than sufficient to answer once and for all the criticism that the development of the Community in the direction of an ever more meaningful European Union demands not so much institutional reforms as a common political will.

[. . .]

The task given to our committee on 9 July of last year by this Parliament was to formulate the major objectives of European Union – of which the Community, political cooperation and the EMS are only partial forms – and redefine institutional competencies and the necessary institutional reforms.

[. . .]

At a time when the Community and the member States are wondering about their own and the Community's future, at a time when the feeling of bewilderment is widespread, when there is a strong temptation to seek inspiration in outdated forms only because there is no courage to speak of new ones, at such a time the present debate and the vote which will conclude it cannot fail to have great political significance. If, as we hope, the outcome is positive, this will mean not only that the European Parliament will have had the courage to lead the way, but also that all those who vote for the guidelines will have committed themselves to explaining these guidelines to their parties. to their electors, to their national parliaments and Governments. It will mean more than the adoption of just one more parliamentary resolution to join the innumerable others; it will signal the beginning of a democratic political battle for the Europe of the 1980s, for a Europe made by Europeans for Europeans.

European Parliament, 'Draft Treaty establishing the European Union', February 1984

Article 1

Creation of the Union

By this Treaty, the High Contracting Parties establish among themselves a European Union.

[. . .]

Article 10

Methods of action

1. To attain these objectives, the Union shall act either by common action or by cooperation between the member States; the fields within which each method applies shall be determined by this Treaty.

2. Common action means all normative, administrative, financial and judicial acts, internal or international, and the programmes and recommendations, issued by the Union itself, originating in its institutions and addressed to those institutions, or to States, or to individuals.

3. Cooperation means all the commitments which the member States undertake within the European Council.

The measures resulting from cooperation shall be implemented by the member States or by the institutions of the Union in accordance with the procedures laid down by the European Council.

[. . .]

Article 12

Competencies

1. Where this Treaty confers exclusive competence on the Union, the institutions of the Union shall have sole power to act; national authorities may only legislate to the extent laid down by the law of the Union. Until the Union has legislated, national legislation shall remain in force.

2. Where this Treaty confers concurrent competence on the Union, the member States shall continue to act so long as the Union has not legislated. The Union shall only act to carry out those tasks which

may be undertaken more effectively in common than by the member States acting separately, in particular those whose execution requires action by the Union because their dimension or effects extend beyond national frontiers. A law which initiates or extends common action in a field where action has not been taken hitherto by the Union or by the Communities must be adopted in accordance with the procedure for organic laws.

[. . .]

Article 23

Majorities in the Council of the Union

1. The Council shall vote by a simple majority, i.e. a majority of the weighted votes cast, abstentions not counted.

2. Where expressly specified by this Treaty, the Council shall vote:

(a) either by an absolute majority, i.e. by a majority of the weighted votes cast, abstentions not counted, comprising at least half of the representations;

(b) or by a qualified majority, i.e. by a majority of two-thirds of the weighted votes cast, abstentions not counted, comprising a majority of the representations. On the second reading of the budget, the qualified majority required shall be a majority of three-fifths of the weighted votes cast, abstentions not counted, comprising a majority of the representations;

(c) or by unanimity of representations, abstentions not counted.

3. During a transitional period of ten years, where a representation invokes a vital national interest which is jeopardized by the decision to be taken and recognized as such by the Commission, the vote shall be postponed so that the matter may be re-examined. The grounds for requesting a postponement shall be published.

[. . .]

Article 25

The Commission

The Commission shall take office within a period of six months following the election of the Parliament.

At the beginning of each parliamentary term, the European Council shall designate the President of the Commission. The President shall constitute the Commission after consulting the European Council.

The Commission shall submit its programme to the Parliament. It shall take office after its investiture by the Parliament. It shall remain in office until the investiture of a new Commission.

[. . .]

Article 31

The European Council

The European Council shall consist of the Heads of State or Government of the member States of the Union and the President of the Commission who shall participate in the work of the European Council except for the debate on the designation of his successor and the drafting of communications and recommendations to the Commission.

Article 32

Functions of the European Council

1. The European Council shall:

- formulate recommendations and undertake commitments in the field of cooperation;
- take decisions in the cases laid down by this Treaty and in accordance with the provisions of Article 11 thereof on the extension of the competencies of the Union;
- designate the President of the Commission;
- address communications to the other institutions of the Union;
- periodically inform the Parliament of the activities of the Union in the fields in which it is competent to act;
- answer written and oral questions tabled by the members of the Parliament;
- exercise the other powers attributed to it by this Treaty.

2. The European Council shall determine its own decision-making procedures.

[. . .]

Article 34

Definition of laws

1. Laws shall lay down the rules governing common action. As far as possible, they shall restrict themselves to determining the fundamental principles governing common action and entrust the

responsible authorities in the Union or the member States with setting out in detail the procedures for their implementation.

[. . .]

Article 47

Internal market and freedom of movement

1. The Union shall have exclusive competence to complete, safeguard and develop the free movement of persons, services, goods and capital within its territory; it shall have exclusive competence for trade between member States.

2. This liberalization process shall take place on the basis of detailed and binding programmes and timetables laid down by the legislative authority in accordance with the procedures for adopting laws. The Commission shall adopt the implementing procedures for those programmes.

3. Through those programmes, the Union must attain:

- within a period of two years following the entry into force of this Treaty, the free movement of persons and goods; this implies in particular the abolition of personal checks at internal frontiers;

- within a period of five years following the entry into force of this Treaty, the free movement of services, including banking and all forms of insurance;

- within a period of ten years following the entry into force of this Treaty, the free movement of capital.

[. . .]

Article 56

Social and health policy

The Union may take action in the field of social and health policy, in particular in matters relating to:

- employment, and in particular the establishment of general comparable conditions for the maintenance and creation of jobs;

- the law on labour and working conditions;

- equality between men and women;

- vocational training and further training;

- social security and welfare;

- protection against occupational accidents and diseases;

- work hygiene;
- trade union rights and collective negotiations between employers and employees, in particular with a view to the conclusion of Union-wide collective agreement;
- forms of worker participation in decisions affecting their working life and the organization of undertakings;
- the determination of the extent to which citizens of non-member States may benefit from equal treatment;
- the approximation of the rules governing research into and the manufacture, properties and marketing of pharmaceutical products;
- the prevention of addiction;
- the coordination of mutual aid in the event of epidemics or disasters.

[. . .]

Article 66

Cooperation

The Union shall conduct its international relations by the method of cooperation . . . where they involve:

- matters directly concerning the interests of several member States of the Union;
- or fields in which the member States acting individually cannot act as efficiently as the Union;
- or fields where a policy of the Union appears necessary to supplement the foreign policies pursued on the responsibility of the member States;
- or matters relating to the political and economic aspects of security.

Article 67

Conduct of cooperation

In the fields referred to in Article 66 of this Treaty:

1. The European Council shall be responsible for cooperation; the Council of the Union shall be responsible for its conduct; the Commission may propose policies and actions which shall be implemented,

at the request of the European Council or the Council of the Union, either by the Commission or by the member States.

2. The Union shall ensure that the international policy guidelines of the member States are consistent.

3. It shall coordinate the positions of the member States during the negotiation of international agreements and within the framework of international organizations.

4. In an emergency, where immediate action is necessary, a member State particularly concerned may act individually after informing the European Council and the Commission.

5. The European Council may call on its President, on the President of the Council of the Union or on the Commission to act as spokesman of the Union.

[. . .]

Documents 44

When the Conservative Government of Mrs Thatcher came to power in Britain in 1979, one of the matters to which it turned its attention was the imbalance between what Britain was paying to the Community budget and what it was getting back. From 1980 on this became a war of words between Britain and its partners.

The latter took the position, somewhat against the evidence, that expenditure 'lay where it fell' and that there was no principle of 'juste retour' (fair return) that Britain could invoke. Nevertheless, in the face of Mrs Thatcher's adamantine insistence, they, and after some upsets, the European Parliament, agreed that the UK should receive ad hoc refunds in 1980 and 1981.

The arguments carried on from 1982 to 1984, sometimes becoming bitter and often crowding out other matters from the agenda and enhancing Mrs Thatcher's reputation as a champion of British interests. The dispute was finally resolved, by French statesmanship, at the meeting of the European Council in Fontainebleau in June 1984.

The agreement then reached on budgetary relief for the UK and to some extent for Germany was without limit of time and could be changed only by a new unanimous agreement, at the level of the European Council. From time to time there are murmurs and louder noises of dissatisfaction, notably as more States join Britain and Germany as the Union's creditors. But Britain can hold what it has until and unless it is ready to renegotiate.

Foreign and Commonwealth Office, 'Britain in the European Community – The Budget Problem', September 1982

The budget problem

For 1980 and 1981, the United Kingdom received special refunds from the European Community budget to reduce its excessive net payments. Refunds are also to be paid for 1982. Discussions will soon start on arrangements for 1983 and later. Despite these decisions by the Community, the case for the refunds has been widely misunderstood and occasionally misrepresented.

This Brief explains the nature of the problem and shows why a lasting solution to it has to be found in the long-term interests of the Community as a whole.

History

During the 1970 negotiations over Britain's accession to the Community, the British negotiators pointed out that the Community's financial arrangements, if unchanged, would leave Britain carrying an excessive burden from the budget after the transitional period. This was because of the dominance of the Common Agricultural Policy (CAP), from which Britain's share of expenditure would be low because of the relatively small size of its agriculture. The Community replied that this would not happen, because the balance of the Community's spending would change. In particular, agriculture would take a much smaller share of budget spending. Other programmes would be developed, from which Britain could expect to benefit much more. However, the Community added that 'should unacceptable situations arise . . . the very survival of the Community would demand that the institutions find equitable solutions'.

There have been some welcome changes in the balance of the Community's spending policies with the growth of the Regional and Social Funds. But these developments have not been nearly enough to solve the budget problem. The existence of such a problem was explicitly recognized in Community legislation as early as 1975, when a financial mechanism was introduced to deal with it. This did not prove effective. The Council of Ministers of the Community therefore agreed in May 1980 that the budgetary burden on Britain required immediate correction through refunds and, for the longer term, pledged itself to find a structural solution (the 30 May Mandate). The refunds are being paid: the longer-term solution has yet to be achieved.

Community problem

The imbalance in the budget is a problem for the Community as a whole. It happens to affect Britain most; but a similar problem has already emerged for Germany; and it could, in future, do so for others, especially after enlargement. At present, eight member States, of which five are more prosperous than the Community average, receive more from the budget than their taxpayers contribute to it. Two, Germany and Britain, make transfers to the others.

How the money flows

The transfers are not an abstraction. They are money actually flowing out of certain countries into others. They arise as follows. Each member State collects the Community's own resources from its taxpayers and pays them into a bank account kept by the Commission in its country. The Commission uses this money to make payments to farmers, industrial enterprises and other beneficiaries of Community programmes in that country. In eight member States, Community expenditure exceeds the resources collected and the accounts have to be topped up by transfers from the other two, Britain and Germany. In these two countries, the payments to beneficiaries of Community programmes are less than the taxes collected. The Commission therefore builds up surplus funds which, from time to time, it transfers to its accounts in other countries and spends there. These transfers are a real benefit to the net recipients and a real cost to the net contributor countries. They are also a charge on taxable capacity, for which Britain and Germany have to make allowance in their national budgets . . .

It is easy to understand why people in the net recipient countries are more satisfied with the Community budget arrangements than those in the net contributor countries. Even Germany, the largest and one of the most prosperous of member States, is beginning to find the size of its net transfer a burden. The British public, knowing that Britain is less prosperous than the average, feels that it is being unjustly exploited.

[. . .]

Basic cause of the problem

The Community gets its revenue from agricultural levies, customs duties, and Value Added Tax within a ceiling of 1%. These revenues are the Community's own resources, used to fund Community policies. Today, the lion's share of Community expenditure still goes to agricultural support, despite encouraging progress in developing other Community programmes (see chart below).

The result is that the Community budget transfers resources from member states with relatively small agricultural sectors to those which are net exporters of agricultural products, regardless of their relative prosperity. The diagram below shows which are the richer and which are the poorer member states – those on the left have above average income per head and those on the right have below average income per head.

If the transfers of money through the Community budget went from richer to poorer, then the pattern might look something like this:

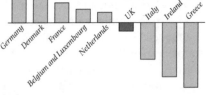

Net payments per head

The actual pattern is quite different. For example, in 1980 and 1981 (leaving out the special refunds to Britain), the pattern was:

To give some idea of the scale of the problem, without refunds the UK would have transferred to other Community countries in 1980 to 1982 some 4.5 billion ecus (£2.5 bn, Dm11 bn, Ff27 bn). That is nearly as large as Britain's entire overseas aid programme in those years.

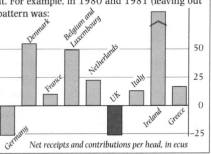

Net receipts and contributions per head, in ecus

Figure 1.

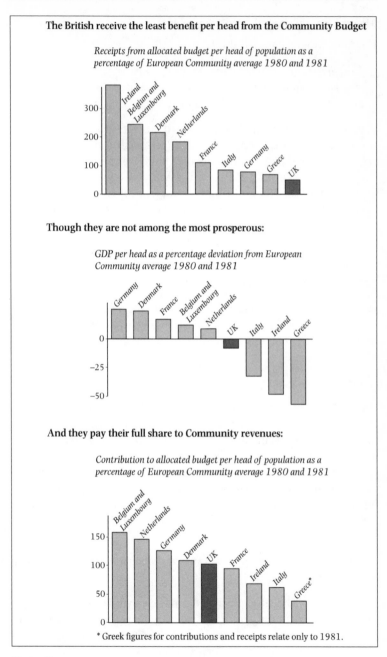

The British receive the least benefit per head from the Community Budget

Receipts from allocated budget per head of population as a percentage of European Community average 1980 and 1981

Though they are not among the most prosperous:

GDP per head as a percentage deviation from European Community average 1980 and 1981

And they pay their full share to Community revenues:

Contribution to allocated budget per head of population as a percentage of European Community average 1980 and 1981

* Greek figures for contributions and receipts relate only to 1981.

Figure 2.

Misunderstanding of the British problem

It is sometimes suggested that:

> *Britain is trying to undermine the common basis of Community financing by insisting on a 'juste retour', i.e. getting back from the budget exactly what the British taxpayers put in.*

Britain is asking for no such thing. It accepts that there may be transfers of resources through the budget. Such transfers, however, should be from the richer to the poorer if the Community is to 'reduce the differences existing between the various regions', as required by the Treaty of Rome. Britain is not one of the richer member States, yet it has made it clear that it is willing to be a modest net contributor.

> *Britain is trying to undermine the Community's revenue system (the 'own resources' system).*

Britain is not challenging the agreed rules of the Community. It was, in fact, one of the first countries to introduce the own resources system in full. All it is asking is that the costs and benefits should be distributed rationally. There is no need to alter the own resources system for this purpose.

> *Britain is trying to undermine the CAP.*

Britain fully accepts the basic principles of the CAP as laid down in the Treaty. It has consistently supported the Commission's efforts to bring about improvements in the operation of the CAP to adjust it to changed conditions. In particular, it shares the Commission's view that the Community must find some way of limiting surplus production and the cost of disposing of it, and that there must be a better balance in the budget with agriculture taking a smaller share. But that can certainly be done without altering the fundamentals of the CAP.

> *Britain is not interested in developing the Community, but only in getting its money back.*

Britain has consistently supported a more rapid development of the Community's regional and social policies. It would like to see more progress made towards completion of the Common Market and its extension to the services sector. It would like to see a more active energy policy, e.g. for coal.

Britain's budget contributions are more than balanced by the gains from trade.

The cost of Community policies to Britain is more than just its net budget contribution. Britain is a net importer of food. It buys food from other member States at Community prices which are higher than world prices because of the price support mechanisms of the CAP. The resulting cost to Britain is not matched by equivalent gains on the industrial side, because the Community does not have a comparable system of price support for industrial products. Britain is, in any case, a net importer of manufactures as well as food from the rest of the Community.

The problem arises from Britain's failure to adapt to Community membership.

Britain has adapted. 43 per cent of its total trade is now with other member States, compared with some 30 per cent before accession. That is a faster change than in any other member State, and brings Britain broadly into line with its partners. Even if Britain were to adapt further, this would do little to reduce the problem, which arises mainly from its small share of receipts from the Community budget.

Wider advantages of the Community membership

Britain is proud to be a partner in the European Community, which has played such a crucial role in the postwar development of Europe. The economic benefits of a massive Common Market and of joint policies are clear enough. Britain values, too, the political benefits of belonging to such an important international grouping. Above all, the Community offers hope for the future development of Europe. But these advantages are not confined to Britain. All member States enjoy them. Yet only Britain and Germany pay more into the budget than they receive from it.

Continuing problem

The refunds for Britain agreed by the Community for 1980–82 were helpful, but only temporary. It has been suggested that they were excessively generous. Yet even after these refunds, Britain is making a net payment over these three years of more than one billion ECU (£600m, Ff 6.4bn, Dm 2.5bn). Eight other member States are far more generously treated by the Community's financial arrangements, even allowing for the cost of refunds.

The development of the Regional and Social Funds in recent years has also been helpful; but the sums in question are far too small to offset the effect on Britain of the CAP.

Future developments in the CAP, such as a widening of the gap between Community and world prices, could make the problem worse. So could the enlargement of the Community which will add two new members well below the Community average in prosperity, who could well expect to be net beneficiaries from the budget.

Conclusion

The Council of Ministers is shortly to begin new negotiations on the new budget problem. It is essential that they should find a lasting solution to it. Failure to do so would prolong the controversy, weaken the Community and divert it from the real challenges and opportunities of the 1980s. The continuing prosperity and development of the European Community, to which Britain is firmly committed, cannot be assured unless the peoples of all the member States believe that the Community gives them a fair deal. A lasting solution to the budget problem must therefore be found. This is the task for the autumn of 1982.

'Conclusions of the Presidency of the European Council', Fontainebleau, June 1984

Budgetary imbalances

1. Expenditure policy is ultimately the essential means of resolving the question of budgetary imbalances.

However, it has been decided that any member State sustaining a budgetary burden which is excessive in relation to its relative prosperity may benefit from a correction at the appropriate time.

The basis for the correction is the gap between the share of VAT payments and the share of expenditure allocated in accordance with the present criteria.

2. As far as the United Kingdom is concerned, the following arrangement is adopted:

(a) for 1984, a lump sum of 1 000 million ECU is fixed;

(b) from 1985 the gap (base of the correction) as defined in paragraph 1 is, for the period referred to in paragraph 4, corrected annually at 66 per cent.

3. The corrections foreseen in paragraph 2 will be deducted from the United Kingdom's normal VAT share in the budget year following the one in respect of which the correction is granted. The resulting cost for the other member States will be shared among them according to their normal VAT share, adjusted to allow the Federal Republic of Germany's share to move to two-thirds of its VAT share.

4. The correction formula foreseen in paragraph 2 (second indent) will be part of the decision to increase the VAT ceiling to 1.4 per cent, their durations being linked.

One year before the new ceiling is reached, the Commission will present to the Council a report setting out the state of play on:

(a) the result of the budgetary discipline;

(b) the Community's financial needs;

(c) the breakdown of the budgetary costs among member States, having regard to their relative prosperity, and the consequences to be drawn from this for the application of the budgetary corrections.

The Council will re-examine the question as a whole and will take the appropriate decisions *ex novo*.

Own resources and enlargement

The maximum rate of mobilization of VAT will be 1.4 per cent on 1 January 1986; this maximum rate applies to every member State and will enter into force as soon as the ratification procedures are completed, and by 1 January 1986 at the latest.

[. . .]

Document 45

The meeting of the European Council in Fontainebleau under French chairmanship on 25–26 June 1984 (See Document 44), also agreed on increasing the Community's 'own resources'.

The French Presidency further obtained agreement to the appointment of an ad hoc Committee on Institutional Affairs, said to be 'on the lines of the Spaak Committee' of 1955. This was not an apt analogy. The Spaak Committee had had a clear task: to give effect to the Messina Declaration.

The new Committee had no similar agenda. The decision to set it up made no mention of a new Treaty.

The Committee chairman was Senator Jim Dooge, friend of Irish Prime Minister Fitzgerald and a former Foreign Minister. The other members were a mixture of independent persons (two of them members of the European Parliament) and serving junior Ministers or high-ranking officials.

Most Committees of this type are expected to seek consensus. The Belgian member, Fernand Herman, a European deputy, proposed, and it was agreed, that the Committee should not even try to reach a high level of agreement. In the event, from the opening word 'Preamble', the report is studded with thirty-seven footnotes and reservations and two dissenting annexes. This may have enhanced its value as a thinkpiece, but it made it less operational.

One of the disputed matters concerned voting. The majority favoured the extension of qualified majority voting. The minority (Denmark, Greece, UK and less vigorously Ireland) emphasized that if a member State considered that very important national interests were at stake, discussion should continue until unanimity was reached.

The majority (Denmark, Greece and UK dissenting) also recommended the convocation of an inter-governmental conference to negotiate a draft Treaty of European Union.

The Dooge Committee reported to the European Council meeting in Brussels on 29–30 March 1985. At the Milan meeting on 28–29 June 1985 the Italian Presidency took a snap vote in which the Belgian, German, French, Irish, Italian, Luxembourg and Netherlands delegations voted in favour of a conference to draft a new Treaty. The material for the conference was to be Franco-German and UK drafts on a 'common foreign and security policy' (which the UK had not intended for a Treaty drafting conference), and especially, the proposals of the Dooge Committee.

'Ad hoc Committee for institutional Affairs: Report to the European Council' [Dooge Report], Brussels, March 1985

Priority objectives

A homogeneous internal economic area. The aim is to create a homogeneous internal economic area, by bringing about the fully integrated internal market envisaged in the Treaty of Rome as an essential step towards the objective of economic and monetary union called for since 1972, thus allowing Europeans to benefit from the dynamic effects of a single market with immense purchasing power. This would mean more jobs, more prosperity and faster growth and would thus make the Community a reality for its citizens.

1. Through the completion of the Treaty.

By creating a genuine internal market by the end of the decade on the basis of a precise timetable.

This involves:

(a) the effective free movement of European citizens;

(b) a favourable climate for investment and innovation through stable and coherent economic, financial and monetary policies in the member States and the Community;

(c) pending the adoption of European standards, the immediate mutual recognition of national standards by establishing the simple principle that all goods lawfully produced and marketed in a member State must be able to circulate without hindrance throughout the Community;

(d) more rapid and coordinated customs procedures, including the introduction as planned of a single administrative document by 1987;

(e) the early introduction of a common transport policy;

(f) the creation at an early date of a genuine Common Market in financial services, including insurance;

(g) the opening of access to public contracts;

(h) the creation of conditions which will favour cooperation between European undertakings and in particular the elimination of taxation differences that impede the achievement of the Community's objectives;

(i) the strengthening of European financial integration, inter alia through the free movement of capital and the creation of a European financial market, hand in hand with the strengthening of the European Monetary System.

[. . .]

2. Through the creation of a technological Community.

The growth capacity of Europe, backed by this genuine internal market, will have to be based, inter alia, on wholehearted participation in technological innovation, and must result in the creation of a technological Community through, among other things, the introduction of faster decision-making procedures. This process must enable European industry to become a powerful competitor internationally in the field of production and application of the advanced technologies.

This means in particular:

(a) that industrial enterprises in the Community must have at their disposal common European standards and suitable procedures for advanced technology products;

(b) that international cooperation during the development phase must be strengthened;

(c) that public and semi-public contract procedures in the Community, concerning inter alia, the supply and use of electronic and communications equipment, must be liberalized;

(d) that the exchange of services connected to the use of advanced technology must be liberalized;

(e) that a successful techno-industrial development in the technological Community depends upon and must increasingly allow for wider scope for individual creativity and performance;

and in addition the following specific activities:

(f) the development of vocational education and training;

(g) the encouragement of universities and research institutes to orient their activities more towards the commercial sector and to ensure the transfer of the results of their work;

(h) the coordination of research and development at national and Community level;

(i) the promotion and support of greater industrial cooperation between European companies including the launching of transnational projects in key sectors;

(j) the furthering of undistorted international exchange of technology and advanced technological products through an active common commercial policy in conformity with GATT obligations.

3. By the strengthening of the European Monetary System (EMS).

The European Monetary System, which was created and set up pending restoration of the conditions for the gradual achievement of economic and monetary union, is one of the achievements of the Community during the last decade. It has enabled the unity of the Common Market to be preserved, reasonable exchange rates to be maintained and the foundations for the Community's monetary identity to be laid.

The time has come, however, to forge ahead towards monetary integration through:

(a) the closer coordination of economic, budgetary and monetary policies with the aim of true convergence of economic performance;

(b) the liberalization of capital movements and the removal of exchange controls;

(c) the strengthening of the European monetary and financial market to make it attractive and capable of supporting the growth and investment effort;

(d) the participation of all member States both in the EMS and in the exchange rate mechanism, provided that the necessary economic and monetary conditions are met;

(e) the increased but non-inflationary use of the ECU in transactions between central banks whether they are members of the system or not;

(f) the elimination consistent with monetary stability of obstacles to the use of the ECU in private transactions;

(g) the promotion of the ECU as an international reserve currency; the coordination of exchange policies with regard to third currencies and in particular the dollar and the strengthening of the role of the European Monetary Cooperation Fund (EMCF) by stages depending in the progress made in the use of the ECU.

Through these measures as a whole it will be possible for the EMS to progress towards the second institutional phase envisaged in the decision of the European Council in Bremen in 1978.
[. . .]

External policy . . . On the diplomatic front several measures could be considered initially which might allow progress to be made towards finding a common voice.

1. The strengthening of political cooperation structure by:

(a) the creation of a permanent political cooperation secretariat to enable successive Presidencies to ensure greater continuity and cohesiveness of action; the secretariat would to a large extent use the back-up facilities of the Council and should help to strengthen the cohesion between political cooperation and the external policies of the Community;

(b) the regular organization of EPC working meetings at the

Community's places of work, while meetings of Ministers should also be arranged in the member States' capitals.

2. The improvement of political cooperation through:

(a) an explicit undertaking by the member States to promote EPC by agreeing to a formalization of the commitments to a prior consultation procedure;

(b) seeking a consensus in keeping with the majority opinion with a view to the prompt adoption of common positions and to facilitating joint measures;

(c) adopting common positions in multilateral and inter-regional relations, particularly at the United Nations.

3. Member States and the Community should examine on a case-by-case basis the desirability of common representation at international institutions, especially in the UN framework and in the countries where only a few member States are represented.

4. Codification of EPC rules and practices.

Security and defence. The aim is to encourage greater awareness on the part of the member States of the common interests of the future European Union in matters of security. The relevant member States will make the fullest contribution both to the maintenance of adequate defences and political solidarity, and to the pursuit of security at the lowest possible level of forces through the negotiation of balanced and verifiable measures of arms control and disarmament.

In any event, this question will have to take account of:

1. The frameworks which already exist (and of which not all partners in the European Community are members) such as the Atlantic Alliance, the framework for and basis of our security, and the Western European Union, the strengthening of which, now under way, would enrich the Alliance with its own contribution.

2. The differing capabilities and responsibilities and the distinctive situations of the Community member States.

3. The existence of interests and objectives which member States, while respecting their individual situations as regards defence and security, recognize as common, in particular the need for the Atlantic Alliance to maintain adequate military strength in Europe for effective deterrence and defence, in order to preserve peace and protect democratic values.

Accordingly, the following measures are proposed:

(a) Developing and strengthening consultation on security problems as part of political cooperation. Such consultation could involve in particular:

  (i) discussion of the nature of external threats to the security of the Union;

  (ii) discussion of the way in which member States' security interests may be affected by the international context, in particular by developments in weapons technology and strategic doctrines, changes in relations between the great powers and the progress of negotiations on disarmament and arms control;

  (iii) an effort to harmonize, whenever possible, the stances to be taken by member States on the major problems posed by the preservation of peace in Europe.

(b) The stepping-up of efforts to draw up and adopt common standards for weapons systems and equipment, taking account of the work being done in the relevant bodies.
  Particular attention is to be paid by member States to:

  (i) rationalizing their military equipment research and development;

  (ii) support for production capacity for high-technology equipment which can strengthen Europe's defensive capabilities.

(c) A commitment by member States to design, develop and produce such systems and equipment jointly.

(d) The will on the part of the member States to create the technological and industrial conditions necessary for their security.

The means: efficient and democratic institutions

Easier decision-making in the Council, which means primarily changes in practice and certain adjustments to existing rules.

1. Less bureaucracy within the institutions, as national authorities have, through their experts, gained too much ground over the last ten years; in particular, the authority of the Permanent Representatives over the various Working Parties must be strengthened in order to improve the preparation of the Council's decisions and to focus its discussions on the most important matters.

2. The growing number of areas of Community activity has led over the years to the Council meeting in a multiplicity of special

compositions. The Council must remain a single institution in which a pre-eminent role of coordination and guidance must be preserved for the ministers with general responsibilities (the 'General Affairs' Council).

3. The rules and procedures governing the Council should be rigorously applied in the interests of its own efficiency and internal cohesion.

4. Concerning principles of voting:

(a) the majority of the Committee favour the adoption of the new general principle that decisions must be taken by a qualified or simple majority. Unanimity will still be required in certain exceptional cases, which will have to be distinctly fewer in number in relation to the present Treaties, the list of such cases being restrictive.

In a spirit of a return to the Treaties, the Presidency must call a vote if the Commission or three member States so request. The vote must be taken within thirty days.

(b) the majority of the Committee considered that more use will need to be made, especially in the context of the enlarged Community, of the majority voting provisions laid down in the Treaties. Once a reasonable time has been devoted to the search for consensus, the Presidency should call for a vote.

Where the Treaties require decisions to be taken by unanimity member States should also make greater use of the possibility of abstention in accordance with Articles 148(3) (EEC), 118 (EAEC) and 28 (ECSC).

When a member State considers that its very important interests are at stake, the discussion should continue until unanimous agreement is reached.

5. In order to ensure the implementation of certain decisions, the use in exceptional circumstances of the method of differentiated Community rules, provided such differentiation is limited in time, is based solely on economic and social considerations and respects the principle of budget unity.

A strengthened Commission. The Commission guarantees autonomous representation of the common interest. Wedded to the general interest whose guarantor it is, the Commission cannot be identified with individual national interests.

If it is to carry out fully the tasks entrusted to it, which make it the lynchpin of the Community, its powers must be increased, in particular through greater delegation of executive responsibility in the context of Community policies.

In the first place, its autonomy must be confirmed so that it can be completely independent in the performance of its duties in accordance with the obligation specifically imposed upon it and on each of its members individually.

To this end it is proposed that the President of the Commission be designated by the European Council.

The other members of the college shall be appointed by common accord of the Governments of the member States, acting on a proposal from the President-designate.

The Commission must not include more than one national from any member State.

At the beginning of its term of office the Commission should receive a vote of investiture on the basis of its programme.

Similarly, the Commission must now be acknowledged as an organ with full powers of initiative, implementation and administration.

The European Parliament as a guarantor of democracy in the European system. A Parliament elected by universal suffrage cannot, if the principles of democracy are logically applied, continue to be restricted to a consultative role or to having cognizance of only a minor part of Community expenditure. That dooms it to oblivion or overstatement, and more often than not to both.

An enhanced role will be sought for it in three areas:

(a) by effective participation in legislative power, the scope of which will be specifically defined, in the form of joint decision-making with the Council; to this end the Commission proposal will be discussed first of all by the European Parliament; the Council will deliberate on the text adopted by the European Parliament; in the event of disagreement, a conciliation procedure will be initiated on the basis of a proposal of the Commission; the Commission will retain its power of initiative throughout the legislative procedure;

(b) by increasing its supervision of the various policies of the Union and its political control over the Commission and over cooperation in the external policy field; the association and accession agreements negotiated by the Union will also be submitted to the European Parliament for approval;

(c) by giving it responsibility in decisions on revenue as the coping-stone of the establishment of a new basic institutional balance;

conciliation between Parliament and the Council would take place at the moment when the frame of reference on the basis of multiannual planning is defined; decisions governing the development of own resources will be taken jointly by the Council and Parliament so that the latter may be able to have a hand in the balancing of expenditure by revenue.

These developments should go hand in hand with increased representativeness of Parliament itself through the standardization of voting procedures to elect its members.

Document 46

As the Dooge Committee was drawing up its Report (See Document 45) the Commission was busy preparing proposals for the single internal market. A frontier free market for goods, services and people is a declared objective of the 1957 Treaty of Rome. Customs duties were abolished among the member States in good time.

Their different degrees of exposure to imports from the rest of the world kept the Common Market created by the Customs Union fragmented by national quotas for such sensitive products as textiles, cars and pineapples. Meanwhile, as the tariffs and other quota barriers disappeared, they brought into relief a vast range of other restrictions on intra-Community trade in goods and services. The characteristics of these measures were that they created at least frontier control formalities, or at worst insurmountable obstacles. A German industrialist was not allowed to insure his premises against fire with a non-German insurer. What British meat traders called 'sausages' could not be sold elsewhere under the name in translations because they were too low in meat. Lorries could not pick up loads outside their State of registration without applying for permits.

Frontiers had powerful economic significance in the so-called Common Market. The cost of 'non-Europe' had been adequately documented. Many different individuals and groups have claimed or deserve credit for the initiatives to create a proper Single Market – the Albert Ball report 'Towards European Economic Recovery in the 1980s' for the European Parliament; the European Parliament itself, and notably Mr Basil de Ferranti; Mr Dekker, the Chief Executive of Philips and the author of a plan for a Single Market; Mr Emile a Campo, a Director-General of the Council who knew everybody and synergized them; Mr K. H. Narjes, a Commissioner in the early 1980s almost a lone voice crying for action; the British Presidency in the second half of 1981, which took up with some success barrier-lifting proposals which had stalled; the author of the Conclusions of the meeting of the European Council in Copenhagen in December 1982; and the European Round Table of top industrialists who added their voices to the demands for Europe to use its strengths.

But the decisive players were the President and Vice-President of the Commission who took office in 1985, M. Jacques Delors and Lord Cockfield. Very different in personality and political philosophy they combined to devise and push through against opposition or faint-heartedness the 300 or so measures needed to make the market single for goods, services, capital and, incompletely, for the movement of people.

The intellectual underpinning was provided by the Cechinni Report, named for its author, a retired Commission senior official, who masterminded an econometric study of the benefits to be won from the completion of the Single Market and wrote the synopsis which became the bible for the sustained promotion campaign which was a feature of the operation.

The ninety page White Paper drafted by Lord Cockfield consists of:

• *an introduction;*

• *a description of each measure required to eliminate a barrier;*

• *a timetable giving dates for each measure in the programme to complete the internal market by the end of 1992.*

Commission White Paper, 'Completing the Internal Market', June 1985

Declarations by the European Council relating to the internal market

'The European Council . . . instructs the Council: to decide, before the end of March 1983, on the priority measures proposed by the Commission to reinforce the internal market', Copenhagen, 3/4 December 1982.

'It asks the Council and the member States to put in hand without delay a study of the measures which could be taken to bring about in the near future . . . the abolition of all police and customs formalities for people crossing intra-Community frontiers', Fontainebleau, 25/26 June 1984.

'The European Council . . . agreed that the Council, in its appropriate formations . . . should take steps to complete the internal market, including implementation of European standards', Dublin, 3/4 December 1984.

'. . . the European Council laid particular emphasis on the following . . . field of action . . . to achieve a single large market by 1992 thereby creating a more favourable environment for stimulating enterprise, competition and trade; it called upon the Commission to draw up a detailed programme with a specific timetable before its next meeting', Brussels, 29/30 March 1985.

Introduction

1. 'Unifying this market (of 320 million) presupposes that member States will agree on the abolition of barriers of all kinds, harmonization of rules, approximation of legislation and tax measures, strengthening of monetary cooperation and the necessary flanking measures to encourage European firms to work together. It is a goal that is well within our reach provided we draw the lessons from the setbacks and delays of the past. The Commission will be asking the European Council to pledge itself to completion of a fully unified internal market by 1992 and to approve the necessary programme together with a realistic and binding timetable'.

2. In such terms did the Commission define its task in the 'Programme of the Commission for 1985' which was presented to the European Parliament on 6 March. On 29 and 30 March, the European Council in Brussels broadly endorsed this view . . .

3. This White Paper is designed to spell out the programme and timetable . . .

4. The Treaty clearly envisaged from the outset the creation of a single integrated internal market free from restrictions on the movement of goods; the abolition of obstacles to the free movement of persons, services and capital; the institution of a system ensuring that competition in the Common Market is not distorted; the approximation of laws as required for the proper functioning of the Common Market; and the approximation of indirect taxation in the interest of the Common Market.

5. In the early days attention concentrated on the common customs tariff, . . .

6. The recession brought another problem. The Treaty specifically required not simply the abolition of customs duties as between the member States, but also the elimination of quantitative restrictions

and of all measures having equivalent effect. Originally it was assumed that such 'non-tariff barriers', as they are commonly called, were of limited importance compared with actual duties. But during the recession they multiplied as each member State endeavoured to protect what it thought was its short term interests – not only against third countries but against fellow member States as well. Member States also increasingly sought to protect national markets and industries through the use of public funds to aid and maintain non-viable companies. The provision in the EEC Treaty that restrictions on the freedom to provide services should 'be progressively abolished during the transitional period' not only failed to be implemented during the transitional period, but over important areas failed to be implemented at all. Disgracefully, that remains the case.

7. But the mood has begun to change, and the commitment to be rediscovered: gradually at first, but now with increasing tempo . . . The time for talk has now passed. The time for action has come. That is what this White Paper is about.

8. The case for the completion of the internal market has been argued elsewhere: and, . . . it has been accepted by the Heads of State and Governments of the member States. But it is worth recalling that the objective of completing the internal market has three aspects:

- first, the welding together of the ten, soon to be twelve, individual markets of the member States into one Single Market of 320 million people;

- second, ensuring that this Single Market is also an expanding market – not static but growing;

- third, to this end, ensuring that the market is flexible so that resources, both of people and materials, and of capital and investment, flow into the areas of greatest economic advantage.

9. While, therefore, the discussion in this Paper will be directed primarily to the first of these objectives there will be a need to keep the other two objectives in mind and to ensure that the measures taken contribute to those ends.

10. For convenience the measures that need to be taken have been classified in this Paper under three headings:

- Part one: the removal of physical barriers;

- Part two: the removal of technical barriers;

- Part three: the removal of fiscal barriers.

11. The most obvious example of the first category are customs posts at frontiers. Indeed most of our citizens would regard the frontier posts as the most visible example of the continued division of the Community and their removal as the clearest sign of the integration of the Community into a Single Market. Yet they continue to exist mainly because of the technical and fiscal divisions between member States. Once we have removed those barriers, and found alternative ways of dealing with other relevant problems such as public security, immigration and drug controls, the reason for the existence of the physical barriers will have been eliminated.

12. The reason for getting rid entirely of physical and other controls between member States is not one of theology or appearance, but the hard practical fact that the maintenance of any internal frontier controls will perpetuate the costs and disadvantages of a divided market; the more the need for such controls diminishes – short of total elimination – the more disproportionate become the costs, expenses and disadvantages of maintaining the frontiers and a divided market.

13. While the elimination of physical barriers provides benefits for traders, particularly through the disappearance of formalities and of frontier delays, it is through the elimination of technical barriers that the Community will give the large market its economic and industrial dimension by enabling industries to make economies of scale and therefore to become more competitive. An example of this second category – technical barriers – are the different standards for individual products adopted in different member States for health or safety reasons, or for environmental or consumer protection. Here the Commission has recently launched a major new initiative which has been welcomed and endorsed by the Council. The barriers to the freedom to provide services could perhaps be regarded as a separate category; but these barriers are analogous to the technical barriers which obstruct the free movement of goods, and they are probably best regarded as part of the same category. There is additional merit in such an approach since the traditional dichotomy between 'goods' and 'services' has fostered an attitude in which 'services' are somehow regarded as inferior and relegated to the bottom of the queue. Technical barriers are technical barriers whether they apply to goods or services and all should be treated on an equal footing. The general thrust of the Commission's approach in this area will be to move away from the concept of harmonization towards that of

mutual recognition and equivalence. But there will be a continuing role for the approximation of member States' laws and regulations, as laid down in Article 100 of the Treaty. Clearly, action under this Article would be quicker and more effective if the Council were to agree not to allow the unanimity requirement to obstruct progress where it could otherwise be made.

14. The removal of fiscal barriers may well be contentious and this despite the fact that the goals laid down in the Treaty are quite explicit and that important steps have already been taken along the road of approximation. This being so, the reasons why approximation of fiscal legislation is an essential and integral element in any programme for completing the internal market are explained in detail . . . Approximation of indirect taxation will raise severe problems for some member States. It may, therefore, be necessary to provide for derogations.

15. We recognize that many of the changes we propose will present considerable difficulties for member States and time will be needed for the necessary adjustments to be made. The benefits to an integrated Community economy of the large, expanding and flexible market are so great that they should not be denied to its citizens because of difficulties faced by individual member States. These difficulties must be recognized, to some degree they must be accommodated, but they should not be allowed permanently to frustrate the achievement of the greater progress, the greater prosperity and the higher level of employment that economic integration can bring to the Community.
[. . .]

23. A detailed timetable for implementing the Commission's proposed programme of measures for the removal of physical, technical and fiscal barriers is to be found in the Annex to this Paper.
[. . .]

Conclusion

219. Europe stands at the crossroads. We either go ahead – with resolution and determination – or we drop back into mediocrity. We can now either resolve to complete the integration of the economies of Europe; or, through a lack of political will to face the immense problems involved, we can simply allow Europe to develop into no more than a free trade area.

220. The difference is crucial. A well developed free trade area offers significant advantages: it is something much better than that which

existed before the Treaty of Rome; better even than that which exists today. But it would fail and fail dismally to release the energies of the people of Europe; it would fail to deploy Europe's immense resources to the maximum advantage; and it would fail to satisfy the aspirations of the people of Europe.

221. The free movement of goods is an important, valuable and possibly indispensable step which has to be taken before economic integration can be achieved. But it is not the ultimate goal; at best it is the indispensable precursor. This philosophy is clearly reflected in the Treaties themselves. The Customs Union was the first objective of the Treaty of Rome. But that it was by no means intended as the last is clearly demonstrated by the fact that what the Treaty established was the European Economic Community. The preamble to the Treaty starts with the declaration: 'Determined to lay the foundations of an ever closer union among the peoples of Europe, resolved to ensure the economic and social progress of their countries by common action to eliminate the barriers which divide Europe'.

222. Just as the Customs Union had to precede Economic Integration, so Economic Integration has to precede European Unity. What this White Paper proposes therefore is that the Community should now take a further step along the road so clearly delineated in the Treaties. To do less would be to fall short of the ambitions of the founders of the Community, incorporated in the Treaties; it would be to betray the trust invested in us; and it would be to offer the peoples of Europe a narrower, less rewarding, less secure, less prosperous future than they could otherwise enjoy. That is the measure of the challenge which faces us. Let it never be said that we were incapable of rising to it.

Document 47

With the resolution of the British budgetary problem at Fontainebleau (See Document 44), there was an opportunity to return to a wider agenda. Fontainebleau set up two committees on the future (See Document 45 on the Dooge Committee). Their reports were considered by the Milan European Council meeting in June 1985. By that time the contents of the Cockfield White Paper were known. The Milan Council, by majority vote (for the first time in a European Council) agreed to convene an intergovernmental conference under Article 236 of the Treaty of Rome to discuss Treaty amendments.

Although it could be convened by a majority, to succeed the conference needed unanimity. The conference did succeed. The Single European Act (SEA) was signed on 17 February 1986 by nine member States, and by Denmark, Greece and Italy on 28 February 1986. It is the 'Single' Act because it contains both the revision of the three founding Treaties of the three Communities and separate Treaty provision (for the first time) on political cooperation in one document. The SEA was the result of a series of compromises and of the political environment. Firstly, there was a convergence of national interests among leading States. Britain was keen on the deregulation seemingly offered by the White Paper, while others were looking for decision-making improvements prior to the accession of Spain and Portugal. Britain also feared exclusion from the first division of developments. Originally Mrs Thatcher famously described the SEA as a 'modest decision'. In fact, it operated as a dynamic for Community development and the goals of the internal market were largely completed by the end of 1992.

The Single Act extended majority voting, formalized Community concern with research and development, introduced the 'cooperation procedure' between the Council and the European Parliament, and gave the Parliament the right to grant or withhold assent on the entry of new members or on new agreements of association. Its major features, however, were the articles providing the basis for the Single Internal Market and the formalization of European Political Cooperation. In the latter the SEA mostly codified the existing system, although it did expand the scope of topics (See Article 30, 6.a), and it did introduce a limited secretariat for this activity (See Article 30, 10.g), something that the French had wished for in the Fouchet era (See Document 27).

'The Single European Act', 1986

Preamble

Moved by the will to continue the work undertaken on the basis of the Treaties establishing the European Communities and to transform relations as a whole among their States into a European Union, in accordance with the Solemn Declaration of Stuttgart.

[. . .]

Provisions relating to the foundations and the policy of the Community: subsection I – internal market

Article 13

The EEC Treaty shall be supplemented by the following provisions: 'Article 8A: The Community shall adopt measures with the aim of progressively establishing the internal market over a period expiring on 31 December 1992, in accordance with the provisions of this Article and of Articles 8D, 8C, 28, 57(2), 70(1), 83, 99, 100A and 100B and without prejudice to the other provisions of this Treaty.

The internal market shall comprise an area without internal frontiers in which the free movement of goods, persons, services and capital is ensured in accordance with the provisions of this Treaty'.
[. . .]

Provisions on European cooperation in the sphere of foreign policy

Article 30

European Cooperation in the sphere of foreign policy shall be governed by the following provisions:

1. The High Contracting Parties, being members of the European Communities, shall endeavour to formulate and implement a European foreign policy.

2. (a) . . . [shall] inform and consult each other.

    (b) . . . shall take full account of the positions of the other partners . . .

    (c) . . . shall ensure that common principles and objectives are gradually developed . . .

[. . .]

5. The external policies of the European Community and the policies agreed in European Political Cooperation must be consistent . . .

6. (a) The High Contracting Parties consider that closer cooperation on questions of European security would contribute in an essential way to the development of a European identity in external policy matters. They are ready to coordinate their positions more closely on the political and economic aspects of security.

[. . .]

10. (g) A Secretariat based in Brussels shall assist the Presidency in

preparing and implementing the activities of European
Political Cooperation and in administrative matters. It shall
carry out its duties under the authority of the Presidency.

[. . .]

Documents 48

*Different visions as to the future of European integration were clearly
revealed in speeches by M. Jacques Delors, President of the Commission of
the European Communities, and Mrs Margaret Thatcher, the British Prime
Minister, in 1988–89.*

The UK had been keen on certain aspects of the SEA, especially the
*emphasis upon deregulation, which fitted in very well with the Conservative
agenda of the 1980s. Other aspects of the SEA had attracted less attention,
and increasingly were regarded as unwelcome, especially the so-called 'social dimension', which as well as new measures to alleviate unemployment,
also gave weight to workers' rights and participation. Indeed, Delors was
arguing that an exclusive emphasis upon liberating market forces risked
alienating voters, and that consequently the Community should build on
1992 to develop common social policies. He felt the Community should
build on 1992 to move towards economic and monetary union.*

*Both of these themes were increasingly highlighted. In the summer of
1988, Delors speaking to the European Parliament about the need to
move towards a European Government, observed that within a few years
80 per cent of legislation in the socio-economic and financial fields would
be 'flowing' from the Community. In September 1988 in a speech to the
British Trades Union Congress he called for measures to be taken on
collective bargaining at the European level. While the social emphasis
encouraged the British Labour Party in its re-appraisal of Community
membership, these speeches were not well received by Mrs Thatcher.*

*In the autumn of 1988 at the College of Europe in Bruges she made her
response to all of these tendencies and gave her 'guiding principles' for the
future. While certain aspects of her speech were unique to the circumstances
of the time, the speech also reflected many traditional features of British
attitudes to European integration, although expressed in Mrs Thatcher's
own distinctive style. Just over a year later Delors gave his response,
choosing to do so in the same forum as that used by Mrs Thatcher. In
his speech Delors used the word 'subsidiarity' ten times, and took the*

opportunity to challenge the assertion that federalism equated with centralization. But he also was clear that federalism or subsidiarity were ways of reconciling loyalty to one's State with the contemporary pressures of global interdependence for common action in many areas of policy.

The fundamentals behind these disputes lived on after both Delors and Thatcher left office.

M. Jacques Delors, President of the European Commission, 'Speech to the European Parliament', June 1988

[B]y 1993 we shall need to have set up the beginnings of European government. I say the beginnings advisedly, . . . something has to be done to ease the decision-making process, in which blockages occur all too often . . . Then we need more democratization: the ways and means are a matter for you. Personally, I set great store by contacts between you and the national parliaments. My impression by and large – and apologies to those whose pride in the keen interest taken by their national parliaments in European affairs might be offended – is that there is an unawareness in many national parliaments of the quiet revolution that is taking place, as a result of which 80 per cent at least of economic, financial and perhaps social legislation will be flowing from the Community by 1993. When the national parliaments eventually wake up to this, there might well be a reaction, a resistance to change. This has already happened in one or two member States. Hence my conviction that the European Parliament has a key role in hastening the development of awareness in the national parliaments. The message has to be got across that together the national parliaments and the European Parliament add up to the democratic expression of the will of the people and they ought to work together . . .

Mrs Margaret Thatcher, Prime Minister, 'Speech at the Opening Ceremony of the 39th Academic Year of the College of Europe', Bruges, September 1988

Britain and Europe

I want to start by disposing of some myths about my country, Britain, and its relationship with Europe. And to do that I must say something about the identity of Europe itself.

Europe is not the creation of the Treaty of Rome. Nor is the European idea the property of any group or institution. We British are as much heirs to the legacy of European culture as any other nation. Our links to the rest of Europe, the continent of Europe, have been the dominant factor in our history . . .

We in Britain are rightly proud of the way in which, since Magna Carta in 1215, we have pioneered and developed representative institutions to stand as bastions of freedom. And proud too of the way in which for centuries Britain was a home for people from the rest of Europe who sought sanctuary from tyranny. But we know that without the European legacy of political ideas we could not have achieved as much as we did. From classical and medieval thought we have borrowed that concept of the rule of law which marks out a civilized society from barbarism. And on that concept of Christendom – for long synonymous with Europe – with its recognition of the unique and spiritual nature of the individual, we still base belief in personal liberty and other human rights.

Too often the history of Europe is described as a series of interminable wars and quarrels. Yet from our perspective today surely what strikes us most is our common experience. For instance, the story of how Europeans explored and colonized and – yes, without apology – civilized much of the world is an extraordinary tale of talent and valour.

We British have in a special way contributed to Europe. For over the centuries we have fought and died for her freedom, fought to prevent Europe falling under the dominance of a single power . . .

It was from our island fortress that the liberation of Europe itself was mounted. And still today, we station 70,000 British servicemen on the mainland of Europe. All these things alone are proof of our commitment to Europe's future . . .

This is no arid chronicle of obscure historical facts. It is the record of nearly two thousand years of British involvement in Europe and contribution to Europe, a contribution which is today as strong as ever. Yes, we have looked also to wider horizons – and so have others – and thank goodness we did, because Europe would never have prospered and never will prosper as a narrow-minded, inward-looking club.

The European Community belongs to all its members, and must reflect the traditions and aspirations of all of them in full measure.

And let me be quite clear. Britain does not dream of an alternative to the European Community, of some cosy, isolated existence on its fringes. Our destiny is in Europe, as part of the Community. That is not to say that it lies only in Europe. But nor does that of France or Spain or indeed any other members.

The Community is not an end in itself. It is not an institutional device to be constantly modified according to the dictates of some abstract theory. Nor must it be ossified by endless regulation. It is the practical means by which Europe can ensure its future prosperity and security of its people in a world in which there are many other powerful nations and groups.

We Europeans cannot afford to waste our energies on internal disputes or arcane institutional debates. They are no substitute for effective action. Europe has to be ready both to contribute in full measure to its own security and to compete – compete in a world in which success goes to the countries which encourage individual initiative and enterprise, rather than to those which attempt to diminish them.

I want this evening to set out some guiding principles for the future which I believe will ensure that Europe does succeed, not just in economic and defence terms but in the quality of life and the influence of its people.

My first guideline is this: willing and active cooperation between independent sovereign states is the best way to build a successful European Community. To try to suppress nationhood and concentrate power at the centre of a European conglomerate would be highly damaging and would jeopardize the objectives we seek to achieve.

Europe will be stronger precisely because it has France as France, Spain as Spain, Britain as Britain, each with its own customs, traditions and identity. It would be folly to try to fit them into some sort of identikit European personality.

Some of the founding fathers of the Community thought that the United States of America might be its model. But the whole history of America is quite different from Europe . . .

I am the first to say that on many great issues the countries of Europe should try to speak with a single voice. I want to see them work more closely on the things we can do better together than alone. Europe is stronger when we do so, whether it be in trade, defence or in our relations with the rest of the world. But working more closely together does not require power to be centralized in Brussels or decisions to be taken by an appointed bureaucracy.

Indeed, it is ironic that just when those countries such as the Soviet Union, which have tried to run everything from the centre, are learning that success depends on dispersing power and decisions away from the centre, some in the Community seem to want to move in the opposite direction.

We have not successfully rolled back the frontiers of the State in Britain, only to see them reimposed at a European level, with a European super-State exercising a new dominance from Brussels.

Certainly we want to see Europe more united and with a greater sense of common purpose. But it must be in a way which preserves the different traditions, Parliamentary powers and sense of national pride in one's own country, for these have been the source of Europe's vitality through the centuries.

My second guiding principle is this. Community policies must tackle present problems in a practical way, however difficult that may be. If we cannot reform those Community policies which are patently wrong or ineffective and which are rightly causing public disquiet, then we shall not get the public's support for the Community's future development.

[. . .]

Those who complained that the Community was spending so much time on financial detail missed the point. You cannot build on unsound foundations and it was the fundamental reforms agreed last winter which paved the way for the remarkable progress which we have since made on the Single Market.

But we cannot rest on what we have achieved so far. For example, the task of reforming the Common Agricultural Policy is far from complete. Certainly, Europe needs a stable and efficient farming industry. But the CAP has become unwieldy, inefficient and grossly expensive. And production of unwanted surpluses safeguards neither the income nor the future of farmers themselves. We must continue to pursue policies which relate supply more closely to market requirements, and which will reduce overproduction and limit costs.

Of course, we must protect the villages and rural areas which are such an important part of our national life – but not by the instrument of agricultural prices.

Tackling these problems requires political courage. The Community will only damage itself in the eyes of its own people and the outside world, if that courage is lacking.

My third guiding principle is the need for Community policies which encourage enterprise if Europe is to flourish and create the jobs of the future. The basic framework is there: the Treaty of Rome itself was intended as a Charter for Economic Liberty. But that is not how it has always been read, still less applied.

The lesson of the economic history of Europe in the 1970s and 1980s is that central planning and detailed control don't work, and that personal endeavour and initiative do. That a State-controlled economy is a recipe for low growth; and that free enterprise within a framework of law brings better results.

The aim of a Europe open for enterprise is the moving force behind the creation of the Single European Market by 1992. By getting rid of barriers, by making it possible for companies to operate on a Europe wide scale, we can best compete with the United States, Japan and the other new economic powers emerging in Asia and elsewhere.

It means action to free markets, to widen choice and to produce greater economic convergence through reduced Government intervention.

Our aim should not be more and more detailed regulation from the centre: it should be to deregulate, to remove the constraints on trade and to open up.

Britain has been in the lead in opening its markets to others.

[. . .]

Consider monetary matters. The key issue is not whether there should be a European Central Bank. The immediate and practical requirements are:

- to implement the Community's commitment to free movement of capital – we have it;

- and to the abolition throughout the Community of the exchange controls – we abolished them in Britain in 1979, so that people can invest wherever they wish;

- to establish a genuinely free market in financial services, in banking, insurance, investment;

- to make greater use of the ECU. Britain is this autumn issuing ECU-denominated Treasury bills, and hopes to see other Community Governments increasingly do the same.

These are the real requirements because they are what Community business and industry need, if they are to compete effectively in the wider world. And they are what the European consumer wants, for they will widen his choice and lower his costs.

It is to such basic practical steps that the Community's attention should be devoted. When those have been achieved, and sustained over a period of time, we shall be in a better position to judge the next moves.

It is the same with the frontiers between our countries. Of course we must make it easier for goods to pass through frontiers. Of course we must make it easier for our people to travel throughout the Community. But it is a matter of plain commonsense that we cannot totally abolish frontier controls if we are also to protect our citizens and stop the movement of drugs, of terrorists, of illegal immigrants . . .

And before I leave the subject of the Single Market, may I say that we emphatically do not need new regulations which raise the cost of employment and make Europe's labour market less flexible and less competitive with overseas suppliers.

If we are to have a European Company Statute, it should contain the minimum regulations. And certainly we in Britain would fight attempts to introduce corporatism at the European level – although what people wish to do in their own countries is a matter for them.

My fourth guiding principle is that Europe should not be protectionist. The expansion of the world economy requires us to continue the process of removing barriers to trade, and to do so in the multilateral negotiations in the GATT.

It would be a betrayal if, while breaking down constraints on trade to create the Single Market, the Community were to erect greater external protection. We must ensure that our approach to world trade is consistent with the liberalization we preach at home.

We have a responsibility to give a lead here, a responsibility which is particularly directed towards the less developed countries. They need not only aid but more than anything they need improved trade opportunities if they are to gain the dignity of growing economic independence and strength.

My last guiding principle concerns the most fundamental issue, the European countries' role in defence. Europe must continue to maintain a sure defence through NATO. There can be no question of relaxing our efforts even if it means taking difficult decisions and meeting heavy costs. We are thankful for the peace that NATO has maintained over forty years. The fact is things are going our way: the democratic model of a free enterprise society has proved itself superior; freedom is on the offensive, a peaceful offensive, the world over for the first time in my life-time.

We must strive to maintain the US commitment to Europe's defence. That means recognizing the burden on their resources of the world role they undertake and their point that their Allies should play a full part in the defence of freedom, particularly as Europe grows wealthier. Increasingly they will look to Europe to play a part in out-of-area defence, as we have recently done in the Gulf.

[. . .]

It's not an institutional problem. It's not a problem of drafting. It's much more simple and more profound: it is a question of political will and political courage, of convincing people in all our countries that we cannot rely for ever on others for our defence but that each member of the Alliance must shoulder a fair share of the burden . . .

We should develop the WEU, not as an alternative to NATO, but as a means of strengthening Europe's contribution to the common defence of the West.

Above all at a time of change and uncertainty, in the Soviet Union and Eastern Europe, we must preserve Europe's unity and resolve, so that whatever may happen our defence is sure. At the same time, we must negotiate on arms control and keep the door wide open to cooperation on the other issues covered by the Helsinki Accords.

But our way of life, our vision, and all that we hope to achieve, is secured not by the rightness of our cause but by the strength of our defence. On this, we must never falter or fail.

I believe it is not enough just to talk in general terms about a European vision or ideal. If you believe in it, you must chart the way ahead . . . This approach does not require new documents: they are all there, the North Atlantic Treaty, the Revised Brussels Treaty, and the Treaty of Rome . . . What we need now is to take decisions on the next steps forward rather than let ourselves be distracted by Utopian goals. However far we may all want to go, the truth is that you can only get there one step at a time.

Let us concentrate on making sure that we get those steps right.

Let Europe be a family of nations, understanding each other better, appreciating each other more, doing more together but relishing our national identity no less than our common European endeavour.

Let us have a Europe which plays its full part in the wider world, which looks outward not inward, and which preserves their Atlantic Community – that Europe on both sides of the Atlantic – which is our greatest inheritance and our greatest strength.

M. Jacques Delors, President of the European Commission, 'Speech at the Opening Ceremony of the 40th Academic Year of the College of Europe', Bruges, October 1989

I often find myself invoking federalism as a method, with the addition of the principle of subsidiarity. I see it as a way of reconciling what for many appears to be irreconcilable: the emergence of a United Europe and loyalty to one's homeland; the need for a European power capable of tackling the problems of our age and the absolute necessity to preserve our roots in the shape of our nations and regions; and decentralization of responsibilities, so that we never entrust to a bigger unit anything that is best done by a smaller one. That is precisely what subsidiarity is about . . .

[My belief] in what I would call working from the bottom up, rebuilding from below, from small entities rooted naturally in a solidarity of interests and a convergence of feeling. That is of course essential, but it is not enough. Others, and I am one of them, must at the same time work from the top down, viewing the paths of integration from above. Otherwise the small streams of solidarity will never converge to form a wide river . . .

Politically speaking, power is not necessarily the obverse of freedom. Neither the European Community – nor the peoples and nations that form it – will truly exist unless it is in a position to defend its values, to act on them for the benefit of all, to be generous. Let us be powerful enough to command respect and to uphold the values of freedom . . .

The time has come, my friends, to revive the ideal.

To get there, however, we must take the path of necessity. At a time when the Community is being courted by some, threatened by others; at a time there are those who, with scant regard for the mortar which already binds us, advocate a headlong dash in the name of a greater Europe, or offer us as an ultimate reference nothing more than the laws of the market; to these we must say that our Community is the fruit not only of history and necessity, but also of political will. Since the turn-around of 1984–87 our achievements are there for all to see . . . Then there is political will. I know that the term has sometimes been abused, as a sort of incantation, but it is precisely political will that led first six, then nine, ten, twelve countries to decide to unite their destinies . . . The contract binding them is clear, involving both rights and obligations.

Last of all history. The Twelve cannot control history, but they are now in a position to influence it once again . . .

The present upheavals in Eastern Europe are changing the nature of our problems . . . Are we going to turn away?

Make no mistake about it. Behind triumphant nationalism and excessive individualism, ethics are making a come-back . . .

The time has come to return to ideals . . . to consider in everything we do in the field of politics, economics and social and cultural life, what will enable every man, every woman, to achieve their full potential in an awareness not only of their rights but also of their obligations to others and to society as a whole . . .

We are creating a model . . .

We owe much to the strength of our institutions because our Community is a Community based on the rule of law. And the condition of success is the joint, transparent exercise of sovereignty.

[. . .]

Let us consider the strength of our institutions . . . beginning with legitimacy. Without legitimacy – as earlier attempts to unite nations have shown – no progress, no permanence is possible. In the Community the progress of history is there for all to see . . .

But effectiveness is another measure of the strength of our institutions . . . the Commission . . . everyone gives it credit for having defined goals and proposed ways and means of revitalizing European integration. The Commission intends to retain this dynamic approach . . . The Commission must never get drunk on its own powers. It must be strict in applying the principle of subsidiarity. It must be aware of the conditions for a dynamic compromise between the Twelve and to that end endeavour to understand each nation and its people. It must draw conclusions from this and be tireless in the pursuit of consensus. It must have the courage to say 'no' when there is a danger of the letter and spirit of the Treaty being ignored. And most important of all, it must have the courage to take a back seat whenever this can serve the European cause.

[. . .]

Despite the success of our Community based on the rule of law, disputes about sovereignty continue. We need to face the issues squarely.

A dogmatic approach will get us nowhere. It will merely complicate the difficult discussions that lie ahead and make it harder to remove the remaining obstacles on the road to the single European market and 1992. The facts speak for themselves. Each nation needs to consider how much room for manoeuvre it genuinely has in today's world. The growing interdependence of our economies, the present or growing influence of the main protagonists on the world stage – all point to a dual conclusion.

First, nations should unite if they feel close to each other in terms of geography, history, values and – dare I say? – necessity.

Secondly – and ideally at the same time – cooperation should develop at world level to deal with such matters as international trade, the monetary system, underdevelopment, the environment and drugs.

The two are complementary rather than concurrent . . .

Europe has little clout as yet . . . It's quite clear that the fault lies in the deliberately fostered fiction of full national sovereignty and hence the absolute effectiveness of national policies.

We are all familiar with the expression 'speaking with a single voice'. This is reality rather than a formula . . . The consequences of the opposite approach prove the point. Think of the shortcomings of our common commercial policy . . . often explained by countries acting alone or failing to identify their own interests correctly . . .

This brings me back to our institutions . . . Since the Single Act and increased recourse to majority voting, there is a new dynamic . . . Thanks to this progress on the institutional front, the Community is advancing rapidly towards the Single European Market and strengthening its rules and common policies. To the advantage of some? No, to the advantage of all: in a sort of positive-sum game . . . We will need to draw conclusions from this experience when the time comes to make further improvements to our institutional apparatus.

And that time is not far off. By its very nature, economic and monetary union is the interface between economic integration and political integration. It is the political crowning of economic convergence. It is a perfect illustration of the joint exercise of sovereignty because a single market for capital and financial services in a world dominated by financial matters calls for a monetary policy which is sufficiently coordinated and sufficiently tight to allow us to make the most of it. Without such a policy we would be prey to international speculation and the instability of dominant currencies.

Monetary union will be acceptable and feasible only if there is parallel progress towards increased convergence of our economies so that policies are more consistent and harnessed to agreed objectives . . . In a democratic society objectives can only be defined by political authorities which have democratic legitimacy.

We therefore need to combine an independent monetary authority – the guarantor of stability – with the subsidiarity which is vital if each nation is to pursue its own policies in areas which are a matter for it alone, and control by our elected representatives in the shape of the European Parliament, our Governments and our national parliaments . . .

Subsidiarity is central to future discussions. The principle is clear but we need to define how it will apply in this particular case . . .

Where does this . . . leave those who argue that economic and monetary union will lead to excessive centralization and *dirigisme?* The fact of the matter is that realistic application of the principle of subsidiarity leaves them without a leg to stand on . . .

Acceptance of subsidiarity implies respect for pluralism and, by implication, diversity . . .

[This is] evident not only in the discussions on economic and monetary union, but also in what we call the Community's social dimension . . . Our twelve countries have differing traditions . . . There can be no question, therefore, of artificially forcing standards upwards or conversely, of provoking the export of social problems. Last but not least, our Governments have differing, and in some cases, opposing points of view . . .

[Regarding the] Charter of Social Rights, . . . when it comes to translating these principles into legislation or collective bargaining, subsidiarity comes into its own, ensuring our different traditions are respected . . . European Company Statute . . . Here again the Commission has been true to the principle of subsidiarity and diversity. Three models are on offer, providing all the flexibility required and corresponding to the three major trends – or, more properly, the three major philosophies – underlying social policy in the Twelve today.

[. . .]

If I turn to the principles of federalism in a bid to find workable solutions, it is precisely because they provide all the necessary guarantees on pluralism and the efficiency of the emergent institutional machinery. Here are two essential rules:

(a) the rule of autonomy, which preserves the identity of each member State and removes any temptation to pursue unification regardless;

(b) the rule of participation, which does not allow one entity to be subordinated to another but, on the contrary, promotes cooperation and synergy, on the basis of the clear and well-defined provisions contained in the Treaty.

This is the starting-point for an original experiment which resists comparisons with any other models, such as the United States of America . . . I have always shied away from such parallels, because I know that our task is to unite old nations with strong traditions and personalities. There is no conspiracy against the nation State. Nobody is being asked to renounce legitimate patriotism. I want only to unite people . . . but also to bring nations together. As the Community develops, as our Governments emphasize the need for a people's Europe, is it heresy to hope that all Europeans could feel that they belong to a Community which they see as a second homeland? If this view is rejected, European integration will founder and the spectre of nationalism will return to haunt us, because the Community will have failed to win the hearts and minds of the people, the first requirement for the success of any human venture. [. . .]

I have no doubt that, if we refuse to face up to these new challenges, not only will we be shirking our responsibilities but the Community will disintegrate, stopped in its tracks by the weight of unresolved contradictions . . . How are we to find a solution except by strengthening the federalist features of the Community which . . . offer the best possible guarantee of survival to all concerned? There, I am quite sure, lies the only acceptable and satisfactory solution to the German question.

I have always favoured the step-by-step approach . . . But today I am moving away from it precisely because time is short. We need a radical change in the way we think of the Community and in the way we act on the world stage . . .

I am concerned that we will never achieve all this with our present decision-making procedures. Thanks to the Single Act, the Council, Parliament and the Commission are a more efficient institutional troika than they were a few years ago. But this is not enough to enable us to keep pace with events . . .

It is time, then, for new political initiative . . . The Commission . . . will propose answers to the questions raised by another quantum leap: who takes the decisions; how do the various levels of decision-making intermesh (subsidiarity again!); who puts decisions into practice; what resources will be available; what will it mean in terms of democracy?

[. . .]

Documents 49

In the negotiations leading to the conclusion of the Single European Act, the Commission and a majority of delegations wanted to lay the Treaty foundations for an economic and monetary union. They were opposed by Germany, which was anxious to protect the independence and continuing existence of the Bundesbank, and by Britain, which had still deferred membership of the European Monetary System 'until the time is right'.

The compromise in the SEA was something of a rebuff of the unionists. There is a reference in the Preamble to the approval by Heads of State and Government in Paris in October 1972 of the objective of the progressive realization of economic and monetary union. A new chapter is added to the EEC Treaty under the sectional heading 'Monetary Capacity', implying that the Community has one. The chapter heading is 'Cooperation in Economic and Monetary Policy (economic and monetary union)'. The content is thin. It requires that if there is to be institutional development – as the unionists wanted, to get away from the hybridity of the EMS – there would need to be a new inter-governmental conference. The compromise was sealed under the Anglo-German threat to insist on the immediate freeing of capital movements.

Mrs Thatcher welcomed her success in beating off more full-blooded versions and was comforted by the dubious proposition that the chapter heading now meant that 'EMU' meant 'cooperation among national authorities'. But in Mrs Thatcher's metaphor, the sleeping dog had started barking. On 8 January 1988, the French Finance Minister circulated a paper on EMU. The German Presidency of the first half of 1988 took up the idea, suggesting the setting up of a committee to study a monetary area, a central bank and a programme of measures. At the meeting of the European Council in Hanover on 27–28 June 1988, the European Council recalled the objective of the progressive realization of EMU and entrusted to a Committee the task of studying and proposing concrete stages leading towards this union. The Committee Chairman was to be the President of the Commission, M. Jacques Delors. All references to what EMU might involve – European Central Bank, locked-in exchange rates, single cur-rency – were excised from the Committee's terms of reference.

The British Government hoped that its representative on the Committee, the Governor of the Bank of England, in alliance with the President of the Bundesbank, Mr Karl Otto Pöhl, would be able to tone down the enthusiasts. They were to be disappointed. The Report was unanimous and set out a scheme for EMU. Mr Pöhl later acknowledged that he had made a mistake.

The substantive section of the Delors Report opens by stating the impli-cations of EMU: complete freedom of movement for people, goods, services and capital; irrevocably fixed exchange rates among national currencies and finally a single currency (although it is not strictly necessary). A transfer of decision-making power from the member States to the Commu-nity would be necessary. Coordination is not enough – responsibility for the single monetary policy would need to be assigned to a new institution, taking centralized and collective decisions.

Meeting in Madrid on 26–27 June 1989, the European Council com-missioned work, to be based on the Delors Report, on the preparation of an inter-governmental conference to lay down the second and third stages of EMU. The British Government did not dissent, but made a unilateral declaration to the effect that there was nothing automatic about the timing and content of the second stage. It then came closer to clarifying what was meant by the 'right time' for British membership of EMS: completion of the Single Market, free movement of capital and inflation down in Britain. According to Mrs Thatcher herself, the 'Madrid conditions' for British entry into the Exchange Rate Mechanism were not to be taken too seriously. On 5 October 1990, Britain joined the ERM, announcing at the same time a 1 per cent cut in interest rates.

The preparatory work ordered by the Madrid European Council was entrusted to national financial experts, meeting under the chairmanship of Mme Elisabeth Guigou, then special adviser to President Mitterrand.

At the meeting of the European Council in Strasbourg on 8–9 December 1989, President Mitterrand concluded that the necessary simple majority in favour of convening a new inter-governmental conference on EMU under Article 236 of the EEC Treaty existed. The British Government was not part of that majority.

By the meeting of the European Council in Rome on 27–28 October 1990, positions had hardened. Eleven member States agreed on a detailed agenda for the inter-governmental conference on EMU, to begin on 14 December 1990. The United Kingdom dissented. Mrs Thatcher dismissed her European Council colleagues as living in 'cloud cuckoo land'.

In her replies to questions following her statement in the House of Commons about the Rome meeting, Mrs Thatcher poured cold water on ideas about currency unions. This in turn provoked the resignation of her longstanding colleague, Sir Geoffrey Howe; the unsuccessful leadership challenge by the reputedly pro-European Mr Michael Heseltine; and the second ballot of Conservative Members of Parliament which gave Mr John Major the leadership.

In 1990 the ERM was regarded as a zone of exchange rate stability – there had been no significant changes in participants' parities since 1985. But in 1992, as recession took hold in Europe, the currency markets began to doubt the resolve or ability of ERM States to maintain their rates. With heavy selling of the Pound and the Lira, and a report that the President of the Bundesbank had said that the Pound was overvalued, pressure proved irresistible, and on 16 September 1992 the Pound and the Lira left the ERM.

The ERM was effectively suspended on 2 August 1993, when the French Franc had come under selling pressure, attributed to high German interest rates. This served to discredit the realism of the Maastricht Treaty provisions and the timetable for economic and monetary union and in particular to distance the British Government further from it.

'Committee for the Study of Economic and Monetary Union: Report on Economic and Monetary Union in the European Community' [Delors Report], 1989

Chapter II: The final stage of economic and monetary union

Section 1

General considerations

16. Economic and monetary union in Europe would imply complete freedom of movement for persons, goods, services and capital, as well as irrevocably fixed exchange rates between national currencies and, finally, a single currency. This, in turn, would imply a common monetary policy and require a high degree of compatibility of economic and monetary policies and consistency in a number of other policy areas, particularly in the fiscal field. These policies should be geared to price stability, balanced growth, converging standards of living, high employment and external equilibrium. Economic and monetary union would represent the final result of the process of progressive economic integration in Europe.

17. Even after attaining economic and monetary union, the Community would continue to consist of individual nations with differing economic, social, cultural and political characteristics. The existence and preservation of this *plurality* would require a degree of autonomy in economic decision-making to remain with individual member countries and a balance to be struck between national and Community competencies. For this reason it would be necessary to develop an innovative and unique approach.

[. . .]

19. Taking into account what is already provided for in the EC Treaties, the need for a transfer of decision-making power from member States to the Community as a whole would arise primarily in the fields of monetary policy and macroeconomic management. A monetary union would require a single monetary policy and responsibility for the formulation of this policy would consequently have to be vested in one decision-making body. In the economic field a wide range of decisions would remain the preserve of national and regional authorities. However, given their potential impact on the overall domestic and external economic situation of the Community and their implications for the conduct of a common monetary policy, such decisions would have to be placed within an agreed macroeconomic framework and be subject to binding procedures and rules. This would permit the determination of an overall policy stance for the Community as a whole, avoid unsustainable differences between individual member countries in public-sector borrowing requirements and place binding constraints on the size and the financing of budget deficits.

20. An essential element in defining the appropriate balance of power within the Community would be adherence to the 'principle of subsidiarity', according to which the functions of higher levels of government should be as limited as possible and should be subsidiary to those of lower levels. Thus, the attribution of competencies to the Community would have to be confined specifically to those areas in which collective decision-making was necessary. All policy functions which could be carried out at national (and regional and local) levels without adverse repercussions on the cohesion and functioning of the economic and monetary union would remain within the competence of the member countries.

21. Economic and monetary union form two integral parts of a single whole and would therefore have to be implemented in parallel. It is only for reasons of expositional clarity that the following sections look

separately at an economic and monetary union . . . But the Committee is fully aware that the process of achieving monetary union is only conceivable if a high degree of economic convergence is attained.

Section 2

The principal features of monetary union:

22. A monetary union constitutes a currency area in which policies are managed jointly with a view to attaining common macro-economic objectives. As already stated in the 1970 Werner Report, there are three necessary conditions for a monetary union:

- the assurance of total and irreversible convertibility of currencies;

- the complete liberalization of capital transactions and full integration of banking and other financial markets; and

- the elimination of margins of fluctuation and the irrevocable locking of exchange rate parities.

The first two of these requirements have already been met, or will be with the completion of the internal market programme. The single most important condition for a monetary union would, however, be fulfilled only when the decisive step was taken to lock exchange rates irrevocably.

As a result of this step, national currencies would become increasingly close substitutes and their interest rates would tend to converge. The pace with which these developments took place would depend critically on the extent to which firms, households, labour unions and other economic agents were convinced that the decision to lock exchange rates would not be reversed. Both coherent monetary management and convincing evidence of an effective coordination of non-monetary policies would be crucial.

23. The three above-mentioned requirements define a single currency area, but their fulfilment would not necessarily mark the end of the process of monetary unification in the Community. The adoption of a single currency, while not strictly necessary for the creation of a monetary union, might be seen – for economic as well as psychological and political reasons – as a natural and desirable further development of the monetary union. A single currency would clearly demonstrate the irreversibility of the move to monetary union, considerably facilitate the monetary management of the Community and avoid the transaction costs of converting currencies. A single currency, provided that its stability is ensured, would also have a much

greater weight relative to other major currencies than any individual Community currency. The replacement of national currencies by a single currency should therefore take place as soon as possible after the locking of parities.

24. The establishment of a monetary union would have far-reaching implications for the formulation and execution of monetary policy in the Community. Once permanently fixed exchange rates had been adopted, there would be a need for a common monetary policy, which would be carried out through new operating procedures. The coordination of as many national monetary policies as there were currencies participating in the union would not be sufficient. The responsibility for the single monetary policy would have to be vested in a new institution, in which centralized and collective decisions would be taken on the supply of money and credit as well as on other instruments of monetary policy, including interest rates.

This shift from national monetary policies to a single monetary policy is an inescapable consequence of monetary union and constitutes one of the principal institutional changes. Although a progressively intensified coordination of national monetary policies would in many respects have prepared the way for the move to a single monetary policy, the implications of such a move would be far-reaching. The permanent fixing of exchange rates would deprive individual countries of an important instrument for the correction of economic imbalances and for independent action in the pursuit of national objectives, especially price stability.

Well before the decision to fix interest rates permanently, the full liberalization of capital movements and financial market integration would have created a situation in which the coordination of monetary policy would have to be strengthened progressively. Once every banking institution in the Community is free to accept deposits from, and grant loans to, any customer in the Community and in any of the national currencies, the large degree of territorial coincidence between a national central bank's area of jurisdiction, the area in which its currency is used and the area in which 'its' banking system operates, will be lost. In these circumstances the effectiveness of national monetary policies will become increasingly dependent on cooperation among central banks. Indeed, the growing coordination of monetary policies will make a positive contribution to financial market integration and will help central banks gain the experience that would be necessary to move to a single monetary policy.

[. . .]

Chapter III: Steps towards economic and monetary union

39. After defining the main features of an economic and monetary union, the Committee has undertaken the 'task of studying and proposing concrete stages leading towards this union'. The Committee agreed that the creation of an economic and monetary union must be viewed as a single process. Although this process is set out in stages which guide the progressive movement to the final objectives, the decision to enter upon the first stage should be a decision to embark on the entire process.

A clear political commitment to the final stage, as described in Chapter II of this Report, would lend credibility to the intention that the measures which constitute stage one should represent not just a useful end in themselves but a firm first step on the road towards economic and monetary union. It would be a strong expression of such a commitment if all members of the Community became full members of the EMS in the course of stage one and undertook the obligations to formulate a convergent economic policy within the existing institutions.

[. . .]

Section 5

The principal steps in stage three:

58. The final stage would commence with the move to irrevocably locked exchange rates and the attribution to Community institutions of the full monetary and economic competencies described in Chapter II of this Report. In the course of the final stage the national currencies would eventually be replaced by a single Community currency.

59. In the economic field, the transition to this final stage would be marked by three developments.

First, there might need to be a further strengthening of Community structural and regional policies. Instruments and resources would be adapted to the needs of the economic and monetary union.

Second, the rules and procedures of the Community in the macro-economic and budgetary field would become binding. In particular, the Council of Ministers, in cooperation with the European Parliament, would have the authority to take directly enforceable decisions, i.e.:

- to impose constraints on national budgets to the extent to which this was necessary to prevent imbalances that might threaten monetary stability;

- to make discretionary changes in Community resources (through a procedure to be defined) to supplement structural transfers to member States or to influence the overall policy stance in the Community;

- to apply to existing Community structural policies and to Community loans (as a substitute for the present medium-term financial assistance facility) terms and conditions that would prompt member countries to intensify their adjustment efforts.

Third, the Community would assume its full role in the process of international policy cooperation, and a new form of representation in arrangements for international policy coordination and in international monetary negotiations would be adopted.

60. In the monetary field, the irrevocable locking of exchange rates would come into effect and the transition to a single monetary policy would be made, with the ESCB assuming all its responsibilities as foreseen in the Treaty and described in Chapter II of this Report. In particular:

- concurrently with the announcement of the irrevocable fixing of parities between Community currencies, the responsibility for the formulation and implementation of monetary policy in the Community would be transferred to the ESCB, with its Council and Board exercising their statutory functions;

- decisions on exchange market interventions in third currencies would be made on the sole responsibility of the ESCB Council in accordance with Community exchange rate policy; the execution of interventions would be entrusted either to national central banks or to the ESCB;

- official reserves would be pooled and managed by the ESCB;

- preparations of a technical or regulatory nature would be made for the transition to a single Community currency.

The change-over to the single currency would take place during this stage.

[. . .]

'Conclusions of the Presidency of the European Council', Madrid, June 1989

Economic and monetary union

The European Council restated its determination progressively to achieve economic and monetary union as provided for in the Single Act and confirmed at the European Council meeting in Hanover. Economic and monetary union must be seen in the perspective of the completion of the internal market and in the context of economic and social cohesion . . .

The European Council felt that its realization would have to take account of the parallelism between economic and monetary aspects, respect the principle of subsidiarity and allow for the diversity of specific situations.

The European Council decided that the first stage of the realization of economic and monetary union would begin on 1 July 1990.

The European Council asked the component bodies:

(a) to adopt the provisions necessary for the launch of the first stage on 1 July 1990;

(b) to carry out the preparatory work for the organization of an inter-governmental conference to lay down the subsequent stages; that conference would meet once the first stage had begun and would be preceded by full and adequate preparation . . .

'Conclusions of the Presidency of the European Council', Strasbourg, December 1989

Economic and monetary union

The European Council examined the work carried out since the European Council meeting in Madrid with a view to a meeting of the inter-governmental conference.

It noted the agreement reached in the Council and the initiatives of the governors of the central banks with a view to strengthening the coordination of economic policies and improving collaboration between central banks. It notes that these decisions will enable the first stage of EMU as defined in the report from the Delors Committee to begin on 1 July 1990.

It took note of the report from the high-level working party, which identified the main technical, institutional and political issues to be discussed with a view to a Treaty on economic and monetary union.

On this basis, and following a discussion on the calling of an inter-governmental conference charged with preparing an amendment to the Treaty with a view to the final stages of EMU, the President of the European Council noted that the necessary majority existed for convening such a conference under Article 236 of the Treaty. That conference will meet, under the auspices of the Italian authorities, before the end of 1990. It will draw up its own agenda and set the timetable for its proceedings. The European Council emphasized, in this context, the need to ensure the proper observance of democratic control in each of the member States . . .

'Conclusions of the Presidency of the European Council', Dublin, June 1990

1.10. The first stage of economic and monetary union will come into effect on 1 July 1990. The European Council considered that this stage should be used to ensure convergence in the economic performance of member States, to advance cohesion and to further the use of the ECU, all of which are of importance for further progress towards EMU.

The European Council reviewed the preparation of the forthcoming inter-governmental conference. It noted that all the relevant issues are now being fully and thoroughly clarified, with the constructive contribution of all member States, and that common ground is emerging in a number of fields. In these circumstances the European Council decided that the inter-governmental conference will open on 13 December 1990 with a view to establishing the final stages of economic and monetary union in the perspective of the completion of the internal market and in the context of economic and social cohesion. The conference should conclude its work rapidly with the objective of ratification of the results by member States before the end of 1992.

'Conclusions of the Presidency of the European Council', Rome, October 1990

Conference on economic and monetary union

For the final phase of economic and monetary union eleven member States consider that the work on the amendment of the Treaty will be directed to the following points:

1. for economic union, an open market system that combines price

stability with growth, employment and environmental protection and is dedicated to sound and sustainable financial and budgetary conditions and to economic and social cohesion. To this end, the ability to act of the Community institutions will be strengthened.

2. for monetary union, the creation of a new monetary institution comprising member States' central banks and a central organ, exercising full responsibility for monetary policy. The monetary institution's prime task will be to maintain price stability; without prejudice to this objective, it will support the general economic policy of the Community. The institution as such, as well as the members of its council, will be independent of instructions. It will report to the institutions which are politically responsible.

With the achievement of the final phase of economic and monetary union, exchange rates will be irrevocably fixed. The Community will have a single currency – a strong and stable ECU – which will be an expression of its identity and unity. During the transitional phase, the ECU will be further strengthened and developed.

The second phase will start on 1 January 1994 after:

(a) the single market programme has been achieved;

(b) the Treaty has been ratified; and, by its provisions;

(c) a process has been set in train designed to ensure the independence of the members of the new monetary institution at the latest when monetary powers have been transferred;

(d) the monetary financing of budget deficits has been prohibited and any responsibility on the part of the Community or its member States for one member State's debt precluded;

(e) the greatest possible number of member States have adhered to the exchange-rate mechanism.

The European Council recalls that, in order to move on to the second phase, further satisfactory and lasting progress towards real and monetary convergence will have to be achieved, especially as regards price stability and the restoration of sound public finances.

At the start of the second phase, the new Community institution will be established. This will make it possible, in particular, to:

(a) strengthen the coordination of monetary policies;

(b) develop the instruments and procedures needed for the future conduct of a single monetary policy;

(c) oversee the development of the ECU.

At the latest within three years of the start of the second phase, the Commission and the council of the monetary institution will report to the Economic and Financial Council and to the General Affairs Council . . . on the progress made in real convergence, in order to prepare the decision concerning the passage to the third phase, which will occur within a reasonable time . . .

The United Kingdom, while ready to move beyond Stage 1 through the creation of a new monetary institution and a common Community currency, believes that decisions on the substance of that move should precede decisions on its timing. It would, however, be prepared to see the approach it advocates come into effect as soon as possible after ratification of the necessary Treaty provision.

Mrs Thatcher, Prime Minister, 'Speech to the House of Commons on Economic and Monetary Union', October 1990

On economic and monetary union, I stressed that we would be ready to move beyond the present position to the creation of a European monetary fund and a common Community currency which we have called a hard ECU. But we would not be prepared to agree to set a date for starting the next stage of economic and monetary union before there is any agreement on what that stage should comprise. And I again emphasized that we would not be prepared to have a single currency imposed upon us, nor to surrender the use of the Pound Sterling as our currency.

The hard ECU would be a parallel currency, not a single currency. If, as time went by, people and Governments chose to use it widely, it could evolve towards a single currency. But our national currency would remain unless a decision to abolish it were freely taken by future generations of Parliament and people. A single currency is not the policy of this Government.

Documents 50

With the decision taken to convoke an inter-governmental conference on economic and monetary union (See Document 49) demands began to be heard for its extension to political union. This was the theme of the first

Martin Report in the European Parliament adopted on 14 March 1990, of a Belgian memorandum of 20 March 1990 and of a letter sent jointly by the German Chancellor and the French President to the Irish Presidency of the European Council on 19 April 1990.

External events impinged upon the Community's reflections about itself. 1989 saw the revolutionary liberation of Eastern and Central Europe. The Berlin Wall was breached on 10 November 1989, foreshadowing German unification on 3 October 1990. This prospect made France and Britain uncomfortable.

With the Soviet bloc breaking up, the foreign and security policies of members of the European Community needed rethinking, some thought best collectively. On 2 August 1989 Iraq invaded Kuwait. In the ensuing Gulf war, the European Community was conspicuously absent. Member States took their own stances.

On the eve of the European Council meeting in Dublin on 28 April 1990, on 19 April President Mitterrand and Chancellor Kohl sent a letter to the Irish Presidency of the European Council. Kohl in November 1989 had echoed Thomas Mann's famous call 'not for a German Europe, but for a European Germany', but others were apprehensive. After initial hostility to the idea of the new Germany, the speed of movement towards German unification persuaded Mitterrand that he needed to work closely with Kohl, and he began to see some advantages in a 'European Germany'. Thus Kohl and Mitterrand began to work together.

The letter also incorporated an attempt to crystallize the issues of a 'common foreign and security policy' and gave serious impetus to the idea of two parallel inter-governmental conferences.

The letter was discussed in Dublin on 28 April 1990, with general agreement to move forward on political union, although the UK and Portugal dissented. The April meeting instructed Foreign Ministers to examine the issue and to report to the June Dublin European Council.

The second European Council under Irish Presidency in June 1990 decided to convene a second conference, on political union, it already having been agreed in April that a second conference would work in parallel with the IGC on EMU.

The meeting of the European Council in Rome on 27–28 October 1990 saw the majority beginning to flesh out an agenda, with the UK demurring and reserving its position on all mention of specific topics. The second Rome meeting witnessed Mr Major's debut. This time a wide-ranging conference agenda was adopted, without explicit UK reserves, even on the mention of a 'social dimension'.

Work in the IGCs was begun by the Luxembourg Presidency at the beginning of 1991 and pursued in the second half of the year by the Dutch Presidency. The IGCs were concluded at the meeting of Heads of State and Government in Maastricht on 9–10 December 1991, and the Treaty on European Union was signed, also in Maastricht, on 7 February 1992.

'Kohl–Mitterrand Letter to the Irish Presidency', April 1990

In the light of far-reaching changes in Europe and in view of the completion of the single market and the realization of economic and monetary union, we consider it necessary to accelerate the political construction of the Europe of the Twelve. We believe that it is time 'to transform relations as a whole among the member States into a European Union . . . and invest this union with the necessary means of action', as envisaged by the Single Act.

With this in mind, we would like to see the European Council deciding as follows on 28 April:

1. The European Council should ask the competent bodies to intensify the preparations for the inter-governmental conference on economic and monetary union, which will be opened by the end of 1990 at the invitation of the Italian Presidency, as decided by the European Council in Strasbourg.

2. The European Council should initiate preparations for an inter-governmental conference on political union. In particular, the objective is to: strengthen the democratic legitimation of the union, render its institutions more efficient, ensure unity and coherence of the union's economic, monetary and political action, define and implement a common foreign and security policy.

The Foreign Ministers should be instructed to prepare an initial report for the meeting of the European Council in June and to submit a final report to the European Council meeting in December. We wish the inter-governmental conference on political union to be held in parallel to the conference on economic and monetary union.

3. Our aim is that these fundamental reforms – economic and monetary union as well as political union – should enter into force on 1 January 1993 after ratification by the national parliaments. [. . .]

'Conclusions of the Presidency of the European Council', Dublin, April 1990

1.3. The Community warmly welcomes German unification . . . We are confident that German unification . . . will be a positive factor in the development of Europe as a whole and of the Community in particular . . .

1.4. A point has now been reached where the continued dynamic development of the Community has become an imperative not only because it corresponds to the direct interests of the twelve member States but also because it has become a crucial element in the progress that is being made in establishing a reliable framework for peace and security in Europe. The European Council therefore agree that further decisive steps should be taken towards European unity as envisaged in the Single European Act.

[. . .]

Political union

1.12. The European Council discussed the proposal of President Mitterrand and Chancellor Kohl on political union, and the paper submitted by the Belgian Government on the same subject.

In this context the European Council confirmed its commitments to political union and decided on the following steps:

(a) A detailed examination will be put in hand forthwith on the need for possible Treaty changes with the aim of strengthening the democratic legitimacy of the union, enabling the Community and its institutions to respond effectively to the demands of the new situation, and assuring unity and coherence in the Community's international action;

(b) Foreign Ministers will undertake this examination and analysis, and prepare proposals to be discussed at the European Council in June with a view to a decision on the holding of a second inter-governmental conference to work in parallel with the conference on economic and monetary union with a view to ratification by member States in the same time-frame.

[. . .]

'Conclusions of the Presidency of the European Council', Dublin, June 1990

Conference on political union

1.11. The European Council had an extensive exchange of views on the basis of the examination and analysis conducted by the Foreign Ministers and the ideas and proposals put forward by the member States and the Commission.

On this basis, and following a discussion on the calling of an inter-governmental conference on political union, the President of the European Council noted the agreement to convene such a conference under Article 236 of the Treaty. The conference will open on 14 December 1990. It will adopt its own agenda, and conclude its work rapidly with the objective of ratification by member States before the end of 1992.

[. . .]

The European Council considered that the necessary coherence in the work of the two conferences should be ensured by the General Affairs Council.

[. . .]

'Conclusions of the Presidency of the European Council', Rome, October 1990

Conference on political union

The European Council confirmed the will progressively to transform the Community into a European Union by developing its political dimension, strengthening its capacity for action and extending its powers to other supplementary sectors of economic integration which are essential for convergence and social cohesion. European Union will be the culmination of a progressive process agreed by common accord among the member States; it will evolve with due regard being paid to national identities and to the principle of subsidiarity, which will allow a distinction to be made between matters which fall within the Union's jurisdiction and those which must remain within national jurisdiction.

Mrs Thatcher, Prime Minister, 'Speech to the House of Commons on Political Union', October 1990

I should like to offer four comments in conclusion.

First, the Community finds it more difficult to take the urgent, detailed decisions than to discuss longer-term concepts. Moreover, no-one should underestimate the extent to which national interests prevail among those who most proclaim their Community credentials.

Secondly, Britain intends to be part of the further political, economic and monetary development of the European Community. That is what the great majority of member States want, too. When we come to negotiate on particular points, rather than concepts or generalities, I believe that solutions will be found which will enable the Community to go forward as Twelve. That will be our objective.

Thirdly, we are fighting in Europe for British farmers, for British consumers, for a new world trade agreement, for help to the newly democratic countries of Eastern Europe, and for the interests and concerns of our people.

Fourthly, while we fully accept our commitments under the Treaties and wish to cooperate more closely with other countries in the European Community, we are determined to retain our fundamental ability to govern ourselves through Parliament. I believe that is the wish of this House, and we on this side will do our best to see that it is fulfilled . . .

Yes, the Commission wants to increase its powers. Yes, it is a non-elected body and I do not want the Commission to increase its powers at the expense of the House, so of course we differ. The President of the Commission, Mr Delors, said at a press conference the other day that he wanted the European Parliament to be the democratic body of the Community, he wanted the Commission to be the Executive and he wanted the Council of Ministers to be the Senate. No. No. No . . .

Document 51

On 2 June 1992 in an obligatory referendum, the Danish electorate narrowly voted against ratification of the Treaty on European Union, by 50.7 per cent to 49.3 per cent, a majority of 46,269. On 20 September 1992, in an optional referendum, French voters gave a 'petit oui' to the

Treaty, by 51.04 per cent to 48.95 per cent. In Britain, the Conservative Government postponed consideration of its ratification Bill in the House of Commons, facing an anti-Maastricht faction within its own ranks. As Presidency for the second half of the year, Britain was responsible for finding a way out of what was becoming known as the Maastricht ratification crisis.

The British Government needed for its own purposes Community decisions which would (in its language) support the argument that it had ensured that the Treaty on European Union would not be centralizing and it needed to find concessions which could justify a second Danish referendum with some chance of success for the Treaty.

In a tour de force, and after a meagre start at a special European Council meeting held in Birmingham in October, the British Presidency successfully concluded negotiations at the regular European Council meeting in Edinburgh on 11–12 December 1992. The Danes obtained new opt-outs on the possible future defence policy and on economic and monetary union. The Danes and the British obtained agreements on the application of subsidiarity and on 'openness', all part of the theme of the Community drawing closer to its citizens. There was and continues to be much discussion as to the legal status of the 'decision' on Denmark, just as many in Denmark wondered what really had been achieved at Edinburgh.

On 18 May 1993 the second Danish referendum gave a clear positive vote, 56.8 per cent now voting in favour of the Treaty. Two days later, the British House of Commons completed its scrutiny of the ratification Bill. But its troubles were not over, and the Government only finally obtained its way by making support for its position a matter of confidence. It also had to overcome a legal challenge over its right to ratify by Royal Prerogative.

'Conclusions of the Presidency of the European Council', Edinburgh, December 1992

In particular the European Council reached agreement on the following major issues:

- the problems raised by Denmark in the light of the outcome of the Danish referendum . . .

- guidelines to implement the subsidiarity principle and measures to increase transparency and openness in the decision-making process of the Community;

- the financing of Community action and policies during the rest of this decade;

- the launching of enlargement negotiations with a number of EFTA countries;

- the establishment of a plan of action by the member States and the Community to promote growth and combat unemployment.

[. . .]

Annex 1 to Part A: Overall approach to the application by the Council of the subsidiarity principle and Article 3b of the Treaty on European Union

Basic principles

1.15. European Union rests on the principle of subsidiarity, as is made clear in Articles A and B of Title 1 of the Treaty on European Union. This principle contributes to the respect for the national identities of member States and safeguards their powers. It aims at decisions within the European Union being taken as closely as possible to the citizen.

Article 3b of the EC Treaty covers three main elements:

- a strict limit on Community action (first paragraph);

- a rule (second paragraph) to answer the question: 'Should the Community act?'. This applies to areas which do not fall within the Community's exclusive competence;

- a rule (third paragraph) to answer the question: 'What should be the intensity or nature of the Community's action?'. This applies whether or not the action is within the Community's exclusive competence.

The three paragraphs cover three distinct legal concepts . . .

- the principle that the Community should only act where given the power to do so . . .

- the principle that the Community should only take action where an objective can be better attained at the level of the Community than at the level of the individual member State . . .

- the principle that the means to be employed by the Community should be proportional to the objective pursued . . .

The implementation of Article 3b should respect the following basic principles:

- making the principle of subsidiarity and Article 3b work is an obligation for all the Community institutions, without affecting the balance between them . . .

- the principle of subsidiarity does not relate to and cannot call into question the powers conferred on the European Community by the Treaty as interpreted by the Court. It provides a guide as to how those powers are to be exercised . . . [It] shall respect the general provisions of the Maastricht Treaty, including maintaining in full the acquis communautaire, and it shall not call into question the primacy of Community law . . .

[. . .]

Guidelines

First paragraph (Limit on Community action): . . . In order to apply this paragraph correctly the institutions need to be satisfied that the proposed action is within the limits of the powers conferred by the Treaty and is aimed at meeting one or more of its objectives . . .

Second paragraph (Should the Community act?): . . . The Council must be satisfied that both aspects of the subsidiarity criterion are met: the objectives of the proposed action cannot be sufficiently achieved by member States' action and they can therefore be better achieved by action on the part of the Community.

The following guidelines should be used in examining whether the above-mentioned condition is fulfilled:

- the issue under consideration has transnational aspects which cannot be satisfactorily regulated by action by member States; and/or

- actions by member States alone or lack of Community action would conflict with the requirements of the Treaty . . .

- the Council must be satisfied that action at Community level would produce clear benefits by reason of its scale or effects compared with action at the level of member States . . .

Third paragraph (Nature and extent of Community action): . . . Any burdens, whether financial or administrative, falling upon the Community, national Governments, local authorities, economic operators and citizens, should be minimized and proportionate to the objective to be achieved.

Community measures should leave as much scope for national decision as possible . . .

Where it is necessary to set standards at Community level, consideration should be given to setting minimum standards, with freedom for member States to set higher national standards . . .

The form of action should be as simple as possible . . . The Community should legislate only to the extent necessary. Other things being equal, directives should be preferred to detailed measures . . .

Where appropriate . . . preference in choosing the type of Community action should be given to encouraging cooperation between member States, coordinating national action or to complementing, supplementing or supporting such action . . .

1.20. The Treaty on European Union obliges all institutions to consider, when examining a Community measure, whether the provisions of Article 3b are observed . . .

[. . .]

Annex 1 to Part B: Decision of the Heads of State or Government, meeting within the European Council, concerning certain problems raised by Denmark on the Treaty on European Union

. . . Have agreed on the following decision:

Section A: Citizenship

1.35. The provisions of Part Two of the Treaty . . . give nationals of the member States additional rights and protection as specified in that Part. They do not in any way take the place of national citizenships. The question of whether an individual possesses the nationality of a member State will be settled solely by reference to the national law of the member State concerned.

Section B: Economic and monetary union

Denmark will not participate in the single currency, will not be bound by the rules concerning economic policy which apply only to the member States participating in Stage III of economic and monetary union, and will retain its existing powers in the field of monetary policy according to its national laws . . .

[. . .]

Section C: Defence policy

1.37. . . . nothing in the Treaty on European Union commits Denmark to become a member of the WEU. Accordingly, Denmark does not participate in the elaboration and the implementation of decisions and actions of the Union which have defence implications, but will not prevent the development of closer cooperation between member States in this area.

Section D: Justice and home affairs

1.38. Denmark will participate fully in cooperation on justice and home affairs on the basis of Title VI of the Treaty on European Union.

Section E: Final provisions

At any time Denmark may, in accordance with its constitutional requirements, inform other member States that it no longer wishes to avail itself of all or part of this decision . . .

Documents 52

Three of the EFTA States were traditional neutrals: Austria, Sweden and Switzerland. It had been believed that Community membership and neutrality were incompatible (See Document 26). Finland, given its location, had been obliged to take closely into account its relations with the USSR. In 1972 Norwegian voters had rejected membership in a referendum.

Internal EC events and events in the wider Europe provoked a re-examination of the reasoning which had held for nearly two decades. The Community's programme for a Single Market by the end of 1992 suggested to the EFTA States that they might face new trade barriers at the Community's external border, and that they would not share in the benefits of the new area without frontiers.

The end of the Cold War challenged most of the principles of foreign and security policy which had held the day since the 1950s and called for at least some new thinking about neutrality. But the Community was also preoccupied by its own future, with several of the existing member States giving priority to 'deepening' rather than to 'widening' – indeed the latter might, it seemed to them, counteract the former.

At the beginning of 1989, the President of the Commission, M. Jacques Delors, threw out the idea that the EFTA States might like to open negotiations leading effectively to their joining the Single Market. The idea took root; negotiations began in June 1990 and were concluded in February 1992. They constructed a European Economic Area, consisting of the European Community and Austria, Sweden, Finland, Norway, Iceland, Switzerland and Liechtenstein. The four freedoms of the Single Market –

movement of goods, services, capital and people – were extended to the Area. In a referendum in December 1992, the Swiss voters opposed membership of the EEA and Switzerland withdrew. The agreement otherwise came into force on 1 January 1994. Switzerland later sought to negotiate a series of sectoral agreements with the Community.

Some observers thought that Delors may have had a mixture of motives – wider European integration yes, but possibly a brake on applications for membership at a time when the Community was busy deepening. If this was intended, it did not achieve the purpose.

Five of the EEA participants applied for membership of the European Communities: Austria in 1989, Sweden in 1991, Finland, Switzerland and Norway in 1992. With the rejection of Swiss membership of the EEA in 1992, the Swiss application for membership of the Communities was frozen.

Meeting in Maastricht in December 1991 to conclude the Treaty on European Union, the European Council agreed that enlargement negotiations should begin as soon as the Community had 'terminated its negotiations on own resources and related issues in 1992'. But in Lisbon in June 1992, with Britain claiming the credit, the European Council decided to quicken the pace. The actual negotiations were subordinate to the ratification of the Treaty on European Union and the 'Delors II package' (own resources and related issues).

Negotiations for the accession of Austria, Finland, Sweden and Norway opened formally on 1 February 1993. In each case the Commission's opinion, and the Austrian case is the example below, started from the hypothesis that all the applicants accepted everything in the Treaty on European Union and all the legislation the Community/Union had already adopted. In its opinions, the Commission reviewed the adaptations which the applicant would have to make to comply with the terms of membership. This review helped to foreshadow the matters which required to be negotiated with the applicants. The four opinions could not fail to be positive. A potential problem, that of neutrality, failed to materialize as the three neutrals accepted the Common Foreign and Security Policy, without looking for any relief. In the autumn of 1994 the four held referendums. The results were:

State	Yes (%)	No (%)	Turnout (%)
Austria	66	34	81
Finland	57	43	74
Norway	48	52	89
Sweden	52	48	82

The Brussels meeting of the European Council, on 10–11 December 1993 settled corollary institutional questions – number of MEPs, voting weights in the Council, number of Commissioners and so on. But the Lisbon meeting had already stipulated that enlargement was to be on the basis of the institutional provisions contained in the Maastricht Treaty, which meant that major institutional reform was put off. There was a declaration of intent that the inter-governmental conference in 1996 would consider these questions. Lisbon and Brussels read together were ambivalent. What was the exact effect of combining the existing institutional provisions and four more Council votes for each of Austria and Sweden and three more for each of Norway and Finland? The British Government made a stand: even with more votes to be cast around the Council table, the existing blocking minority of twenty-three votes in the twelve member State Community should remain unchanged. All the other member States thought that 'no change' meant that the size of the blocking minority should be increased proportionately, to twenty-seven votes. Since unanimity is needed for decisions of this kind, an impasse developed.

It was resolved by the 'Ioannina Agreement', which unlike the Luxembourg Agreement, became a formal Council decision (of 29 March 1994). This created a grey zone between twenty-three and twenty-six opposing votes, in which the Council would try to find a solution acceptable to the majority, not of sixty-four votes, which would be the new figure after enlargement, but of sixty-eight. At Ioannina the Foreign Ministers also agreed that the question of voting weights and of qualified majorities would be examined in preparation for the 1996 inter-governmental conference.

When the Norwegian referendum of 1994 followed the first of 1972 in rejecting membership, the Ioannina figures were adjusted. The grey zone in the Union of fifteen was twenty-three–twenty-five (replacing twenty-three–twenty-six) out of a total of sixty-five votes (replacing sixty-eight).

The European Council meeting in Corfu on 24–25 June 1994 noted that the 'next phase of the enlargement of the Union will involve Cyprus and Malta'. On Turkey it confined itself to noting the convening of the Association Council under the 1964 Agreement (with the aim of completing the Customs Union). No accession negotiations with Turkey are contemplated.

The Lisbon meeting in June 1992 laid down that all future enlargements must meet the prior conditions that there must be further progress in the internal development of the Union – that is, via the 1996 IGC – and that the candidates must be adequately prepared by means of closer cooperation between them and the Union.

As regards the states of Central and Eastern Europe, the ruling enlargement *texts are the Preambles to the 'Europe Agreements' with them, all of which note that the objective is their membership of the Union. In December 1990 association negotiations opened with Czechoslovakia, Hungary and Poland, which came later to be known as the Visegrad countries from the town in which they agreed on their own mutual cooperation. The first so-called 'Europe Agreements' were signed in December 1991. These were criticized for being too restrictive on the Community side and allowing insufficient trade opportunities to the three States. The Agreement at the Copenhagen meeting of the European Council (21–22 June 1993) that the 'associated countries in Central and Eastern Europe that so desire shall become members of the European Union' was an important step forward and was followed at the end of the year by a series of 'Europe Agreements'. A typical example is given below, that between the Community and Hungary.*

Mission de l'Autriche auprès des Communautés Européennes

Austria forms part of the very core of Europe; Austria's image of itself has been shaped by history; it is inseparably linked with the idea of transnational European solutions. This background explains the particular commitment of the Austrian people to the ideas and ideals of European integration that have inspired the Treaties establishing the European Communities.

Since the end of the Second World War, Austria has consistently participated in efforts towards European cooperation and the integration of Western European democracies, even at a time when such a commitment by a country still under Four-Power occupation required courage and determination.

By virtue of its political, social and economic system Austria has always considered itself an integral part of the family of Western European democracies ever since it regained its freedom after the Second World War.

Based on these considerations, the applications for membership . . . assert Austria's political claim to become a member of the Community on an equal footing. Austria thereby expresses its readiness to accept the rights and obligations resulting from such a membership . . .

In the Preamble of the EEC Treaty the member States express their resolution 'by thus pooling their resources to preserve and strengthen peace and liberty' and call 'upon the other peoples of Europe who share their ideal to join in their efforts'. Austria considers its permanent neutrality, which it declared in 1955, to constitute its specific contribution to the preservation of peace and security in Europe.

At a time when confrontation is being replaced by cooperation, neutral Austria, thanks to its historical experience and its contacts with neighbouring countries in Central and Eastern Europe, can give the European Community additional profile and force of gravity and constitute an element of additional strength. Austria's wish to become a member of the Community is based on a broad political consensus . . .

The position of the Federal Government thus rests on a sound basis and the European Community can be assured that, as a member of the Community, Austria will be a reliable partner and will demonstrate the solidarity required for the accomplishment of European unification.

Due to its economic system and its social structures Austria can be regarded as a factor which will strengthen the Community from a socio-economic point of view. The country fits into the existing structures of the Community harmoniously; already today the Community is a partner for more than 70 per cent of Austria's foreign trade (including trade in services).

The Austrian gross national product per capita is higher than the Community average so that the country will be a net contributor to the EC budget and can thus make an important contribution towards an improved economic and social cohesion of the Community.

Austria's membership in the Community will also improve the Community's 'geographical cohesion'. The integration of Austria would make it easier to benefit by the advantages and opportunities of the EC – 'Internal Market' and a 'Citizens' Europe'.

On account of its highly developed economy, well balanced social structures, intellectual resources, highly qualified workers and employees, high level of productivity and strong currency Austria can become a partner who will broaden and fortify the basis of the Community's competitiveness in the world economy.

Last but not least, Austria's intellectual and cultural heritage is an inseparable component of the history of European culture and thought. Austria sees its own identity as a major element of the European identity which the European Community aims to create. [. . .]

Austria is interested that its desire to become a member of the Community shall be realized as soon as possible. This objective should not

be delayed by any new priorities which the Community might set
itself.

The experience gained and the success achieved by the European
Communities ever since their establishment permit the conclusion
that the processes of deepening and enlargement of the Community
do not contradict each other.

'The Challenge of Enlargement: Commission Opinion on Austria's Application for Membership', April 1992

Foreword

The Community has to reconcile two requirements. First, it must
unhesitatingly and in accordance with the procedures laid down in
Article 237 of the EEC Treaty confirm its openness towards applicant
European countries whose economic and political situation are such
as to make accession possible. In addition, the Community must take
care to strengthen its own structures sufficiently to maintain the
impetus of its own integration. This forward movement must be safeguarded, even in an enlarged Community.

The Community is at present engaged in completing the internal
market and is seeking at the same time, through the two inter-governmental conferences that are now underway, to establish an
economic and a political union. By 1 January 1993 the internal
market will be completed and the results of the two inter-governmental conferences should also have been approved. The
Commission is therefore convinced that no negotiations on a fresh
enlargement should be initiated before that date . . . Once that date
is passed, the Community should be ready and willing to open negotiations with applicant countries meeting economic and political
conditions for accession. It is clear that in this context the Community will also have to take account, where some of the countries
which have already applied or may apply are concerned, of the
implications of the concept of neutrality. This concept of neutrality
is, moreover, steadily evolving in the light of developments in Europe
and worldwide.

In the accession negotiations, the Community will have to take as
a basis the Community rules and structures as they emerge from the
two inter-governmental conferences . . . including the results concerning foreign policy and security, which will have the effect of
establishing a stronger identity to which the applicant countries will
have to adjust . . .

The Community must . . . seek in its future partners the necessary willingness to join with it in the further continuation of the integration process . . .

Introduction

In its letters, dated 14 July 1989, the [Austrian] Government emphasizes that it submits the application for accession on the understanding that its internationally recognized status of permanent neutrality will be maintained. The text reads: 'Austria submits this application on the understanding that its internationally recognized status of permanent neutrality, based on the Federal and Constitutional Law of 26 October 1955, will be maintained and that, as a member of the European Communities by virtue of the Treaty of Accession, it will be able to fulfil its legal obligations arising out of its status as a permanently neutral State and to continue its policy of neutrality as a specific contribution towards the maintenance of peace and security in Europe'.

[. . .]

The Austrian economy and the Community

Although its economy is medium-sized, as a member State Austria would form part of the group of member States that are the most stable and the strongest economically in the Community. In view of the degree of convergence of its economy with that of the Community, Austria will be able to participate fully in the major Community projects, establishment of the internal market and EMU and strengthening economic and social cohesion, without fundamentally changing the economic policies pursued up to now . . .

Problems posed for the Community by Austria's perpetual neutrality by reference to the existing Treaties: The common commercial policy clearly poses problems . . . Particularly true in the case of the Community's now consistent practice of imposing economic sanctions against certain non-Community countries under Article 113 of the EEC Treaty after a consensus has been reached with political cooperation . . . In the event of war such sanctions would be incompatible with the obligations of neutrality . . . In peacetime the imposition of 'political' sanctions might be at odds with Austria's policy of neutrality but no legal obligations would cramp Austria's freedom to determine where it stood on issues under discussion in the Community institutions except for the very general ones in the Neutrality Act . . .

Problems which could arise in the context of the future common foreign and security policy: . . . Even on the hypothesis that the process of reaching decisions on implementing the common foreign and security policy would rest on a consensus of agreement with regard to decisions of principle, the present member States would require a minimum level of legal certainty with regard to Austria's capacity to join in such a consensus without running into constitutional barriers . . .

Possible solutions to problems arising in connection with Austria's neutrality: Solutions to the legal difficulties . . . will have to be sought in the accession negotiations, either through a redefinition by Austria of its neutral status (with its partners being notified of such a redefinition), or through the inclusion in the Act of accession of a derogation from the EEC Treaty.

Under Article 224 of the EEC Treaty member States may obtain a general derogation from Treaty rules, in two sets of circumstances that are relevant . . . Namely in the event of war or to enable a member State to carry out 'obligations it has accepted for the purpose of maintaining peace and international security'. Given the strictness of the interpretation which, according to the Court of Justice ruling, is necessary where exceptions under Article 224 are concerned, it is not possible to accept the argument put forward by the Austrian authorities to the effect that Austria's neutrality represents a contribution to maintaining peace and international security and that Austria would thereby be able to exempt itself from certain Treaty obligations.

On the other hand, it will be necessary to reach agreement in the accession negotiations themselves on an approved interpretation of general exceptions pursuant to Article 224.

[. . .]

Developments in the negotiations within the inter-governmental conference on political union would also require the Community to seek specific assurances from the Austrian authorities with regard to their capacity to undertake obligations entailed by the future common foreign and security policy.

It is clear from the foregoing that Austria's permanent neutrality creates problems for both the Community and Austria . . . these problems should not however prove to be legally insurmountable in the context of the accession negotiations.

Conclusions

From both the economic and political points of view, Austria's application for accession is in a quite different category from those of previous applicants.

From the economic point of view, no previous applicant has started from a position where, by virtue of numerous agreements, it already had completely free trade in industrial products with the Community, or had already committed itself to apply a substantial part of the acquis communautaire, or where its degree of economic integration with the Community was so advanced . . .

The Community will on the whole benefit from the accession of Austria . . .

'Conclusions of the Presidency of the European Council', Lisbon, June 1992

Enlargement

The European Council considers that the EEA Agreement has paved the way for opening enlargement negotiations with a view to an early conclusion with EFTA countries seeking membership of the European Union. It invites the institutions to speed up preparatory work needed to ensure rapid progress including the preparation before the European Council in Edinburgh of the Union's general negotiation framework. The official negotiations will be opened immediately after the Treaty on European Union is ratified and the agreement has been achieved on the Delors II package.

Negotiations with the candidate countries will, to the extent possible, be conducted in parallel, while dealing with each candidature on its own merit. The European Council agrees that this enlargement is possible on the basis of the institutional provisions contained in the Treaty on the Union and attached declarations.

The European Council considers that, if the challenges of a European Union composed of a larger number of member States are to be met successfully, parallel progress is needed as regards the internal development of the Union and in preparation for membership of other countries.

In this context the European Council discussed the applications which have been submitted by Turkey, Cyprus and Malta. The European Council agrees that each of these applications must be considered on its merits . . .

As regards relations with Central and Eastern Europe, the European Council reaffirms the Community's will to develop its partnership with these countries within the framework of the Europe Agreements in their efforts to restructure their economies and institutions. The political dialogue will be intensified and extended to include meetings at the highest political level. Cooperation will be focused systematically on assisting their efforts to prepare the accession to the Union which they seek. The Commission will evaluate progress made in this respect and report to the European Council in Edinburgh suggesting further steps as appropriate . . .

'Conclusions of the Presidency of the European Council', Edinburgh, December 1992

1.6. The European Council in Lisbon agreed that official negotiations with EFTA countries seeking membership of the Union will be opened immediately after the Treaty on European Union is ratified and agreement has been reached on the Delors II package.

Given the agreement reached on future financing and prospects for early ratification of the Treaty on European Union by all member States, the European Council agreed that enlargement negotiations will start with Austria, Sweden, and Finland at the beginning of 1993. These negotiations will be based on the general negotiation framework of which the General Affairs Council took note on 7 December. They will be transformed into negotiations under Article O of the Treaty on European Union once it enters into force, and can only be concluded once the Treaty on European Union has been ratified by all member States. The conditions of admission will be based on the acceptance in full of the Treaty on European Union and the acquis communautaire, subject to possible transitional measures to be agreed in the negotiations . . .

'Conclusions of the Presidency of the European Council', Copenhagen, June 1993

Relations with the countries of Central and Eastern Europe

1.2. The European Council today agreed that the associated countries in Central and Eastern Europe that so desire shall become members of the European Union. Accession will take place as soon as the associated country is able to assume the obligations of membership by satisfying the economic and political conditions required.

Membership requires that the candidate country has achieved stability of institutions guaranteeing democracy, the rule of law, human rights and respect for and protection of minorities, the existence of a functioning market economy as well as the capacity to cope with competitive pressure and market forces within the Union. Membership presupposes the candidate's ability to take on the obligations of membership including adherence to the aims of political, economic and monetary union.

The Union's capacity to absorb new members, while maintaining the momentum of European integration, is also an important consideration in the general interest of both the Union and the candidate countries.

[. . .]

1.4 The European Council agreed that the future cooperation with the associated countries shall be geared to the objective of membership which has now been established . . .

- The Community proposes that the associated countries enter into a structured relationship with the Institutions of the Union within the framework of a reinforced and extended multilateral dialogue and concertation on matters of common interest . . . Where appropriate . . . Joint meeting of all the Heads of State and Government can be held to discuss specific predetermined issues.

- The European Council, recognizing the crucial importance of trade in the transition to a market economy, agreed to accelerate the Community's efforts to open up its markets . . .

- The Community will continue to devote a considerable part of the budgetary resources foreseen for external action to the Central and Eastern European Countries, in particular through the PHARE programme . . .

'Europe Agreement establishing an Association between the European Communities and their Member States, of the One Part, and the Republic of Hungary, of the Other Part', December 1991

- Considering the importance of the existing traditional links between the Community, its member States and Hungary and the common values that they share;

- recognizing that the Community and Hungary wish to strengthen these links and to establish close and lasting relations, based on mutual interests, which would facilitate the participation of Hungary in the process of European integration, thus strengthening and widening the relations established in the past notably by the Agreement on Trade and Commercial and Economic Cooperation, signed on 26 September 1988;

- considering the opportunities for a relationship of a new quality by the emergence of a new democracy in Hungary;

- reaffirming their commitment to pluralist democracy based on the rule of law, human rights and fundamental freedoms, a multiparty system involving free and democratic elections, to the principles of market economy and to social justice, which constitute the basis for the association;

- recalling the firm commitment of the Community and its member States and of Hungary to the process of the Conference on Security and Cooperation in Europe (CSCE), including the full implementation of the all provisions and principles therein, in particular the Helsinki Final Act, the concluding documents of the Madrid and Vienna follow-up meetings and the Charter of Paris for a new Europe;

- conscious of the importance of the association agreement in building the structures of a peaceful, prosperous and stable Europe, with the Community as one of its cornerstones;

- believing that full implementation of the association will be facilitated by further actual progress in Hungary towards a market economy, inter alia in the light of the conclusions of the CSCE Bonn Conference, and genuine rapprochement of the Contracting Parties' economic systems;

- desirous of establishing regular political dialogue on bilateral and international issues of mutual interests, to enhance and complete associations;

- taking account of the Community's willingness to provide decisive support for the completion of the process towards a market economy in Hungary and to help it cope with the economic and social consequences of structural readjustment;

- taking account furthermore of the Community's willingness to set up instruments of cooperation and economic, technical and financial assistance on a global and multiannual basis;

- bearing in mind the economic and social disparities between the Community and Hungary and thus recognizing that the objectives of this association should be reached through appropriate provisions of this Agreement;

- convinced that the Association Agreement will create a new climate for their economic relations and in particular for the development of trade and investments, instruments which are indispensable for economic restructuring and technological modernization;

- desirous of establishing cultural cooperation and developing exchanges of information;

- considering Hungary's firm intention to seek full integration in the political, economic and security order of a new Europe;

- having in mind that the final objective of Hungary is to become a member of the Community and that this association, in the view of the Parties, will help to achieve this objective.

Have agreed as follows:

Article 1

An association is hereby established between the Community and its member States on the one part and Hungary on the other part. The objectives of this association are:

- to provide an appropriate framework for the political dialogue between the Parties, allowing the development of close political relations;

- to establish gradually a free trade area between the Community and Hungary, covering substantially all trade between them;

- to make progress towards realizing between them the other economic freedoms on which the Community is based;

- to establish new rules, policies and practices as a basis for Hungary's integration into the Community;

- to promote economic, financial and cultural cooperation on the widest possible foundation;

- to support Hungary's efforts to develop its economy and to complete the conversion into a market economy;

- to set up institutions suitable to make the association effective.

[. . .]

'Declaration by the Twelve Member States at the End of the Inter-governmental Conferences concerning the Accession of Norway, Austria, Sweden and Finland to the European Union', Ioaninna, March 1994

The twelve present member States of the European Union agreed that if four new member States join the Union, the threshold necessary for the qualified majority fixed by the Treaties will be fixed at sixty-four votes. They have also agreed that the question of the reform of the institutions, including the weighting of votes and the threshold for the qualified majority in the Council, will be examined at the Conference of representatives of the Governments of the member States which will be convened in 1996, in accordance with Article N(2) of the Treaty on European Union.

They have further agreed to invite the European Parliament, the Council and the Commission to draw up a report on the functioning of the Treaty on European Union. These reports will provide input for the work of a discussion group of representatives of the Ministers for Foreign Affairs, which shall be set up by the European Council in Corfu and shall start work in mid-1995 . . .

They take note that the Council has decided that, if members of the Council representing a total of twenty-three to twenty-six votes indicate their intention to oppose the adoption by the Council of a decision by qualified majority, the Council will do all within its power to reach, within a reasonable time and without prejudicing the obligatory time-limits laid down by the Treaties and by secondary legislation, such as those in Articles 189b and 189c of the Treaty establishing the European Community, a satisfactory solution that can be adopted by at least sixty-eight votes. During this period, and in full regard for the Rules of Procedure of the Council, the President, with the assistance of the Commission, will undertake any initiatives necessary to facilitate a wider basis of agreement in the Council. The members of the Council will lend him their assistance.

Lastly, they agree that the various elements of this Declaration will continue to apply until the entry into force of an amendment to the Treaties, following the 1996 Conference.

[Norway, Austria, Sweden and Finland expressed their agreement to this text]

Documents 53

During the campaign for the European elections which took place in June 1994, the British Prime Minister announced what was billed as a new doctrine. European integration did not mean that every member State had to do the same thing. This was an innovation for his Government, although the principle of 'variable geometry' had been recognized and acted upon in the Treaty on European Union. It co-existed, in British Conservative Party Euro-thinking, with the insistence that Britain must be 'in the heart of Europe'. The doctrine helped to reconcile some of the divergences among party supporters. When pressed, Government spokesmen gave different explanations – the extreme version being that Mr Major was not talking about mature members, but about newcomers. In September 1994 the Christian Democratic party of Germany, in the context of the German Presidency of the EU and of the federal elections coming up in October, published a statement of the party position (not the Government position) on European policy. This contained some disarmingly frank observations.

The principal proposal in the paper was that the hard core of the EU should be strengthened. It comprised 'five or six countries' (Italy being the uncertain member). They must all participate in all policy fields. The implication was that the others would not or could not. No country should use a veto to block the will of the others to deepen integration.

Mr Major immediately responded that he 'recoiled' from the idea of the hard core and the corollary that some countries were more equal than others. Britain probably would prefer a Europe where there were several circles of overlapping and different memberships; it did not wish to see an 'inner' circle of fixed membership, which might force it to choose between whole-hearted participation or exclusion from the heart of Europe.

Wolfgang Schäuble and Karl Lamers, CDU/CSU, 'Reflections on European Policy', Bonn, September 1994

Reflections on European policy

The situation

The process of European unification has reached a critical juncture in its development. If, in the next two to four years, no solution to the causes of this critical development is found, the Union, contrary to the goal of ever closer union invoked in the Maastricht Treaty, will in essence become a loosely knit grouping of States restricted to certain economic aspects and composed of various sub-groupings. It would then be no more than a 'sophisticated' free trade area incapable of overcoming either the existential internal problems of the European societies, or the external challenges they face.

The main causes are:

- Overextension of the EU's institutions which, originally set up for six member countries, must now cater for a membership of twelve – soon (it is to be expected) to rise to sixteen.

- A growing differentiation of interests, fuelled by differences in the level of socio-economic development, which threatens to obscure the basic commonality of interests.

- Different perceptions of internal and, above all, external priorities (e.g. Maghreb/Eastern Europe) in a European Union stretching from the North Cape to Gibraltar.

- A process of profound structural economic change. With its mass unemployment, which it will be impossible to overcome in the short term, this crisis poses a threat to already overstretched social systems and to social stability. The economic crisis is one aspect of the general crisis of modern society in the West.

- An increase in 'regressive nationalism' in (almost) all member countries, which is the product of deep-seated fears and anxieties caused by the internal crisis of modern society and by external threats, such as migration. Fear and anxiety tempt people to seek, if not a solution, then at least refuge in a return to the nation State and all things national.

- The highly debilitating effect of the enormous demands placed on national Governments and parliaments by the above problems.

- The open question, at least as regards the 'when' and 'how', of the involvement of the countries of (Eastern) Central Europe in the European Union. For the present members of the European Union, eastward expansion constitutes both a challenge and a test not only in terms of the material contribution they are able and willing to make but also in terms of their moral and spiritual self-conception. The Union's response will show whether it is able and willing to become the main pillar of a continental order, alongside a democratized and once again stable Russia and in alliance with the USA.

Germany's interests

Owing to its geographical location, its size and its history Germany has a special interest in preventing Europe from drifting apart. If Europe were to drift apart, Germany would once again find itself caught in the middle between East and West, a position which throughout its history has made it difficult for Germany to give a clear orientation to its internal order and to establish a stable and lasting balance in its external relations . . .

Now that the East–West conflict has come to an end, a stable order must be found for the eastern half of the continent too. This is in the interest of Germany in particular since, owing to its position, it would suffer the effects of instability in the East more quickly and directly than others. The only solution which will prevent a return to the unstable prewar system, with Germany once again caught in the middle between East and West, is to integrate Germany's Central and Eastern European neighbours into the (West) European postwar system and to establish a wide-ranging partnership between this system and Russia. Never again must there be a destabilizing vacuum of power in Central Europe. If (West) European integration were not to progress, Germany might be called upon, or be tempted by its own security constraints, to try to effect the stabilization of Eastern Europe on its own and in the traditional way. However, this would far exceed its capacities and, at the same time, erode the cohesion of the European Union, especially since everywhere memories are still very much alive that historically German policy towards the East concentrated on closer cooperation with Russia at the expense of the countries in between. Hence, Germany has a fundamental interest both in widening the Union to the East and in strengthening it through further deepening. Indeed, deepening is a precondition for widening. Without such further internal strengthening, the Union would be unable to meet the enormous challenge of eastward expansion. It might fall apart and once again become no more than a loose grouping of States unable to guarantee stability . . . Owing to its position, its size and its close relations with France, Germany bears a special responsibility and has a major opportunity to play a leading part in promoting a course of development which will benefit both it and Europe . . .

What must be done? Proposals

The above goal can only be achieved through a combination of measures in the institutional sphere and in a number of policy fields. The following five proposals are mutually dependent and reinforcing, and form an integrated whole:

- further develop the EU's institutions and put subsidiarity into effect, including the retransfer of powers;
- further strengthen the EU's hard core;
- raise the quality of Franco-German relations to a new level;
- improve the Union's capacity for effective action in the field of foreign and security policy;
- expand the Union towards the East.

It goes without saying that, especially with a view to enhancing public acceptance of European integration, these measures must be accompanied by efforts to combat organized crime, establish a common policy on migration, fight unemployment, establish a common social policy, ensure Europe's continued competitiveness and protect the environment.

Further developing the EU's institutions. The further development of the EU's institutions, which is on the agenda of the inter-governmental conference in 1996, should be based on the following principles:

- The goal must be to strengthen the EU's capacity to act and to make its structures and procedures more democratic and federal.

- To this end, the question of who does what must be answered. This should be done in a quasi-constitutional document which, in a clear language, describes the division of powers between the EU, the nation States and the regions, and defines the fundamental values on which the Union is based.

- This document must be oriented to the model of a 'federal State' and to the principle of subsidiarity. This applies not only to the division of powers but also to the question of whether public authorities, including those of the Union, should perform certain functions or should leave them to groups in society . . .

- All existing institutions – the Council, the Commission, the Presidency and the European Parliament – must be reformed . . . The reforms must be geared to concepts for a new institutional balance, according to which the European Parliament will increasingly become a genuine law-making body with the same rights as the Council; the Council, in addition to performing tasks in the inter-governmental field in particular, will assume the functions of a second chamber, i.e. a chamber of the member States; and the Commission will take on features of a European Government.

In addition to greater efficiency, democratization must be acknowledged as the guiding principle of all reforms. Naturally, this applies first and foremost to the European Parliament . . . This should be accompanied – not preceded – by efforts to enhance participation by national parliaments in the decision-making process within the EU. With regard to the Council, democratization means striking a better balance between the basic equality of all member States, on the one hand, and the ratio of population size to number of votes in the Council, on the other.

The further development of the EU's institutions must combine coherence and consistency with elasticity and flexibility. On the one hand, they must be flexible enough to absorb and compensate for the tensions inherent in a Community stretching from the North Cape to Gibraltar and differentiated enough to cope with differences in member countries' ability (and willingness) to pursue further integration. On the other, they must be strong enough to ensure that, even in the face of tremendous challenges, the Union retains its ability to act.

To achieve this, the 'variable geometry' or 'multi-speed' approach should as far as possible be sanctioned and institutionalized in the Union Treaty or the new quasi-constitutional document, despite the considerable legal and practical difficulties involved. Otherwise, this approach will continue to be limited to inter-governmental cooperation, which might well encourage a trend towards a 'Europe à la carte'. It must therefore be decided whether, in the case of amendments to the Maastricht Treaty, the principle of unanimity laid down in Article N should be replaced by a quorum yet to be more clearly specified. It is essential that no country should be allowed to use its right of veto to block the efforts of other countries more able and willing to intensify their cooperation and deepen integration.

Developing flexible approaches to integration, as envisaged for monetary union in the Maastricht Treaty and as already practised outside the Treaty within the framework of the Schengen Agreement, appears all the more imperative in view of the immense difficulties the above institutional changes will cause even with membership at its present level . . .

Further strengthening the EU's hard core. In addition to ensuring that the decision-making process within the European Union becomes more efficient and democratic, the existing hard core of countries oriented to greater integration and closer cooperation must be further strengthened. At present, the core comprises five or six countries. This core must not be closed to other member States; rather, it must be open to every member State willing and able to meet its requirements.

The task of the hard core is, by giving the Union a strong centre, to counteract the centrifugal forces generated by constant enlargement and, thereby, to prevent a South-West grouping, more inclined to protectionism and headed in a certain sense by France, drifting apart from a North-East grouping, more in favour of free world trade and headed in a certain sense by Germany.

To this end, the countries of the hard core must not only participate as a matter of course in all policy fields, but should also be recognizably more Community-spirited in their joint action than others, and launch common initiatives aimed at promoting the development of the Union. Belgium, Luxembourg and the Netherlands must therefore be more closely involved in Franco-German cooperation – especially since the Netherlands, too, has revised its earlier sceptical attitude towards the essential function of these two countries as the driving force behind European integration. Cooperation among the core countries must focus in particular on the new policy fields added to the Treaty of Rome by the Maastricht Treaty.

In the monetary field, too, there are strong signs that a hard core of five countries is emerging. They (together with Denmark and Ireland) are the ones which come closest to meeting the convergence criteria stipulated in the Maastricht Treaty. This is especially important since monetary union is the cornerstone of political union (and not, as is often believed in Germany, an additional element of integration alongside political union).

If monetary union is to be completed within the set timetable, it will encompass probably no more than a small number of countries in line with the procedure outlined in the Maastricht Treaty. Even so, it will be completed only if the hard core of five work towards this objective systematically and with great determination. To this end, in the fields of:

- monetary policy
- fiscal and budgetary policy
- economic and social policy

they should strive for ever closer coordination and aim to establish common policies, thereby irrespective of the formal decisions taken in 1997 or 1999 – laying the foundations for monetary union among themselves by that time.

The core countries must convince all the other members of the EU, in particular founder member Italy, but also Spain and, of course, Great Britain – of their unreserved willingness to involve them more closely as soon as they have overcome their current problems and in so far as they themselves are willing to work towards the common objectives. The formation of a core group of countries is not an end in itself but a means of reconciling the two ostensibly conflicting goals of widening and deepening the European Union.

[. . .]

Excursus

To propose the formation of a hard core in Europe and the further intensification of Franco-German cooperation does not, however, imply the abandoning of hopes that Great Britain will assume its role 'in the heart of Europe' and thus in its core. Rather, these proposals are born of the conviction that determined efforts to spur on the further development of Europe are the best means of exerting a positive influence on the clarification of Great Britain's relationship to Europe and on its willingness to participate in further steps towards integration.

[. . .]

John Major, Prime Minister, 'Speech', Leiden, September 1994

Europe: a future that works

Tasks for the future

I see two pre-eminent tasks for the period ahead:

- within the existing Union, to rebuild the cohesion and confidence which has diminished in the past few years;

- in external policy, to extend security and prosperity to the countries to our East.

[. . .]

The European Union now needs to regain public support by making a success of what is already on its agenda.

Let me touch on some of the key points in this process.

Flexibility

First, cohesion within a Community of twelve to sixteen requires flexibility, as I argued consistently throughout the recent European elections. So I am glad a debate on this matter is now developing, and I have read with great interest recent contributions by Edouard Balladur and by Wolfgang Schäuble and Karl Lamers. I welcome their emphasis on a more flexible Europe. Diversity is not a weakness to be suppressed: it is a strength to be harnessed. If we try to force all European countries into the same mould we shall end up cracking that mould. Greater flexibility is the only way in which we shall be able to build a Union rising to sixteen and ultimately to twenty or more member States.

The way the Union develops must be acceptable to all member States. It seems to me perfectly healthy for all member States to agree that some should integrate more closely or more quickly in certain areas. There's nothing novel in this. It is the principle we agreed on economic and monetary union at Maastricht. It may also happen on defence.

But the corollary is that no member State should be excluded from an area of policy in which it wants and is qualified to participate. To choose not to participate is one thing. To be prevented from doing so is quite another – and likely to lead to the sort of damaging divisions which, above all, we must avoid.

So I see a real danger, in talk of a 'hard core', inner and outer circles, a two-tier Europe. I recoil from ideas for a union in which some would be more equal than others. There is not, and should never be, an exclusive hard core either of countries or of policies. The European Union involves a wide range of common policies and areas of close cooperation. No member States should lay claim to a privileged status on the basis of their participation in some of them. For nearly forty years now, the member States of the European Union, first six, then nine, ten, twelve, soon to be sixteen, have worked to reduce divisions in Europe. We must not see them reintroduced.

That is why an essential component of the future European construction must be flexibility. We need a debate about it.

By flexibility, of course, I do not advocate chaotic nonconformity . . . There are areas where conformity is right and necessary – in the rules which govern international trade and the Single Market and the environment, for example. But conformity can never be right as an automatic principle. Flexibility is essential to get the best out of Europe – and to respect the wishes of our peoples. The European

Monetary Union is a case in point. The arrangements in the Maastricht Treaty for progress towards EMU do not simply allow, but require a differentiated approach. This is essential. Whatever one's view of EMU Stage 3 – and I have thought it right to reserve the United Kingdom's position, and still do – the introduction of a common currency without proper prior economic convergence would be calamitous. But Maastricht recognized that. In general, the Maastricht Treaty's flexible arrangements allow countries freedom and choice on how they decide to participate in the pursuit of our shared aims.

The inter-governmental conference

In developing Britain's approach to the IGC, I will be guided by four considerations:

- The first is my sense of what Britain's Parliament wants and what people actually need.

- Secondly, I shall want to see greater flexibility in the European Union, and greater tolerance of diversity.

- But that makes it all the more important, thirdly, that Europe maintains a strong sense of shared purpose and common enterprise. The IGC must be the anvil on which we forge a stronger Union.

- And fourthly, that any proposals for change are workable and effective. The European Union has never lacked for ideas for its development. But it needs ideas which work.

[. . .]

Conclusion

We want to ensure that common policies are adopted only where they offer real common benefit. We want to ensure our Union is not a directorate of the larger countries, at the expense of the smaller.

We don't want Europe to go off the road. When we see a proposal that could have this effect, we'll say so, in a frank and realistic way. And when we have positive proposals to put forward, we'll do so vigorously. That is a positive attitude we have. An attitude to help Europe towards a future – a future that works.

Document 54

By early 1994 unemployment in the twelve member States of the European Union had reached 17 million. If the enterprise were to be judged by its success in 'promoting . . . a high level of employment' (Treaty establishing the European Community, Principles, Article 2), it would be found to be failing.

At the end of 1993 the Commission responded to a request from the European Council meeting in Copenhagen in June 1993 to produce a White Paper on 'Growth, Competitiveness and Employment'. It opens with: 'Why this White Paper? The one and only reason is unemployment'.

It dismisses protectionism, a quick fix of Government spending, a cut in working hours along with job-sharing and cuts in wage rates. It sets out a list of possible positive actions.

Although the European Council greeted the White Paper favourably (after the British Chancellor of the Exchequer had begun by disparaging it), tangible progress was scant by the time M. Delors left office on 23 January 1995.

Meanwhile, in most of the member States, and despite signs that the recession was ending, unemployment continued to rise.

European Commission, 'Growth, Competitiveness, Employment: The Challenges and Ways Forward into the 21st Century: White Paper', 1994

There is no miracle cure.

- *Neither protectionism*, which would be suicidal for the European Union, the world's largest trading power, and would run counter to its proclaimed objectives, in particular that of encouraging the economies of the poorest countries to take off;

- *nor a dash for economic freedom*: turning on the tap of Government spending and creating money can, like a narcotic, produce a short-lived illusion of well-being. But the return to reality would be all the more painful when we had to repair the damage wreaked by inflation and external imbalances. The worst damage would be higher unemployment;

- *nor a generalized reduction in working hours and job-sharing at national level*: this would result in a slowing-down of production due to the difficulty of striking the right balances between the demand for skilled workers, the optimum utilization of plant and the supply of labour;

- *nor a drastic cut in wages to align our costs on those of our competitors in the developing countries*: socially unacceptable and politically untenable, such an approach would only worsen the crisis by depressing domestic demand, which also contributes to growth and the maintenance of employment.

[. . .]

Ways forward into the 21st century

In order to reverse the disastrous course which our societies, bedevilled by unemployment, are taking, the European Union should set itself the target of creating 15 million jobs by the end of the century . . .

The White Paper is, . . . consistent with the guidelines submitted to the European Council, in accordance with the new Treaty (Article 103), to mark the beginning of the second stage of European economic union, which must be successful if a single currency is to be achieved. We must therefore place our thinking within a macroeconomic reference framework for both economic and monetary convergence which will increase the opportunities available to our economies.

[. . .]

The gradual reduction in public deficits is necessary during the initial phase in order to bring indebtedness under control and to continue to increase public saving during the second phase. This will call for increased efforts to restructure spending – and in particular to curb operating expenditure – in favour of public resources allocated to tangible and intangible investment and to an active employment policy.

Stable monetary policies consistent with the aim of low inflation will be a constant benchmark throughout the period. They would lead to further interest-rate cuts that would make more attractive the investment essential to the modernization and competitiveness of our economies. Investment in infrastructures, housing and environmental improvement projects would thus be given a particular boost.

Finally, the trends of all categories of income should be made consistent with the objectives of monetary stability and cost moderation. During the first phase, the task would be to avert an acceleration which would frustrate the reduction of interest rates in the long term; during the second, it would be necessary to guarantee an adequate rate of return to permit an increase in the investment ratio and hence in growth.

An open economy

Only properly managed interdependence can guarantee a positive outcome for everybody.

Each of the major bursts of growth in the European economies started with a qualitative leap in international trade. The most spectacular contribution probably came from the establishment of the multilateral trading system resulting from the Bretton Woods Agreements after the Second World War. Today we are perhaps seeing the beginnings of an equally important leap forward with the very rapid integration into world trade of developing countries and former Communist countries.

The Community must be open and prepare itself for this prospect. This is why the conclusion of the Uruguay Round negotiations is of such importance for it too. For the first time, these negotiations will produce a global agreement between industrialized and developing countries containing balanced concessions aimed at fair access to all markets.

[. . .]

Decentralized economy

The market economy has a decentralizing effect. This was the reasoning behind the 'Single Market' project (Objective 92). Its aim was not only to achieve economies of scale but also to set free the dynamism and the creativity inherent in competition.

Decentralization now also reflects a radical change in the organization of our societies, which are all confronted with the growing complexity of economic and social phenomena and the legislative or regulatory framework.

Hence the growing importance of the local level at which all the ingredients of political action blend together most successfully.

Hence also the decentralization movement affecting the business world. SMEs [Small and medium sized enterprises] are often cited as models because they embody operational flexibility and a capacity for integration which the units which make up the big companies are now trying to imitate. Hierarchical and linear empires are gradually giving way to interactive organizations.

[. . .]

A more competitive economy

Drawing maximum benefit from the Single Market. While industrial policy continues to be controversial no one is in any doubt as to the responsibility of Governments and of the Community to create as favourable an environment as possible for company competitiveness. Compliance with the competition rules is an important element. It helps to ensure that the Single Market is a living reality. However, where companies are concerned, progress is needed in three areas.

The first concerns the body of rules (laws, regulations, standards, certification processes) which ensure the smooth functioning of the market. The rules have to be supplemented in line with the initial target (whether they concern intellectual property or company law, for example). It must also be simplified and alleviated. But, above all, how it then develops has to be guaranteed against the risk of inconsistency between national and Community laws. This means fresh cooperation between Governments at the legislative drafting stage. Likewise, care should be taken to ensure that the Community legislation affecting companies is consistent, especially the environmental legislation.

The second condition revolves around small and medium-sized enterprises. While they are a model of flexibility for big companies, they are also increasingly a factor of competitiveness as a result of 'farming-out' and subcontracting. Hence the measures taken on the initiative of big companies to galvanize their suppliers and clients. However, the 'demography' of SMEs, i.e. their birth, growth and regeneration, is also a matter of national policy. In some countries it will be necessary to adapt their tax systems, rights of succession and access to equity and to simplify inter-company credit regulations and practices. While most of the work has to be done at national level, the Community, for its part, must help to fit SMEs into the dynamics of the Single Market. The immediate task, therefore, is to work towards simplification and information. An initiative will shortly be proposed in this connection.

The third condition concerns the accelerated establishment of trans-European infrastructure networks . . .

In order to establish these networks, promote the information society, and develop new environmental improvement projects, the Commission proposes to accelerate the administrative procedures, act as a catalyst, to use the existing financial instruments and to supplement them through recourse to saving . . .

Stepping up the research effort and cooperation . . . As part of an increase in the overall research effort, cooperation between the different countries' research policies and between companies will be encouraged. This cooperation will gradually become a basic principle and not just one 'aspect' of Community research and development policy. This principle will help to identify major priorities and to promote meetings between operators and especially between producers and users concerning important issues of common interest, this being the only guarantee that market potential is taken into account when defining research priorities.

[. . .]

Action on jobs

As we have seen, the Community has failed to match the substantial increase in generated wealth with parallel improvements in job opportunities. Looked at more closely, however, the performances of individual States differ quite considerably. For instance, Germany and Spain have enjoyed a comparable rate of growth over the last fifteen years of around 2.3 per cent, yet their average levels of unemployment are 6 and 16 per cent respectively. Over the same period, meanwhile, the United Kingdom, France, Belgium and Italy have all had an unemployment rate of around 9 per cent of the active population, but with growth rates ranging from 1.8 to 2.5 per cent on average. These disparities tell us a lot.

In a general manner, they show that growth is not in itself the solution to unemployment, that vigorous action is needed to create jobs. However, such action must take account of national circumstances. More specifically, the inflexibility of the labour market, which is responsible for a large part of Europe's structural unemployment, can be traced back to specific institutional, legal and contractual circumstances in each country. The educational system, labour laws, work contracts, contractual negotiation systems and the social security system form the pillars of the various 'national employment environment' and combine to give each of them a distinctive appearance. In each case, the entire system must be mobilized to improve the functioning of the labour market. This goes to show, once again, that there is no miracle solution, nothing short of coordinated action by the various players responsible for the components of these systems can effect the necessary transformation.

Moreover, in each country the methods of social dialogue will reflect national traditions.

Investment in education and training: knowledge and know-how throughout life. Our countries' education systems are faced with major difficulties, and not only of a budgetary nature. These problems are rooted in social ills: the breakdown of the family and the demotivation bred by unemployment. They also reflect a change in the very nature of what is being taught. Preparation for life in tomorrow's world cannot be satisfied by a once-and-for-all acquisition of knowledge and know-how. Every bit as essential is the ability to learn, to communicate, to work in a group and to assess one's own situation. On the other hand, if tomorrow's trades require the ability to make diagnoses and propose improvements at all levels, the autonomy, independence of spirit and analytical ability which come of knowledge will once again be indispensable.

Lifelong education is therefore the overall objective to which the national educational communities can make their own contributions. Difficult choices will have to be made, between increasing university capacity or quality, between higher education and vocational paths. However, each country should be aiming towards universally accessible advanced vocational training.

[. . .]

The need for double flexibility – both internal and external – in labour markets. Generally speaking, the flexibility of the labour market has deteriorated under the effects of an accretion of partial measures designed to reduce registered unemployment. All of these measures now need to be re-examined by all the players with a view to removing obstacles to employment.

The question of labour flexibility needs to be examined from two angles: that of the external labour market, where supply meets demand, and that of the market internal to each business, i.e. the human resources at its disposal which it adjusts according to its needs.

Improving external flexibility means making it possible for more unemployed persons to meet the identified requirements of businesses. The first step here is to improve geographical mobility. This could be encouraged by injecting new impetus into the accommodation market and, in particular, by removing obstacles to the construction of rented accommodation.

The provision of a framework for exercising the right to advanced vocational training has already been mentioned. This is a major pillar of flexibility, which also calls for initiatives, sometimes radical, from the two sides of industry in cooperation with the public authorities:

[. . .]

Internal flexibility is the result of optimum management of a company's human resources. The aim is to adjust the workforce without making people redundant wherever this can be avoided. Focusing on the continuity of the link between the company and the worker, it maximizes the investment in human resources and staff involvement. It is up to individual companies to improve internal flexibility by means of staff versatility, the integrated organization of work, flexible working hours, and performance-related pay. Tailored to the European company model, it should be central to negotiations within the company.

The virtues of decentralization and initiative. The optimum operation of the labour market calls for a large degree of decentralization within 'employment areas'. In return, the national authorities should focus on the quality of training and the homogeneity of qualifications.

The successful experience of several member States shows the importance of effective participation of the social partners in the decentralized management of employment areas.

Likewise, it is only by a decentralized approach, i.e. at company level, that adjustments to working hours can lead to improved competitiveness, and thereby encourage job creation and job retention.

[. . .]

Reducing the relative cost of unskilled and semi-skilled labour. The problem of social security contributions has to be seen in the broader context . . . In most countries of the Union, labour costs have to bear the heavy burden of statutory charges. It should be remembered that between 1970 and 1991 they rose from 34 per cent to 40 per cent of GDP whereas, for example, they remained stable in the United States below 30 per cent. Are we not to see this as a cause of the economic slowdown and especially of the increase in unemployment?

To return to unskilled and semi-skilled labour, which is very closely linked to long-term unemployment, it should be noted that, in eight out of the twelve countries of the European Union, social security contributions are relatively more onerous on low incomes. These countries suffer the most from what is one of the most severe structural causes of unemployment and undeclared employment in the Community.

Studies have been carried out in several countries with very high levels of security contributions. These studies show that a reduction of 30 to 40 per cent in social security contributions for low-paid workers would increase employment by 2 per cent. In other countries, the possibility of replacing existing forms of income guarantee payments with a system of negative tax deserves close attention.

For most countries of the Union, it is essential to reduce the non-wage costs of unskilled and semi-skilled labour by an amount equivalent to 1 or 2 points of GNP by the year 2000. The improvement in tax revenue resulting from this measure would offset the cost by up to 30 per cent. The remainder should be financed by savings or other revenue. Irrespective of its intrinsic merits, the CO_2/energy tax proposed by the Commission is one of the best ways of offsetting reductions in the cost of employment. Homogeneous taxation at source of investment income as proposed by the Commission since 1989 would be another possibility.

[. . .]

Call for action

The analyses set out in this document and the possible solutions identified should guide us towards a sustainable development model, both from the viewpoint of the effectiveness of the triangular relationship, growth–competitiveness–employment, and as regards the environment and the improvement in the quality of life.

The effort to be made calls for adaptations in behaviour and policies at all levels: the Community level, the national level, and the local level. Since we are aware of the differing situations in member States, we deemed it preferable not to formulate the possible solutions in unduly concise terms. It will be for each member State to take from the document the elements it regards as making a positive contribution to its own action.

Nevertheless, in the Commission's view, the individual chapters of Part B should provide the basis for work in the various specialized meetings of the Council of Ministers. If a conclusion along these lines were reached at the forthcoming European Council meeting, this would facilitate and actually set in motion the mobilization of the Community institutions in the pursuit of the objectives set.

As for Community action proper, it is proposed to impart a new impetus or give a new form, but only in accordance with five priorities:

- making the most of the Single Market;

- supporting the development and adaptation of small and medium-sized enterprises;

- pursuing the social dialogue that has, to date, made for fruitful cooperation and joint decision-making by the two sides of industry, thereby assisting the work of the Community;

- creating the major European infrastructure networks;

- preparing forthwith and laying the foundations for the information society.

These last two priorities hold the key to enhanced competitiveness and will enable us to exploit technical progress in the interests of employment and an improvement in living conditions.

It needs to be stressed that the implementation of these two priorities in no way calls into question the financial decisions taken as part of Package II by the Edinburgh European Council. There is, therefore, no need to review the ceilings on resources.

Recourse to saving is the only other source of financing. It would be modest in magnitude since the borrowings envisaged would account for less than 2 per cent of total market issues.

For the rest, what we are advocating is not only economically indispensable but also financially viable and hence carries no risk of adding to national public deficits.

Through these forward-looking measures, the Community will lay the foundations for sound and lasting economic growth the benefits of which will far outweigh the cost of raising the funds required.

As a parallel development, and this is also one of the far-reaching changes made to our growth model, the new-found consistency between macroeconomic policy and an active employment policy will eliminate all the behavioural or structural rigidities that are partly to blame for the underemployment with which we are having to contend. It will then be possible to satisfy the numerous needs that have not yet been met as well as those to which the changes both in the organization of our societies and in the organization and sharing-out of work will give rise.

The Commission thus calls on everyone to conduct a lucid analysis of our strengths and weaknesses and to adapt behaviour to the rapid changes taking place in today's world, setting our sights and focusing our determination on what the future holds.

Documents 55

The movement towards the inter-governmental conference (IGC) of 1996 was driven by two forces. The first was that Maastricht clearly left several matters unresolved or fudged, and it was agreed, therefore, and written into the Treaty on European Union, Article N, to hold another IGC. Secondly, the member States had been confronted with the prospect of the further enlargement of the Union, especially towards the East.

The delay in the ratification of the Treaty on European Union, which did not enter into force until 1 November 1993, left only eighteen months or so of hands-on experience of European Union before preparation began for the review. Enlargement, an agreed objective and priority, confirmed in the Europe Agreements (See Document 52) was tied to the reforms expected from the conference.

An IGC is for Treaty reform. Policy reform is for the institutions. But high level policy reform might creep into the conference, which brings together the same personalities as compose the European Council. However, given criticism that the 1990–91 IGC on political union was not well prepared in advance of 1996, the member States set up a Reflection Group to prepare the way. The Reflection Group consisted of representatives of the fifteen member States, under a Spanish President, Carlos Westendorp, a Commissioner, Marcelino Oreja (ironically also from Spain), and two MEPs. The explicit terms of reference of the Reflection Group, which was set up by the Corfu European Council of June 1994, steer clear of policy and have more to say about institutions and procedures. But the continuing functioning of the Union and its further enlargement impinge on two policy blocks: the cost of farm policy and the single currency.

In the Reflection Group itself, the institutional questions debated were divisive. In the Interim Report, produced over the summer of 1995, Mr Westendorp, making no effort to disguise the differences, without naming names, and faithful to the Group's terms of reference, presented options rather than solutions or compromises.

The European Council met informally in Majorca in September 1995 for an initial consideration of key IGC issues, the informal nature of the meeting meaning that there were no formal conclusions. Conclusions would have been difficult in any case because of the level of disagreement among the member States.

Many members were irritated by French nuclear testing, some were *irritated by the German Finance Minister briefing his parliamentarians to the effect that Italy would not be able to join the single currency in 1999 and that there were problems over the Dutch and Belgians. A week before the meeting in his first major speech on European policy since becoming Foreign Secretary, Mr Malcolm Rifkind, a veteran of the Dooge Committee (See Document 45), took as his inspiration Palmerston's dictum that the object of a British Foreign Minister is British interests. This could mean that Britain might not join in some of the Euro-harmonization, with a corresponding loss of influence over developments.*

In sum, it appeared as if there was no time, inclination, material or political will to sketch out the next stages in European Union. The fate of the 1996 IGC depended on all of these being present.

Mr Carlos Westendorp, 'Progress Report from the Chairman of the Reflection Group on the 1996 Inter-governmental Conference', September 1995

Topic 1: Basic points

Reasons for reform: the challenges facing Europe

In addition to the explicit reasons set out in the TEU itself, which relate to completion of the Maastricht venture, and the commitments subsequently entered into by both the Council and the European Council in connection with the most recent enlargement and with a view to the next, there are also implicit reasons for holding the 1996 inter-governmental conference which the Reflection Group has been instructed to prepare. The Group has identified two fundamental reasons, namely improving the functioning of the Union and equipping it with the means to cope with the internal and external challenges facing it, such as the next enlargement.

A key challenge facing the Union internally is the need to ensure that European construction becomes a venture to which its citizens can relate. The growing popular dissatisfaction with public matters in general and European construction in particular is partly due to economic, political and institutional reasons: a high level of unemployment, which is particularly serious in the case of young people and the long-term unemployed, social rejection and exclusion, the crisis in relations between representatives and those represented, the European Union's growing complexity and the lack of information on, and understanding of, its raison d'etre, as well as worrying developments in organized crime (drug trafficking, money laundering, terrorism) which are prompting a growing call for public security, that cannot be met by States acting alone, and is likewise receiving no satisfactory response from the Union because of the gaps or shortcomings in its mechanisms.

There are also major challenges resulting from the profound changes taking place outside the Union as the end of the century approaches: major political instability in the European region following the end of the Cold War, major migrations of populations which are particularly acute in Europe, risks of ecological imbalances which the Union cannot ignore etc., coupled with an increasing globalization of the economy which highlights Europe's loss of some of the comparative historical advantages gained through its social and technological innovations, and which can only be met by adopting an equally global approach.

The responses

The new internal and external context in Europe calls for responses that will ensure greater political stability while simultaneously allowing economic development and a social climate of solidarity to be safeguarded within an open, global and competitive economy, in other words responses that will put the European Union in a position to continue acting as the principal factor of peace and prosperity on the European continent.

Europe's responses to the above challenges have already been partly determined, as in the case of economic and monetary union (although some members of the Group see a case for adjusting the balance between social and economic aspects on the one hand and monetary aspects on the other, without however altering the original timetable and convergence criteria) or of the next enlargement, which will present its own challenges. As stated above, other responses have already been formulated either by the Treaty itself or by subsequent European Councils: it is the Reflection Group, however, that has been tasked with working out their details and giving them concrete form. The Group's initial analysis led to the following conclusions:

If, as stated above, the Union's principal internal challenge is to reconcile itself with its citizens, enhancing its legitimacy in their eyes will have to be the prime objective of the coming reform.

Achieving this goal will require a clear definition of the Union's objectives, i.e. the joint goals sought, ensuring the credibility of policies and/or the cooperation machinery designed to attain those objectives (or, to put it another way, adapting the instruments with a view to reaching the objectives set) and preserving the Union's internal cohesion. The Group has come to the conclusion that the coming reform must give priority to the 'real' problems, i.e. those which preoccupy Europeans most. A majority of personal representatives include unemployment, internal security and environmental degradation among the problems to be tackled as a matter of immediate urgency.

A further response to the challenge posed by citizens' alienation from the Union would be a correct and systematic application of the principles of efficiency, democracy, transparency and solidarity to relations between the Union's Institutions and between its member States, and also between the member States and the Institutions. These principles should be put into practice through concrete measures, such as improved application of the subsidiarity principle ('who does what?'); simplification (of texts and procedures); bolstering the rights of the Union's citizens; greater political responsibility for the Institutions combined with increased accountability on their part, with national parliaments assuming a more prominent role in this connection; and greater transparency in the functioning of the Institutions, which should be given the means to take decisions with the broadest possible backing from citizens. The machinery designed to preserve the Union's internal cohesion also needs to be adapted and strengthened, this step being particularly important with a view to the next enlargement.

The responses to the challenges posed by the profound changes which have taken place outside the Union, in the political and security context as well as in the economic and commercial sphere, need to be based on reinforcement of the instruments set up to achieve the highest possible levels of external stability and security. The key task here, therefore, is to take all the steps necessary to provide the Union with a genuine external identity that will enable it to become a world force in international relations, so that it can promote its values, defend its interests and help shape a new world order. This will clearly only be possible if the Foreign Policy really functions, with full consistency being ensured between the political and economic aspects of the Union's external action. To cope with the new challenges that have arisen with regard to security in Europe, it is also necessary to face up to the question of whether the Union should provide itself with a real common defence policy.

The next enlargement represents both a moral imperative and a major opportunity for Europe. At the same time, however, it presents the Union with a major challenge requiring an adequate response both at the inter-governmental conference itself, through the reforms designed to improve the Union's functioning in general and institutional reform in particular, and in the margins of that conference, in view of the impact which enlargement will have on applicant countries and on the Union's policies. The next enlargement will be different from the previous ones because of the large numbers of applicant countries and the heterogeneity of their political, economic and social situations. To ensure that the next enlargement does not weaken or actually break up the Union, the changes needed to cope with the challenge involved must first be made. Sure though they may be, the benefits deriving from enlargement cannot be reaped until the 1996 conference has been concluded satisfactorily. The success of the former thus depends on the success of the latter.

Principles and objectives

The Group unanimously emphasizes the need to continue and strengthen European integration in this new end-of-century context. Preservation of a common core formed by the principles and objectives of the Union, the single institutional framework and the 'acquis communautaire', which characterizes the European Community as an entity based on the rule of law, represent the principal guarantee of peace and prosperity for the citizens of the Union. The Group emphasizes that this peace guarantee is not perpetual and that it would be a grave error to underestimate the Community's main contribution to the member States and their citizens, namely a shared view of life that has ruled out war as a means of settling differences. The Group accordingly feels that the conference must endorse and reinforce the Union's common principles and objectives, i.e. peace and freedom, internal and external security and prosperity for Europe and solidarity between them . . .

Mr Malcolm Rifkind, Secretary of State for Foreign and Commonwealth Affairs, 'Principles and Practice of British Foreign Policy', September 1995

Let us start with first principles. I am not preoccupied with agonized soul-searching about Britain's historical vocation . . .

The best starting-point is Lord Palmerston's dictum: 'the furtherance of British interests should be the only object of a British Foreign

Secretary'. Thus we must identify first what interests do we have as a nation, and second, how do we best further them.

The answer to the first question is clear. Our most important interest is our own territorial security and the maintenance of peace in Europe. For some countries that might constitute a complete answer. For us it is only part. Britain's interests overseas are substantial and they are wide. In part that is a legacy of an imperial past . . . But our internationalism is more than the residue of history. Modern Britain remains pre-eminently a nation of traders and travellers . . .

Britain's economy is open and international. Only the US attracts more foreign investment . . . So Britain's interests spread across the globe. These considerations give us an even greater interest than most other countries in political stability, freedom of trade, and freedom of passage throughout the world, not just in our own continent . . . It follows that our foreign policy must be global . . .

What of the modern setting . . .? How do we best promote our interests . . .? Most importantly, the nation state remains the basic building block of the international system. It is nation states to which most people feel their first allegiance. International relations are still principally about dealings between states. The conduct of foreign policy must reflect this.

But it must also reflect new global realities. The electronic media, both instant and multinational, serve as a powerful focus for bringing public opinion immediately to bear on policy-makers . . .

Take the environment . . . Or take the global market. In commerce and the media we are near the end of geography . . .

So even the most powerful sovereign states have lost some of their freedom of action . . . We live in a less controllable, more interdependent world . . .

That does not mean the end of sovereignty. It does not make policy-making futile. It does demand new approaches. It means accepting the limits on what Governments can do by themselves and working within them. Above all, it means nations must work together more to defend their security, their prosperity and their environment . . .

If maintaining the 'balance of power' is not and cannot be any longer the basis of our foreign policy in Europe, it is not the case that the only alternative is a single foreign policy shared with all our neighbours and partners. That may evolve one day but we have not got it yet nor are we likely to in the foreseeable future.

A common foreign and security policy implies an identity of interests, and although we do have much in common we have a long way to go. The current controversy over French nuclear tests, the residual colonial obligations of the United Kingdom and France, the differences between Greece and Turkey, the self-imposed constraints on Germany's contribution to peacekeeping, are examples of a continuing diversity of interests and, therefore, of policy.

This need not depress us nor should it lead us to reject those many areas where our interests are the same and where the pursuit of them will be strengthened by a common approach. Where there is a genuine identity of interests British objectives can be furthered by being part of a European consensus with the weight and influence that that provides. What we must not do is suppress important national interests in order to construct an artificial consensus, a bogus unity, that lacks credibility or conviction.

It is not the case, as is often argued, that failure to obtain a single foreign policy would lead us back to a diplomacy in Europe based on the balance of power. Rather, modern Europe will see close cooperation as its primary feature. The conflict of the past replaced by a willing and natural cooperation will be the basis on which we build security, prosperity and freedom. These considerations are relevant to the debate about the future of the European Union and Britain's role in it . . .

Variable geometry is already well established. Some members of the Union cherish their neutral status. Others have shared their defence for years in NATO and the Western European Union. Some members take part in the Schengen Agreement. For others, like Britain, monitoring border controls remains an effective way to counter the risks of drug traffic and illegal immigration. It is clear that full economic and monetary union will not be a sensible option for all members in the foreseeable future.

Sometimes one hears this described as a potential two-speed Europe. But that is unwise. It implies a common destination arrived at in different timescales. That is certainly relevant to enlargement but may not be appropriate to social policy or to a Single Currency. There may be some areas of integration that even in the long term will not be attractive or acceptable to a number of member States. As the European Union increases from fifteen to twenty and then, perhaps, to twenty-five States that is bound to become more and more likely.

If this reflects the reality of different interests, then the European Union will need to respond in a sensitive and flexible manner. Europe has such a rich tapestry of culture, history and language that it would be extraordinary if each country was as comfortable as every other with a given degree of integration.

There is often anxiety expressed at the loss of influence that Britain might incur if it did not join an area of integration which our partners in Europe had concluded was desirable. One has heard this argument with regard to the Social Charter and the Schengen Agreement. It is relevant to the future debates over a Single Currency and other matters. It is not an unreasonable point. If one is not part of an organization one does lose influence and this can inhibit us in the pursuit of our national objectives. Our long delay in joining the European Community is a good example. But one must not take this argument too far. While the accretion of influence is the stuff of diplomatic life and particulary important to a power like Britain, we must constantly remind ourselves that influence is a means not an end in itself. Occasionally it may be appropriate to accept a loss of influence if that is the only way we can protect our interests.

Other countries have had to face this dilemma. The French since de Gaulle, have been in NATO but outside the integrated military structure. This may have irritated their Allies but it has not undermined the Alliance nor severely damaged the French where it really matters to them. Their influence in certain areas has been reduced but they judge that is a sacrifice they are willing to make to protect their interests . . .

How then should Britain respond to proposals for further integration in the European Union? It should, in my view, do so by a cool assessment of the British interest. The criterion we should apply is the net effect of integration as opposed to cooperation in that particular area of policy. Would there be a significant benefit to the prosperity, security, or quality of life of the people of the United Kingdom that would justify the loss of national control over decision-making in that area? If harmonization would be harmful to the United Kingdom, or if it were being pursued for ideological rather than practical reasons, we should oppose it with courtesy, courage and conviction.

In the case of the Single Market the net benefit of harmonization was clear. That is why we championed this major reform. We have reached the same conclusion in many other cases. In these areas, we take the lead in insisting that the rules must be properly obeyed – by all. But, as with other countries, there will undoubtedly be occasions when integration is not acceptable. For example, as far as the Social Chapter is concerned or the removal of frontier controls, the balance for Britain would be a significant disadvantage. Hence the opt-out negotiated by the Prime Minister.

This pragmatic approach should not be interpreted as implying a lack of enthusiasm or commitment to the European Union. We are as committed as France or Germany or the Netherlands to our membership of the Union. It has brought and will continue to bring major benefits to all the peoples of Europe. It was a French statesman who called for a 'Europe des patries' and that is close to our vision.

A further challenge for Europe is its relationship with the United States and Canada. We must build a new partnership between Europe and North America . . . Our renewed partnership must go beyond commerce. We need a much closer dialogue between Congress and the parliaments of Western Europe.

We have all benefited from the close and constant dialogue between American and European administrations; between the US military and our own armed forces; between the diplomats on both sides of the Atlantic. That experience needs to be applied to our legislatures and parliamentarians if occasional differences are to be reduced and resolved.

Sources

The documents which we have selected have been published already, several of them in different places, and in different versions. In some cases we began with the language in which they were originally drafted. Unless official translations have been published, we have made our own. They may differ from those of other translators. We have standardized the spelling and presentation of the documents.

Crown copyright is reproduced with the permission of the Controller of H.M.S.O. We gratefully acknowledge the copyright of the Irish State Paper Office and for the documents published by Official Publications of the European Communities (OOP) for the copyright of the European Communities. Again, we apologize if any material herein is subject to copyright and will be pleased to include appropriate acknowledgements in any further edition.

Document 1

Joseph Besse ed., *A Collection of the Works of William Penn* (London, 1726)

Document 2

Pan-europe: Publications de l'institut universitaire d'études européennes (Geneva, Presse universitaire de France, 1988)

Documents 3

International Conciliation: Documents for the Year 1930, Special Bulletin (Worcester, Carnegie, June 1930) pp. 325–46

E. L. Woodward and Rohan Butler eds, *Documents on British Foreign Policy 1919–39*, Second Series (London, H.M.S.O., 1946) Vol. I

International Conciliation: 'European Federal Union: Replies of Twenty-Six Governments of Europe to M. Briand's Memorandum of May 17, 1930' (Worcester, Carnegie, December 1930) No. 265

Document 4

Pascal Fontaine ed., *Jean Monnet: A Grand Design for Europe* (Luxembourg, OOP, 1988)

Documents 5

The Manifesto of Ventotene (Rome, Associazione Italiana per il consiglio

dei Communi d'Europa, the Centro Italiano Formazione Europea, and Movimento Federalista Europea, 1981)
Altiero Spinelli and Ernesto Rossi, 'Gli Stati Uniti d'Europa e le varie tendenze politiche' in Eugenio Corloni ed., *Altiero Spinelli and Ernesto Rossi, Problemi della federazione europea* (Rome, 1944)

Document 6

German Mosaic (Suhrkamp Verlag,1972)

Document 7

Fontaine, *Jean Monnet*

Document 8

W. Lipgens ed., *Documents on the History of European Integration, Vol. I: Continental Plans for European Union, 1939–1945* (Berlin, Walter de Grutyer, 1985)

Document 9

W. Eichler ed., *Europe Speaks* (London, Militant Socialist International, 1944)

Document 10

Randolph S. Churchill ed., *The Sinews of Peace* (London, Cassell, 1948). Reproduced by permission of Curtis Brown Ltd, London on behalf of The Estate of Sir Winston S. Churchill. Copyright Winston S. Churchill, 1946.

Document 11

United States Department of State Bulletin, 15 June 1947

Documents 12

Command Paper 7599 (London, H.M.S.O., 1949)
Command Paper 9304 (London, H.M.S.O., 1954)

Documents 13

A. and F. Boyd, *Western Union* (London, United Nations Association, 1948)
Ibid.

Document 14

Command Paper 7778 (London, H.M.S.O., 1949)

Documents 15

Jean Monnet, *Mémoires, Vol. 2* (Fayard Press, 1976) pp. 423–8
Fontaine, *Jean Monnet*
Command Paper 7970 (London, H.M.S.O., 1950)

Document 16

Command Paper 4863 (London, H.M.S.O., 1972)

Documents 17

Consultative Assembly, Council of Europe, 11 August 1950, *Proceedings*
Command Paper 9127 (London, H.M.S.O., 1954)

Document 18

European Parliament: Committee on Institutional Affairs: Selection of Texts Concerning Institutional Matters of the Community from 1950 to 1982 (Luxembourg, European Parliament, 1982) [Hereafter *EP Texts*]

Document 19

Ibid.

Documents 20

William Slany ed., *Foreign Relations of the United States 1955–1957, Vol. IV: Western European Security and Integration* (Washington D.C., US Government Printing Office, 1986)
Ibid.

Document 21

The Guardian, 2 January 1989

Document 22

Command Paper 648 (London, H.M.S.O., 1959–60)

Documents 23

Hansard Fifth Series, Vol. 645, cols 1480–1507 (2 August 1961)
Conservative Political Centre (London, 1962)

Document 24

Mimeograph

Document 25

Parliamentary Debates: Dail Eireann Official Reports, 1961, Vol. 191, cols 204–32

Document 26

Documents of Swedish Foreign Policy 1961 (Stockholm, Royal Ministry for Foreign Affairs, 1962)

Documents 27

EP Texts
Ibid.

Document 28

Walter Hallstein, *Die Europäische Gemeinschaft* (Econ Verlag, 1973)

Document 29

Ambassade de France Service de Presse et d'Information, London, 1963 (mimeograph)

Documents 30

Edmond Jouve, *Général de Gaulle et la Construction Européenne, Vol. II* (Librairie Generale de Droit et de Jurisprudence, 1967) Annexes and *EP Texts*

Document 31

Hansard Fifth Series, Vol. 746, cols 1061–97 (8 May 1967)

Document 32

Ambassade de France Service de Presse et d'Information, London 1967 (mimeograph)

Documents 33

Bulletin of the European Communities 1–1970 (Luxembourg, OOP, 1970) [Hereafter *Bull. EC.*]
Ibid. 11–1970
Bull. EC. Supplement 11–1970 [Hereafter *Bull. EC/S.*]

Document 34

H.M.S.O., pamphlet, 1971

Document 35

Bull. EC. 10–1972

Document 36

Bull. EC. 12–1973

Documents 37

Command Paper 6003 (London, H.M.S.O., 1975)
Pamphlet

Document 38

Bull. EC/S. 2/76

Document 39

Bull. EC/S. 2/76

Documents 40

Mimeograph
Bull. EC. 6–1978
Bull. EC. 12–1978

Document 41

Council of the European Communities 1980 (Luxembourg, OOP, 1980)

Document 42

EP Texts

Document 43

Battling for the Union, Altiero Spinelli (European Parliament, May 1987)
Draft Treaty Establishing the European Union (*EP Texts*)

Document 44

Britain in the European Community: The Budget Problem (Central Office of
   Information for F.C.O., H.M.S.O., September 1982)
Bull. EC. 6–1984

Document 45

Council of the European Communities 1985 (Luxembourg, OOP, 1985)

Document 46

COM (85) 310 (Document Series, Luxembourg, OOP, 1985)

Document 47

Bull. EC/S. 2/86

Documents 48

Debates of the European Parliament, No. 2–366/155–157 (15 June 1988)
British Embassy – Press Service – Brussels 20 September 1988, mimeo-
    graph
Bull. EC. 10–1989

Documents 49

Committee for the Study of Economic and Monetary Union (Luxembourg,
    OOP, 1989)
Bull. EC. 6–1989
Bull. EC. 12–1989
Bull. EC. 6–1990
Bull. EC. 10–1990
Hansard Sixth Series Vol. 178, cols 869–92 (30 October 1990)

Documents 50

Agence Europe, 20 April 1990
Bull. EC. 4–1990
Bull. EC. 6–1990
Bull. EC. 10–1990
Hansard Sixth Series Vol. 178, cols 869–92 (October 1990)

Document 51

Bull. EC. 12–1992

Document 52

Mission de l'Autrichie Auprès des Communautés Européennes, Aide Mémoire,
    16 February 1990, mimeograph
Bull. EC/S4/92
Bull. EC. 12–1992
Bull. EC. 6–1993
Official Journal L 347 31.12.93
Bull. EC. 3–1994

Documents 53

CDU/CSU – Fraktion des Deutschen Bundestages (Bonn, September 1994)
British Embassy Press Service, The Hague, 7 September 1994, mimeo-
    graph

Document 54

Growth, Competitiveness, Employment: European Commission (Luxembourg, OOP, 1994)

Documents 55

SN 509/1/95 REV 1 (REFLEX 10) OR. es. (Madrid, September 1995) Mimeograph

Index